SECOND EDITION

D1488187

Teaching Self-Control Through Management and Discipline

Tom V. Savage
California State University, Fullerton

Allyn and Bacon

Boston • London • Toronto • Sydney • Tokyo • Singapore

Vice President, Editor in Chief, Education: Sean W. Wakely
Editorial Assistant: Jessica Barnard
Marketing Manager: Joyce Nilsen
Editorial Production Service: Chestnut Hill Enterprises, Inc.
Manufacturing Buyer: Megan Cochran
Cover Administrator: Jennifer Hart

Internet: www.abacon.com

Between the time Website information is gathered and published, some sites may have
closed. Also, the transcription of URLs can result in typographical errors. The publisher
would appreciate notification where these occur so that they may be corrected.

Library of Congress Cataloging-in-Publication Data

Savage, Tom V.
    Teaching self-control through management and discipline / by Tom V. Savage.
      p.   cm.
    Rev. ed. of: Discipline for self-control. c1991.
    Includes bibliographical references and index.
    ISBN 0-205-28819-7
    1. Classroom management—United States. 2. School discipline—
United States. 3. Self-control—United States. I. Savage, Tom V.
Discipline for self-control.   II. Title.
LB3012.2.S38   1998
371.102'4—dc21   98-25985
                                                           CIP

Printed in the United States of America

10 9 8 7 6 5 4 3   03 02 01 00

Photo Credits: Pages 1, 21, 40, 98, 210/Will Hart; pages 60, 78, 117, 135, 157, 185/Will
Faller/page 231: Robert Harbison.

Contents

Preface

The inability to manage the classroom continues to be a major reason for teacher failure. Numerous teachers experience acute job dissatisfaction and burnout because of the constant struggle with students. The tendency of many is to point the finger of blame to a permissive society that has not taught respect for others or the value of education. While there may be some truth to this assertion, the fact is that managing the classroom has been an issue for teachers for generations.

There is no shortage of proposed solutions. Many of these proposals have been tried and found to be effective for some teachers and ineffective for others. Because an approach does not solve all problems, it is discarded only to be replaced by another method. The sobering fact is that there is no one solution that will work for all students and all problems. Discipline in the schools is a complex problem that will not be solved with simple solutions. Proposed solutions often touch on only one part of the issue. Some offer suggestions on how to prevent problems, while others provide suggested actions when problems occur. What is needed is an understanding of both the prevention and the response.

The purpose of *Teaching Self-Control Through Management and Discipline,* Second Edition, is to provide an overview of the domain by investigating both the prevention, that is, the management dimension, and the response, the discipline dimension. Some of the basic concepts of classroom management and discipline are provided to help each reader select and design an approach that is consistent with his or her own philosophy and the needs of the specific situation.

A major factor that needs to be considered is the purpose of management and discipline. The purpose that ought to guide the decisions of all teachers is that of helping students learn self-control. Understanding this purpose can help individuals design and evaluate effective management and discipline programs.

This book is written for those who deal with students on a daily basis. It is hoped that the application of these ideas will help more individuals achieve satisfaction and fulfillment as teachers. Its content is the result of an ongoing quest for understanding how to relate to students and to deal with the problems they bring to school. This quest began years ago with the challenges provided by a classroom of behaviorally disordered students in East Los Angeles and has expanded to include hundreds of teachers and classrooms across several states. It is hoped that the fruits of this quest will provide a foundation on which others can build.

There are many individuals who have made valuable contributions to the content of the book. Those individuals include the in-service teachers who continue to ask hard questions and challenge superficial answers and preservice teachers who enthusiastically seek new answers. I am indebted to the graduate and credential candidates at California State University, Fullerton, and California Baptist College who have provided suggestions and encouragement based on their use of the first edition. I am most indebted to my wife, Marsha. She has been a valuable colleague and critic. Her advice and encouragement have been vital in helping to bring this project to completion.

T.V.S.

1 Understanding Management and Discipline in the Classroom

Chapter Objectives

After reading this chapter you should be able to:

- State your personal definition of the terms management and discipline
- Define the various components of the management and discipline domain
- Explain the relationship between management and discipline and the academic program of the school
- State the basic purpose of management and discipline
- Explain the implications of the basic purposes of management and discipline on teacher actions

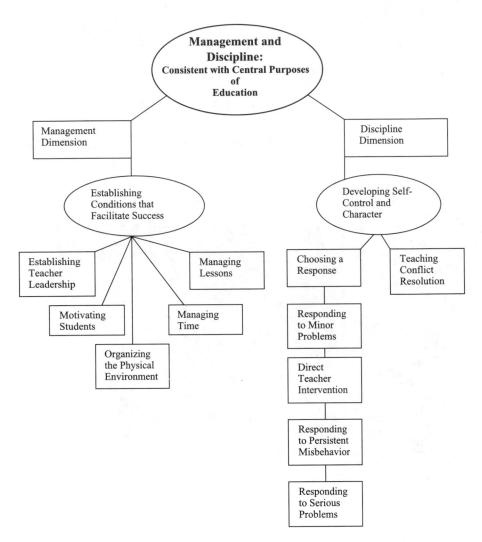

FIGURE 1-1 **Graphic Organizer of the Management and Discipline Domain**

Teachers have two primary roles, instructing students and managing the classroom. The instructing role involves planning, implementing the plans, and assessing learning outcomes. The management role involves creating an environment that facilitates learning and responding to incidents of misbehavior, or what is commonly termed "discipline."

Much effort and attention is directed toward helping teachers develop knowledge and skill in fulfilling the instructional role. Time is spent helping prospective teachers understand learning theory and develop instructional approaches. However, much less emphasis is placed on the knowledge and skill required for fulfilling the management and discipline role. Yet, it is the management and discipline role that is most troublesome for many teachers. There are several reasons for this lack of emphasis on the management and discipline role.

One reason is that the management and discipline role has been poorly defined and inadequately understood. It is sometimes often defined very simplistically. On the one hand, you are advised to love or trust the students and all problems will disappear. On the other hand, you are advised to "be tough and not smile till Christmas." Still others try to provide you with a simple set of responses or prescriptions designed to insure student compliance. The fact is that management and discipline is a complex issue involving a number of possible variables and is relatively immune to a "quick fix." Slee (1995) contends that implementing discipline programs in an effort to find a quick fix actually generates further educational problems and rarely meets with much success.

These inadequate definitions have led to proposed solutions that are often based on a series of "myths" about discipline (Hoover and Kindsvetter, 1997). These myths often have great appeal because they are based on conventional wisdom and therefore appear to be believable. These myths need to be subjected to critical appraisal. The development of solid definitions and understanding the management and discipline dimension of education can help us examine these myths and move toward more productive and useful approaches.

Another perception that has resulted in a lack of emphasis in preparing teachers for the management and discipline role is the view that success in managing a classroom is basically the result of a teacher's personality and, therefore, cannot be taught or learned. There is certainly an element of truth to this perception. In fact, Hoover and Kindsvetter (1997) claim that the personality of the teacher is probably the most crucial factor in determining success in the management and discipline role (p. 11). Some individuals do have personality characteristics as well as beliefs and values that provide them with a good foundation for success. However, there are elements of teacher leadership—understanding group processes, clarification of beliefs and attitudes, as well as concepts and skills—that can be learned so that individuals act more purposefully and attain higher degrees of success.

There is also the belief that the management role is something that can only be learned through experience and, therefore, that efforts to "teach" management are ineffective. Once again, there is an element of truth in this belief. There is no substitute for experience. However, throwing inexperienced teachers into the sometimes turbulent waters of the classroom and watching to see if they "sink or swim" results in too high a cost for both teachers and students. Too many teachers become frustrated or simply fail and leave the profession, not having experienced the personal and professional rewards they had anticipated.

ACTIVITY 1-1 WHAT ARE YOUR CONCERNS?

Directions: When learning something new it is helpful to take some time to reflect on what you already know, the concerns you have and the steps you think you can take to learn what you think you need to know. Take a sheet of paper and divide it into four columns. Label the four columns as shown below. Take some time to reflect and write some comments in each column. You should keep this sheet of paper and add to it as new concerns occur to you.

What do I know?	What do I want to learn	How can I learn it?	How will I know I have learned?
What do I already know/believe about classroom management and discipline?	What are my concerns and what do I want to learn about classroom management and discipline?	Where can I go to get the information I need to address my concerns and identify what I want to learn?	How can I evaluate what I learn?

WHAT ARE THE CAUSES OF DISCIPLINE PROBLEMS?

As with many complex issues, there are multiple causes for what are often termed "discipline problems." An understanding of these multiple causes can help us identify what needs to be changed and how to change it. Some of the causes are subject to teacher control and others are not. However, some teachers do not seem to have many problems relating to management and discipline. Why is this so? This provides us with a hint that the behavior of the teacher does have an important impact on the classroom and we should not use societal conditions as an excuse.

To be sure, there are conditions outside the classroom that have a direct relationship to education. Schools mirror society and problems in society will manifest themselves in the classroom. Mendler and Curwin (1983) identify four factors that contribute to problems in the schools: the presence of violence in society, the influence of the media, the values of the "me" generation, and the lack of a secure family environment.

Students are confronted daily with examples of individuals who attempt to solve conflict through violence. Many students arrive at school with no knowledge of any other way to respond. The media presents students with many images and perspectives that tell them that core values, such as honesty, respect for others, the need to put forth effort, and the value of education, are no longer important. Currently, generational values tend to place a high priority on permissiveness, immediate gratification, and placing oneself first. The lack of a secure family environment means that many students are coming to school lacking the sense of security and support that they need. Students cannot be expected to leave these factors at the classroom door. They will affect the classroom.

However, rather than viewing these as insoluble problems and giving up, we need to view such situations as opportunities. Students can be taught alternative ways of resolving conflict and most welcome alternatives. Most students are afraid of violence. In a permissive society and one in which there is a lack of a secure family environment, people often lose their sense of security and find themselves searching for meaning and a purpose in life. They are drawn to people and places that treat them with respect, offer them a sense of security and belongingness, and provide them with opportunities to get their needs met. Teachers who implement fair and consistent management and discipline in the classroom help create the perception that someone does care and someone can offer guidance for difficult times. Teachers who are able to create a learning environment based on mutual respect and concern, one in which individuals feel safe from physical and emotional threat and rules are logical and consistently enforced, discover that schools become attractive places where students want to be.

There are, however, too many schools and classrooms that are not viewed as attractive places, that are not places students want to go to and their needs are met (Glasser, 1986). Students go to school each day with the prospect of facing additional failure and humiliation. They seldom have the opportunity for meaningful input and participation. The curriculum is viewed as largely irrelevant to them, something determined by someone outside of school. Rather than having choices, they are told what to learn and how to learn it. Individual interests and strengths are given second priority to covering the prescribed curriculum and passing tests. They are told about the values of democracy and the skills of responsible citizens but these values do not apply to them in school.

Students, like all people, respond with disrespect to these signs of hypocrisy. They are individuals who deserve respect and who want to have some control over their lives. They have needs that must be met, needs for belonging, affection, achievement, power, and fun. If these needs cannot be met in ways that the school has determined are appropriate, they will seek to meet them in ways that might be considered inappropriate and destructive.

As we begin to search for the causes of discipline problems, we need to begin with ourselves. Are we creating educational environments that do respect students and do allow them input and decisions in their own education? Is our curriculum culturally relevant and worthwhile? Does the school offer opportunities for students to achieve success rather than pose threats of failure? Is the school a place where students feel like they belong? Does their educational experience offer them opportunities to have fun? Seeking answers to these questions will provide us with many solutions to management and discipline problems.

DEFINING MANAGEMENT AND DISCIPLINE

Before we progress any further in our discussion, we need clear definitions of *management* and *discipline*. Our definitions will influence the decisions we make and how we define what is appropriate and inappropriate practice. This will require you to engage in some serious reflection. It requires that you make your beliefs and theories public so that you can review and challenge them. Your success as a teacher requires that you engage in constant problem solving and decision making.

One of the first beliefs that you might need to challenge is that there are easy or simple solutions to complex educational problems. If there were simple, easy answers, problems related to classroom management and discipline would not be some of the most serious ones that teachers face. This book will not provide you with simple prescriptions and easy answers. To understand the ideas outlined in the rest of the book, you will need to begin with an understanding of *management* and *discipline*.

The management role includes two interrelated dimensions. One is the prevention dimension, the other the response dimension. The prevention dimension refers to the management of the physical and social environment. The reaction dimension refers to the actions that are taken when misbehavior occurs. These two dimensions must be considered together. Frequently, teachers who need help want to focus on the reaction dimension, "tell me what to do when someone misbehaves." These problems, however, often have roots in the management area.

It is important to begin by defining *management* and *discipline*. Slee (1995, p. 12) points out that how we use language and how we define terms frame our understanding and the responses we generate. This is especially true in the case of classroom management and discipline. Discussions with teachers, a review of a number of academic papers and books, and examination of statements by the public reveal that individuals define these terms very differently. This leads to numerous difficulties as we seek solutions to educational problems. If a solid knowledge base for management and discipline is to be constructed and a productive search for solutions begun, we must begin with a definition of terms. When this is done, your actions and beliefs can be more productively defined and examined, and some of the contradictory and confusing advise can be evaluated. One of your first challenges will be to evaluate the definitions and understanding you have of these terms and consider the implications for educational practice. Many individuals use terms such as *classroom management, discipline, control, behavior modification,* and *punishment* as interchangeable terms. This then leads to misunderstandings and confusion (Slee, 1995). In this book, these terms are defined very differently.

Management

Management is defined as that aspect of your teaching role that focuses on creating an environment and establishing conditions that facilitate student success in achieving both academic and social goals. This involves your exercise of classroom leadership, the facilitation of student motivation, the arrangement of the physical environment, management of time and lessons, and attendance to principles of group dynamics.

Some educators are troubled by the term *management* because they define it as something that reinforces autocratic behavior. They see it as communicating the assumption of controlling and directing the behavior of others (Kohn, 1996). They equate it with top-down, hierarchical power relationships between "boss" and "employee" roles in business. In this context, power rests with those in authority and it is the prerogative of the boss to establish all of the rules and the role of the employees to follow with unquestioned obedience. This definition of *management* and the inferences that it communicates have led individuals like Kohn (1996) to reject the concept of classroom management as one that is inappropriate for education.

The definition of *management* in this book also rejects the preceding definition and its related assumptions. In fact, much of the business community has rejected this definition and has focused on more collaborative, humane, noncoercive, and democratic models of management (Kouzes and Posner, 1987). Rather than rejecting the term *management* (it is still a useful concept), we need to define it so that it does communicate to classroom teachers important information regarding their role in the classroom.

Rather than defining *management* as a term denoting power relationships, it is more appropriately defined as organizing responsibilities. For example, when I say that I am managing my affairs, it indicates that I am carefully ordering and organiz-ing my priorities, my time, and my economic responsibilities. *Management* is a tool to help accomplish my personal goals. Classroom management should refer to the process of organizing the environment in order to help students achieve worthwhile and important goals. Glasser, in *The Quality School* (1990), defines this type of class-room management in detail. He points out that it is the role of the teacher to manage so that students can easily see the connection between what they are being asked to do and how to find quality ways to satisfy their basic needs (p. 8). By doing this, the effective teacher can manage the classroom without resorting to coercion.

Rather than inferring that classroom management indicates the right of a person to exercise power over others, it needs to be understood as a means of organizing, so that sharing of power among the classroom participants is facilitated. Power is used in service to others rather than in service to oneself. Glasser (1990) uses the term *lead manager* rather than *boss manager* to indicate this type of relationship. *Boss man-agement* is defined as having four basic elements:

- The teacher sets the tasks and the standards for what students are to do with lit-tle or no consultation with them. The boss does not compromise; the students must adjust to the teacher.
- The teacher tells rather than shows the students what to do and rarely asks for stu-dent input on how they might do better.
- The teacher inspects and grades the work and does not involve the students in the evaluation.
- When the students resist, the teacher uses coercion to make them do what they are told and, as a result, creates an environment where the teacher and students are adversaries.

(Glasser, 1990, pp. 25–26)

In contrast to this style of management, *lead management* has the following characteristics:

- The teacher involves the students and gets their input in discussions of the work to be done and the conditions under which it is to be completed.
- The teacher communicates expectations clearly and models the task. Student input is continuously solicited.
- The students are asked to inspect and evaluate their own work for quality and the teacher is willing to listen to students and accept that they do know a good deal about how to produce high quality.
- The teacher is a facilitator who tries to provide the students with the best tools in a workplace that is non-coercive and non-adversarial.

(Glasser, 1990, pp. 31–32)

Lead management leads to some important changes in the way power is defined and used in the classroom. In the traditional, or boss management, style, which fosters an adversarial and coercive atmosphere, there is a constant struggle for power and power is seen as a fixed sum commodity. Therefore, one loses power if it is shared with others. However, lead managers realize that power is actually an expandable pie, and the more everyone feels a sense of power and influence, the greater ownership and investment they have and the stronger the attachment to the leader. This then means that the leader actually has more power and influence. For example, Kouzes and Posner quote an executive of Ford Motor Company as saying, "I had to give up power to gain power" (1987, p. 164).

The importance of the definition of *management* that you hold and its relationship to the discipline dimension is readily apparent to students. If they do not feel a sense of ownership in the classroom, do not feel that they are respected, that their needs are being addressed, and believe that they must constantly engage you in a power struggle in order to feel significant, there are going to be more behaviors that will be defined as inappropriate that will require your intervention. If, on the other hand, students believe that you respect them, that you are seeking to help them reach important goals and helping them fulfill their needs, and that they have a voice in the classroom, many problems will be prevented.

Discipline

A general use of the term *discipline* is as a synonym for *control*. Discipline is frequently viewed as an unfortunate by-product of education. The emphasis is on dealing with problems quickly and efficiently so that the goals of the prescribed curriculum can be accomplished. In this context, the purpose of discipline is to minimize disruption so that academic goals can be met. Discipline then means the set of rules and punishments applied in order to keep students on task. It implies that your primary concern is to promote conformity and obedience (Hoover and Kindsvetter, 1997). Subjection to the will of an authority is implicit.

While maintaining a focus on the achievement of academic goals is an important outcome of education and the establishment of rules is important, there are other goals and purposes for discipline. The implications of a definition that relies on conformity to the will of an authority and unquestioned obedience are clearly in opposition to our views of the role of a citizen in a democratic society and are in opposition to many of the stated purposes of education.

Furthermore, this definition casts students and teachers as adversaries and creates conditions that lead to conflict and power struggles. The role of the teacher is to make students "toe the line" and it is the role of the students to "test the limits." It is clear that adversarial relationships between teachers and students are an impediment to learning and constant power struggles are a threat to a classroom environment that is supposed to produce a sense of cooperation and community.

However, there is an alternative definition of *discipline*. *Discipline* is also defined as the development of self-control, character, orderliness, and efficiency. This definition indicates that discipline is more than a response to misbehavior that is concerned primarily with rules and punishments. It implies that compliance and conformity are not the main goals, and that discipline is a process of growing toward self-control, developing character, and learning orderly and productive ways of living. These positive outcomes result in a satisfying and productive life, not one based on fear and blind conformity to rules. This alternative definition is consistent with accepting the responsibility required of individuals living in a democratic society. It is consistent with the highest and noblest goals of education. This alternative and more positive view of discipline is the one that is used in this book.

DISCIPLINE AS A CENTRAL EDUCATIONAL CONCEPT

In order to refine your understanding of discipline and to reflect on your role in the classroom, you need to consider discipline as a central educational concept, a basic element in the entire fabric of education. Discipline should not be considered apart from the basic goals and purposes of the school and the curriculum. If the goal of education is to create individuals who are thinking, questioning problem-solvers, individuals who are willing to challenge injustice when it occurs and who are participants in a democratic society, then discipline in the classroom needs to be consistent with those goals. Discipline needs to be viewed as an essential component of everyone's education and absolutely critical to the development of healthy individuals. We need to recognize that how we operate and manage our classroom affects the lessons that students learn. This can be viewed as a part of the "hidden curriculum," those things that students learn that are not intended to be taught or a part of the formal curriculum. The way we conduct our classroom is constantly sending students messages about their role in society and correct relationships among people. Therefore, we should not have management and discipline approaches that are contrary to the fundamental purposes of education.

What this implies is that you need to conceptualize how you view management and discipline in your classroom. You need to begin thinking of it as an important part of the curriculum you are teaching and not separate from it. The goals and purposes of discipline need to be clearly defined as stated and progress toward then constantly evaluated. For example, if a central purpose of education is to help individuals learn their roles as citizens of a democracy, how do the discipline approaches we use contribute to that goal? If you believe that you need to be educating individuals for lifelong learning, do your discipline techniques further that goal?

An additional implication of discipline as a central educational concept means that we need to consider the needs of the students and what we know about growth and learning. This implies that there is a developmental aspect that must be considered. Therefore, the same approach to incidents of misbehavior may not be appropriate for all students and all developmental levels.

THE GOAL OF DISCIPLINE

This discussion of discipline as a central educational concept leads to a consideration of the goals and purposes of discipline that extend beyond that of obtaining student conformity and compliance. The most fundamental purpose of discipline is the development of self-control. Hyman and d'Allesandro (1986) point out that in a democracy discipline needs to originate from within rather than from a fear of punishment. Therefore, self-control is one of the most important outcomes of education and a basic prerequisite for a democratic society. Academic knowledge and technological skill will be of little consequence if those who possess them lack self-control. The lack of self-control is an important component in many of the ills of society. We cannot legislate rules fast enough or punishments harsh enough if there is little self-control.

How is self-control learned? Students are taught self-control by being allowed to make choices, organizing their time, setting priorities, being peacemakers when others engage in disputes, engaging in collaborative learning experiences, and learning to trust each other (Rogers and Frieberg, 1994). Developing self-control means that students choose to act in ways that are consistent with self-chosen beliefs and principles. Individuals who exercise self-control demonstrate what Glasser (1965) calls *responsibility*. They are fulfilling their own needs without interfering with the ability of others to fulfill needs. Self-control involves a consideration of individual motivations as well as the impact of the action on those in the social environment. It places individual needs in the context of a broader societal context.

In this context, the development of self-control requires something more than a method or set of actions to be learned when misbehavior occurs. Rather, it is basically a philosophy (Good and Brophy, 1997) grounded in the belief that students can be trusted with responsibility and that they need to be given freedom to make choices and mistakes. This philosophy also recognizes that learning self-control is not something that is done quickly. It involves growth and development and is therefore acquired through a series of small steps. Once again, there are no "quick fixes" or easy answers; it takes effort and patience. Good and Brophy (1997) point out that there have been remarkable improvements in both school climate and student achievement in urban schools that have implemented this philosophy.

Acceptance of self-control as an important goal of education and discipline provides a perspective that influences the decisions that we make concerning the classroom climate we want and identifying appropriate responses to misbehavior. This goal pushes us to examine what we mean by effective management and control. *Effectiveness* is not defined as obtaining obedience and compliance. Effective management and discipline are evaluated by determining whether students are moving toward greater self-control and self-discipline. Therefore, students who have been in your classroom for some time should be demonstrating progress in exercising increased self-control. If they are not, you need to reflect on your management and discipline approach.

ACTIVITY 1-2   WHAT IS SELF-CONTROL?

A major premise of this book is that the purpose of discipline in the classroom is to help learners develop self-control. Take a few minutes to reflect on that premise and its implications for your role as a teacher.

1. How much self-control do you think students of the age you plan to teach have?

2. Do you think that lack of self-control is a serious problem that needs to be addressed?

3. Do you think that teachers can have an impact on helping students learn self-control? If so, what are some specific ways they can have an impact?

4. How do you think individuals learn self-control?

5. If you accept the premise that modeling is an important method of learning, what are the implications for you as you attempt to teach self-control?

———

Acceptance of the goal of self-control also implies that students need to be given the opportunity to participate in rule making and to question those rules that they do not understand or perceive as unreasonable. It means that misbehavior requires a teacher response that helps the student grow toward self-control, not merely a response to stop the behavior so that other educational goals can be achieved.

It is important at this point to clarify the role of the teacher. I do not mean to imply that the teacher is merely an observer standing off to the side and allowing students to do whatever they desire, or that "anything goes." There are times when teachers need to say "no." A teacher's role is to help students reflect on their behavior and begin to consider the impact of their actions on themselves and on others. What I am talking about here is not a teacher who "demands" obedience and compliance, but one who earns the respect of the students so that they value and trust his or her leadership. This respect is not earned by insisting on blind obedience but by making that an exception rather than the rule. Kohn contends that in this type of classroom teachers actually have more success in getting students to comply when it is really necessary for them to do so (Kohn, 1996).

Neither am I implying that when students are left entirely on their own they will always make the best choices. We know from our own experience that this is simply not true. We all make poor choices. We are all assisted by being involved with responsible and caring people who help us reflect on their choices and understand the relationship between behavior and consequences. You, as a teacher, have the opportunity to be that responsible and caring person. This carries some specific implications for you as a teacher and how you view your role and the assumptions you make about students.

You need to be a caring and responsible person who cares enough about students not to allow them to engage in self-destructive behaviors. You care enough about them to help them learn lessons that will enable them to achieve satisfying and productive relationships with others. This means that there are times when you will be firm and you will insist that students behave responsibly. This does not mean, however, that you are arbitrary, harsh, and use your power as a teacher to show that you are the boss.

Part of your role as a teacher (and for some of us as parents) means that we make sure that students experience the consequences of their actions. Individuals who have been allowed to escape reflection on their choices or who have been shielded from the consequences of their actions have trouble exercising self-control and are destined to a life of frustration and anger. However, we need to make sure that the consequences are appropriate and related to the action and the age and development of the student. Consequences are not arbitrary punishments intended to impress the students with your power.

THE MANAGEMENT AND DISCIPLINE DOMAIN

The preceding discussion of the definitions of *management* and *discipline* and the purpose of discipline as the development of self-control forms the basis for understanding the discipline and management domain and the discussions in the following chapters.

Management and discipline can be divided into two related dimensions. The first dimension relates to the prevention of problems and focuses on the management aspect. The second dimension, success in implementing the management dimension, is what often distinguishes successful teachers from unsuccessful ones.

However, misbehavior will always occur. It cannot be entirely prevented. Your task as a teacher will be to develop a range of responses so that you can choose the one that will be acceptable for the situation and most likely to assist the student in growth toward self-control. When viewed in this context, misbehavior becomes a valuable learning experience rather than an event that creates hostile adversarial relationships. When hostility occurs, learning is the casualty and neither the teacher nor the students have a satisfying experience.

The Management Dimension

The next five chapters of this book will focus on the management or prevention dimension. Systematic attention to these topics can help you avoid many problems and create a positive classroom environment in which your needs and those of your students are being met.

Teacher Leadership and Authority

One of the first and most important tasks you have as a teacher is to establish your leadership and authority in the classroom. The style of leadership you establish and the values and beliefs that you convey through your leadership style will have an important impact on the attitudes of the students and their willingness to cooperate with you and follow your directions. Teacher leadership and authority are communicated in the way you establish classroom rules and procedures, how you share power with students, the manner in which you establish your authority, the respect you show toward the students, and your consistency in the treatment of students.

Motivation

Motivation and discipline are closely linked because there is a strong tie between the motivation of individuals and their behavior. Individuals who believe that their needs are being met in school will have fewer problems than those individuals who believe that school is interfering with their ability to satisfy their needs. There is probably no situation more likely to result in severe behavior problems than boredom in the classroom. An understanding of the principles of motivation and how they can be applied to the classroom are key ingredients in creating a productive classroom that is relatively free of serious behavior problems.

Organizing the Physical Environment

All behavior occurs in a setting. We all know that the physical setting establishes a context for our actions. Psychologists and architects have developed a concept labeled *behavioral setting,* which focuses on the ways the physical environment influences the behavior of its inhabitants. Because schools and classrooms are places where individuals spend a considerable amount of time, it is useful to consider them as behavioral settings and figure out how the physical properties of the setting might influence the behavior of the teacher and the students. The use of color and light, the arrangement of the desks, the amount of noise, and the physical attractiveness of the space are attributes that will influence behavior. They need to be considered as you plan and create an environment that will help you accomplish important educational outcomes and minimize disruptive behavior.

Managing Instructional Time

The efficient and productive use of the time when students are in the classroom is another key to the prevention of problems and the development of student and teacher satisfaction. Many experienced and successful teachers indicate that they keep the students so busy that they don't have the opportunity to misbehave. There is much wisdom in this approach. Individuals who are busy, preferably on tasks they perceive to be interesting and important, are seldom disruptive. A goal of broadcast media is to try and eliminate "dead air space" in which nothing is being broadcast. You should also try to reduce the "dead air space" that occurs in the classroom when students have nothing to do. Studies have shown that improvement in achievement is directly related to increasing the amount of time students spend on a learning task. During a typical day in a classroom, a substantial amount of time is spent on noninstructional tasks and the students are not actively engaged in learning. When students are not on-task, not only are they not learning, they are more likely to be engaged in misbehavior.

Managing Lessons

Delivering effective lessons is a complex task. The classroom is a multidimensional, fast-paced, unpredictable environment. Teaching demands more than simply reading a lesson plan. While you are teaching a lesson you need to be aware of the behavior of students throughout the classroom. The lesson needs to be focused on an objective, delivered with clarity and smoothness, at a pace that is appropriate for the students in the class. If the lesson is too slow, boredom will cause discipline problems. If the lesson is too fast, frustration will set in. To focus exclusively on the management dimension is also inadequate. No matter how much effort is spent on prevention, some misbehavior will occur. This is because we are dealing with human beings and everybody (even parents and teachers) misbehaves from time to time.

The Discipline Dimension

There will be behavioral problems that will occur in even the best managed classrooms. Therefore, you need to consider what you will do when problems do occur in the classroom. One important step is to deliberately teach students conflict resolution skills. They will be faced with conflict situations throughout their lives. Many of the problems that occur in the school will occur outside the view of the teacher. Among the most valuable tools we can give students are conscious approaches they can use to deal with conflict when it does arise.

You will also need to think about the decision you must make when you are called on to respond to misbehavior. I suggest that there are two criteria that you should use when making this decision. The first is the ability of the student to exercise self-control. Students will vary in their ability to exercise self-control. Some may have little self-control and others considerable self-control. It is not likely that the same response will be appropriate for every student. We need to remember that our goal is to help students develop self-control. We should then select responses that will provide each student with the opportunity to learn and move toward increased self-control.

Secondly, the seriousness of the misbehavior should be considered when selecting a response. Minor incidents or those that are the result of carelessness or immaturity should be handled differently than those that have the potential to harm others or that are deliberate attempts to disrupt the classroom.

In trying to assist you in making these decisions, a range of possible responses is suggested. Understanding a range of alternative responses will provide you with some flexibility as you respond to problems and increase the likelihood that you can help students move toward self-control. The next five chapters will deal with the response dimension.

Responses to Minor Problems and Supporting Self-Control

The first category of responses are unobtrusive actions that are designed to provide students with cues that prompt them to evaluate their own behavior and provide them with an opportunity to self-correct their behavior. Responsibility for correction is placed on the student. As students learn how to self-correct they become more responsible. Responses in this category preserve respect for the dignity of the student, and are very effective for those who generally have some self-control and for addressing minor problems.

Direct Teacher Intervention

If students do not respond to attempts that allow them to exercise self-control or the problems are more serious ones, then more intrusive and systematic responses need to be used. This often requires the identification of the causes of the misbehavior and using classroom meetings to identify the logical and natural consequences of the behavior. Student desks may be rearranged so that students can go to a time-out area in order to reflect on their actions and gain some self-control.

Responding to Persistent Misbehavior

Persistent misbehavior and more serious misbehavior require even more direct and intrusive measures. These involve the use of behavior modification techniques, the development of behavioral contracts, loss of privileges, and parent–teacher conferences. Persistent problems may also require that the classroom teacher begin to involve other professionals, such as the school administrator, counselor, or psychologist. Students who have serious and persistent behavioral problems are usually students who are experiencing serious problems that require considerable effort in order to overcome them. The focus of the teacher when dealing with these types of students must remain on identifying the causes of the misbehavior and removing them. The goal is to help the student make better choices rather than to punish him or her.

Responding to Serious Behavior Problems

The majority of the problems that are encountered in the classroom are relatively minor ones. However, serious problems, such as intimidation, fighting, bullying, chronic truancy, cheating, and drug abuse require serious responses. This type of misbehavior is a clear indication that the student has lost self-control and serious and well-planned interventions are necessary. Because these serious misbehaviors often involve factors that exist outside the classroom, attempts to solve these problems will almost always require the involvement of parents and other trained professionals who have skills beyond those possessed by the classroom teacher. Once again, the focus is on helping students who are in trouble and helping them develop a healthy life. Because these problems are serious, it often requires a considerable amount of time and effort to bring about improvement. However, as a teacher who taught classes of students with these serious problems, I can attest that the rewards make the efforts worthwhile.

Teaching Conflict Resolution in the Classroom

Conflict is natural and is a part of the human condition. All of us experience a variety of conflicts in our lives. We cannot always count on having someone else, such as a teacher, handle our conflicts for us. We need to learn how to confront and handle conflicts independently. Unfortunately, many individuals do not learn how to deal with conflict in a productive manner. They may attempt to withdraw or may impulsively respond in fear and anger. The results of both approaches can be disastrous. Students need to be taught specific approaches that they can use when confronted with conflict situations. Learning conflict resolution skills not only provides important skills to students, it gives them a role in responding to incidents and shares responsibility with them.

SUMMARY

Success in teaching requires that teachers attend to two interrelated and complementary tasks: instructing students and managing a learning environment in which learning is possible. Evidence suggests that the management task is the one that causes the most difficulty. Failure in this domain results in high personal and economic costs. It is one of the major causes of teacher burnout and turnover. The loss of learning in classes in which there is persistent misbehavior is considerable.

Understanding the management and discipline domain requires that you first begin by defining how you understand those terms. Management and discipline need to be considered in conjunction with the goals of the curriculum. The goal of helping students develop self-control is the primary purpose that is to be achieved and the actions that teachers take should be evaluated in terms of how well they help students learn self-control.

There are no easy answers or quick fixes. If there were, this would not be a serious concern of educators. Much of what needs to be learned must be learned through experience. There are, however, some basic principles and concepts that can be used to organize that experience and minimize the problems that you might experience in the classroom. It is the purpose of this book to provide you with some of those concepts so that your progress toward achieving the personal and professional satisfactions of teaching can be enhanced.

The first section of this book will focus on the prevention of problems through management. The second half of the book will focus specifically on those actions that can be taken when misbehavior occurs.

SUGGESTED APPLICATIONS

1. The first step you need to take is to clarify your values and beliefs regarding the role of the teacher in management and discipline. One way to do this is to begin a journal that you will keep as you read the subsequent chapters and reflect on them. Before reading Chapter 1, what did you view as the purpose for discipline? How did you define *management* and *discipline*? How have you changed

as a result of reading this chapter? What questions came to your mind about the role of a teacher as you read the chapter? What might be other points of view that could be expressed? What do you think you need to learn in order to achieve success in this important aspect of teaching?.

2. Interview a new teacher or a student teacher to get his or her perspective on the topic. How serious do they think the problem is? What was most surprising to them as they entered the classroom? What do they think you need to know in order to achieve success? How are their responses similar to or different from those expressed in the chapter?

3. Interview two or three students at the age level you are interested in teaching. What are their views of the seriousness of discipline problems in schools? What do they see as the causes of problems? What do they think is most effective for teachers to do? What do they think is ineffective?

4. Now that you have written your views, have interviewed a new teacher and some students, reflect on these three different perspectives. Do you see any themes that recur? What differences do you note? How has this information changed your personal theories and beliefs?

SUGGESTED READINGS

Glasser, W. (1965). *Reality therapy: A new approach to psychiatry.* New York: Harper & Row.

Glasser, W. (1986). *Control Theory in the Classroom.* New York: Harper & Row.

Glasser, W. (1990). *The quality school: Managing students without coercion.* New York: Harper & Row.

Good, T. L. & Brophy, J. E. (1997). *Looking in Classrooms* (7th Ed.). New York: Longman.

Hoover, R. L. & Kindsvetter, R. (1997). *Democratic discipline: Foundation and practice.* Columbus, OH: Merrill.

Hyman, I. & D'Alleesandro, J. (1986). Good old-fashioned discipline: The politics of punitiveness. *Phi Delta Kappan,* 66, 39–45.

Kohn, A. (1996). *Beyond discipline: From compliance to community.* Alexandria, VA: Association for Supervision and Curriculum Development.

Kouzes, J. L. & Posner, B. Z. (1987). *The leadership challenge: How to get extraordinary things done in organizations.* San Francisco, CA: Jossey-Bass.

Mendler, A. N. & Curwin, R. L. (1983). *Taking charge in the classroom: A practical guide to effective discipline.* Reston, VA: Reston Publishing Company.

Rogers, C. & Freiberg, H. J. (1994). *Freedom to learn* (3rd Ed.). Columbus, OH: Merrill.

Slee, R. (1995). *Changing theories and practices of discipline.* Washington, DC: Falmer Press.

PART ONE

Effective Classroom Management

CHAPTER

2 Establishing Teacher Leadership and Authority

Chapter Objectives

After reading this chapter you should be able to:

- Define leadership and apply it to teaching
- Define different types of authority
- Compare the advantages and disadvantages of authoritarian and democratic methods to establishing rules
- List steps to be followed when establishing classroom rules
- Identify the importance of teacher consistency

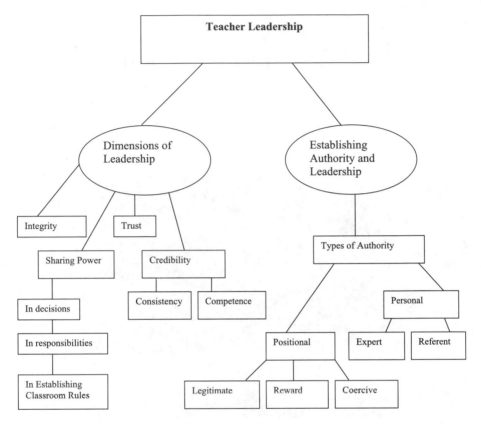

FIGURE 2-1   **Graphic Organizer for Establishing Teacher Leadership**

Teacher leadership is an elusive ingredient that often spells the difference between success and failure in classroom management. Cronbach (1977) points out that it is the responsibility of the teacher to establish an enthusiastic and purposeful work atmosphere. As a teacher, you are expected to be the leader of the classroom. The students look to you to determine the direction of the classroom. You will need to assist many different students, from different backgrounds, and with different motivations, to move forward and willingly cooperate with you. How can that be done? What are the elements of leadership? Can it be learned? These are some of the questions addressed in this chapter.

Leadership is an essential component if any group is to be productive. Although learners do influence a teacher's leadership style, studies have shown that patterns of leadership remain relatively stable over time. This leads to the conclusion that teachers establish the patterns of leadership behavior in the classroom rather than merely responding to the students (Soar and Soar, 1987).

DISCIPLINE SCENARIO 2-1 **Show Them You're the Boss**

Kelly was a new teacher getting ready to face her first class of students. She was understandably nervous about the experience. An experienced teacher stopped by to chat and sensing Kelly's nervousness, she gave the following advice:

> *You have to establish yourself as the person in charge from day one. Don't try to be friends with the students and don't worry about being viewed as mean. Start right off with some rules and come down hard on the first person who violates them. Make an example of him or her so that the rest of the students will know that you mean business. This will lead them to respect your authority as a teacher and will prevent lots of problems.*

What is your reaction?

1. Do you agree with this advice?

2. Are there some points that you think are valid?

3. Which points do you agree with?

4. What will you do to establish your authority in the classroom?

Boles and Davenport (1975) emphasize that leadership exists only when the leader–follower relationship is such that the followers accept a particular person as leader. In a classroom context, it is important that learners accept the teacher as the leader. When they do, many problems are prevented. When this acceptance of the teacher as a leader is not present, a perpetual power struggle ensues.

WHAT IS LEADERSHIP?

Simply having a role and a title does not make a person a leader. Perhaps it is most useful to understand that leadership is a process, not a position. It involves skills and abilities that can be applied to a variety of situations (Kouzes and Posner, 1987). Moving toward exercising this important role in the classroom requires an understanding of the essential elements of leadership.

It is useful to begin the search for classroom leadership by reviewing the concept of *lead management* introduced in Chapter 1. This concept has important implications for the role of the leader and it is consistent with studies of leadership. An important element of lead management is the focus it places on the uses of power and control. Effective leaders understand that wise uses of power are important. Leaders do not use power to control; they use it to enable others to act. They give power to others and create a sense of shared ownership (Kouzes and Posner, 1987).

Studies of leadership in areas outside of education can provide us with some insight into the essential ingredients of teacher leadership. Kouzes and Posner (1987) conducted a study of characteristics of successful leaders and their finding are especially useful. One major characteristic they found was that leaders had a deep respect for the aspirations of others.

Another important component of leadership they emphasize is credibility. People must be able to believe in their leaders. A major test of credibility is consistency between words and actions. If behavior is not consistent with stated beliefs, respect and credibility are lost. False promises, deceptions, and inconsistent behavior destroy a person's credibility. When individuals lose their credibility, it is almost impossible to regain it.

The majority of us want leaders who are honest, competent, inspiring, and who have a clear sense of direction. People are drawn to leaders who demonstrate genuine acts of caring. We respect leaders who inspire a commitment by breathing life into our hopes and dreams. It is a part of the job of the leader to help individuals believe they can "win."

Trust is another important dimension of leadership. Leaders are people who are trusted. Trust, however, appears to be a two-way street. It appears that the leader must be the first to trust. When others are viewed as trusted, they can then return that trust to the leader.

Some additional findings on the characteristics of leadership indicate that the leader also needs to be viewed as a competent person, a good model, one who recognizes and supports good ideas, and one who provides for an element of fun. Leaders are also learners; they learn from mistakes as well as successes. Most importantly, Kouzes and Posner contend that leadership can be learned.

These characteristics certainly have important applications for teachers. You need to realize that sharing power with students and creating a sense of ownership in the classroom is important. Demonstrating trust in the ability of students and accepting their ideas and contributions establishes conditions of trust and respect for the teacher as a leader. When you have respect for the aspirations and dreams of the students, you send them the message that they are important. Helping students clarify their goals and communicate the positive expectation that they can attain them creates a positive environment in which learning can occur. This can be a difficult challenge when some students have all but given up hope and have developed helplessness.

An atmosphere of fun needs to be created. This does not mean that everything needs to be fun, but that the opportunity exists and that it does occur. Classrooms can be businesslike and fun places at the same time. You also need to be a model of learning and enthusiasm. If you are not interested in learning, the student will not be interested in learning. If you are bored with teaching, you can expect the students to be bored with learning.

Most importantly, you need to establish your credibility in the classroom. Credibility is developed by demonstrating that you care about the students you teach, by being well-prepared and competent, and by making sure that your actions are consistent with your words. This is directly related to the point made in Chapter 1 that classroom discipline needs to be consistent with the basic goals of the school and the curriculum. If you profess something in the curriculum, it needs to be reflected in the ways you relate to students in the classroom. In developing teacher leadership, consistency and sharing power are especially important.

TEACHER CONSISTENCY

Consistency is an especially important aspect of developing teacher credibility. Teacher consistency in the classroom is something that is often misunderstood. Consistency is not the mindless application of rules. There are several aspects to teacher consistency. One aspect is the consistent application of the rules on a day-to-day basis. Day-to-day consistency means that if a behavior is unacceptable it is always unacceptable. That means that acceptable or unacceptable behavior does not change according to the moods of the teacher, for example, when a teacher excuses inappropriate behavior when in a good mood and is especially severe when in a bad mood. Rule enforcement should be based on established rules and procedures understood by all rather than on the mood of the teacher. Teachers who complain that the class is constantly testing their authority are often those do not have a clear set of classroom standards or enforce rules inconsistently. As a result, students enter the classroom each day uncertain as to the teacher's expectations and feeling they must "test" him or her in order to discover the limits. Then they frequently become angry and hostile when corrected because they believe they are being treated unfairly.

Application of consequences to all students in the classroom is another dimension of teacher consistency. A rule for one student is a rule for all students. A common complaint of students who have persistent behavior problems is that they are not treated the same as other students. Because they have a reputation as a "problem," teachers are quick to punish even their slightest rule violation. High achievers or usually well-behaved students, however, are just as quickly excused for rule violations. This selective enforcement creates hostility not only between teacher and student but also among students. Students resent those who seem to be accorded special favors. Selective enforcement of rules interferes with teacher credibility and undermines teacher leadership.

Teacher consistency also includes consistent application of rewards when students do follow rules, as well as consistent application of consequences when they do not. Consistency in rewarding appropriate behaviors creates a positive environment that emphasizes productive behavior, and it is an essential ingredient in helping students develop self-control. It lets them know that their productive behavior has a payoff.

SHARING POWER AND RESPONSIBILITY

A willingness to share responsibility is another important aspect of teacher leadership. Research indicates that effective schools provide many opportunities for learners to assume responsibility and to participate in making decisions regarding their school. Increased student participation has been found to be associated with higher levels of academic achievement and less disruptive behavior (Rutter, 1983).

Many tasks are involved in operating a classroom, and quite a few are routine and repetitive. Delegating these tasks to students allows the teacher more time to focus on important tasks related to teaching. Additionally, many students enjoy doing them and get much satisfaction out of helping the teacher.

You need to consider the ways you can provide the students you will be teaching with responsibility and ownership in the classroom. Doing this is somewhat easier in the elementary school, where you have the same students all day. It is somewhat more difficult in the middle schools and high schools where you may only have a group of students for one period during the day. However, older students are able to perform more independently and should be allowed opportunities to be involved.

For example, younger children enjoy doing tasks, such as helping clean up the room, that might not be appealing to older students. However, older students can assist in operating audiovisual equipment, working as assistants to the teacher, being in charge of classroom supplies, or being a part of a school governance group that hears and decides cases of student misbehavior.

One activity that teachers of older students have used to get students involved in classroom responsibilities is listing all of those areas in which students can be involved. This list is discussed with the class and they are allowed to apply for one of the jobs. This can take the form of a formal lesson in which students learn how to make a job application. Another approach is that of having the students list their first three choices of jobs. The teacher reviews these and task assignments are then made based on student preferences. Care needs be taken to ensure fairness in assigning the responsibilities. Also, responsibilities can be changed every few weeks so that different students have the opportunity to have some of the favored responsibilities.

Assigning responsibility to students empowers them and helps them develop a sense of belonging. They feel that they are important and that the school belongs to them, not just to the school authorities. Allowing students the opportunity to participate in the operation of the classroom and decision making gives them an opportunity to exercise power in constructive ways. They are then less inclined to try and show their power and importance by challenging the authority of the teacher. Assigning responsibilities to students not only demonstrates to the learners that the teacher has enough confidence to share responsibility and respects their views, it also makes good sense and helps students learn responsibility.

ESTABLISHING AUTHORITY AND LEADERSHIP

One of your most important goals is to establish yourself as an authority in the classroom. Authority is defined as the right to give commands, enforce obedience, or make decisions. Authority may be the result of a position that carries with it certain authority or it may be the influence that results from knowledge or prestige. Authority is an empty concept, however, if others do not recognize it. As a teacher, it is important that students accept your authority or little will be accomplished. The way in which you develop your leadership in the classroom influences student acceptance of your authority.

As you consider how to go about establishing your classroom leadership, it is useful to consider a framework that defines different types of authority and the uses of each type. French and Raven (1959) defined a framework based on the differences between earned authority and ascribed authority. The importance of understanding these different types of authority is emphasized by Boles and Davenport (1975): Teachers need to earn the respect of students. They contend that admiration, affection, liking, and respect for the moral integrity of the teacher form the psychological basis on which student acceptance of teacher leadership is built.

The French and Raven framework defines five different types of authority: expert, referent, legitimate, reward, and coercive. Each of these five types of authority has some application in the classroom. The problem arises when teachers are unaware of the limitations of different types of authority and rely on those that might be least effective in developing teacher leadership. Understanding these different types of authority can help you understand how to apply those concepts of leadership discussed earlier in the chapter.

Legitimate Authority

Some roles carry with them authority regardless of the person filling that role. This type of authority is sometimes called *positional authority*. It is authority that comes with a position and is therefore ascribed or assumed. The person who fills the position is given the "legitimate" right to make certain decisions. For example, the position President of the United States always has the authority or right to make certain decisions and exercise certain powers, regardless of who the person is that occupies that position.

The role of teacher carries a certain amount of legitimate authority. There are decisions and leadership roles that are expected of a person who assumes the position of teacher. This is expected of teachers by the public, the administrators, and, to some extent, the students.

There are, however, some problems related to the uses of legitimate authority in teaching. First of all, unquestioned obedience is not something that is taught or valued in our society. Even the legitimate authority of those in highest offices is frequently challenged. The public does not hesitate to call into question the legitimate authority of the president, elected representatives, or law enforcement officers. In fact, a fundamental purpose of education is to teach students to resist blindly following the leadership of others (Render, Padilla, and Krank, 1988).

Secondly, although authority is conferred on the teacher by state and local school officials, the students have no input in the decision. They have not voluntarily given authority to the teacher. In fact, many of them seem bent on challenging the authority of the teacher. While the lack of student assent may not have been a serious problem in the past, when there might have been more widespread appreciation of the role of the teacher, it can certainly be a problem today. Throughout society the role of teaching is denigrated and criticized. Teachers are often pictured as ineffective, incompetent, poorly educated, and weak. Students who come to school having been immersed in a culture where the authority of teachers is questioned are not likely to view them as having much legitimate authority.

Gender issues have also influenced the legitimate authority of teachers. Teaching has long been regarded as a "feminine profession." For many decades it was one of the few professions women were allowed to enter. The teaching force is still largely female and teaching is still regarded as acceptable for women but somewhat inappropriate for "strong" males. Because our society has been reluctant to grant females leadership roles, the authority ascribed to the role of teacher has traditionally been weak.

Some problems arise because some beginning teachers have higher expectations of their legitimate authority than actually exists. They expect that students will obey simply because they are told to do so by the teacher. As someone who has worked with numerous student teachers in several regions of the country, I have observed the frustration and bitterness that often occurs when a student teacher realizes the limitations of legitimate authority. They cannot understand why students do not listen to them, do not obey their commands, and deliberately challenge their authority. Tauber (1985) states that it can no longer be taken for granted that learners come to school with an automatic respect for teachers' legitimate power. This is one of the issues you must consider as you reflect on your role as a teacher. If you are under the impression that legitimate teacher authority is quite strong and that students will obey you simply because you are the teacher, you need to rethink this perception.

Another difficulty with legitimate authority is that some people interpret it in ways that are harmful to the development of a productive classroom environment. Hoover and Kindsvetter (1997) point out that some people are drawn to teaching because it provides access to power and authority. These may well be individuals with inadequate self-concepts searching for social environments where they can feel significant. This type of individual attempts to use legitimate power in an authoritarian manner that is contrary to the basic goals of education and discipline. This misuse of legitimate authority actually increases problems and makes management and discipline more difficult.

The foregoing discussion, however, does not imply that you cannot use legitimate authority. Legitimate power can be most helpful at the beginning of the school year, when the majority of students enter the classroom with little or no knowledge of the teacher. They are temporarily willing to submit to the legitimate authority of the teacher. They will follow reasonable rules and teacher requests. During this beginning phase, when students are often on their best behavior, legitimate power

ACTIVITY 2-1   TEACHERS NEED MORE AUTHORITY

Some educators claim that the seriousness of discipline in the classroom is related to an erosion of teacher authority. They contend that education needs to return to the time when the authority of the teacher was unquestioned. Students and parents need to understand that the teacher is the authority in the classroom. Individuals who are unwilling to respect the professional judgment of the teacher should go elsewhere. This business of always questioning the judgment of the teacher and pushing the rights of the students must stop. Teachers are hired to do a difficult task and it cannot be done if 30+ students are always clamoring for their "rights."

What do you think?

1. What are the rights of teachers and the rights of students in the classroom? Do some checking on the legal rights of teachers in establishing an educational environment. How can the rights of students and the rights of teachers be balanced?

2. State your position on the issue of teacher authority in the classroom. What should be the boundaries of teacher rights?

---

can be used to establish teacher leadership that is built around earned authority and respect. As students develop their understanding of the teacher, other types of authority begin to replace the legitimate or positional authority of the teacher.

Reward Authority

Another type of authority, one related to legitimate authority, is what is called "reward authority." Reward authority is based on the power to give rewards or incentives that accompanies a given position. The position of teacher grants the person filling that role the authority to provide rewards and benefits to students. There are many ways that teachers give rewards. There are the tangible awards, such as grades, special responsibilities, and privileges. There are social rewards, such as attention, praise, status, and prestige. Teachers are constantly giving out rewards in one form or another. Everyone enjoys getting a reward, and the person who possesses the ability to give rewards has considerable authority. However, like legitimate authority, there are some limits to the reward authority of teachers.

One of the serious limitations is that reward authority is not earned. If the class does not respect the person giving the rewards, the rewards may even become a disincentive to cooperation. For example, teacher praise from an unpopular teacher is something that may be more embarrassing than reinforcing.

A critical aspect of the effective use of reward authority is the way in which the rewards are administered. If they are administered in a fair manner and are given for legitimate efforts, then reward authority is enhanced. However, if the rewards are viewed as only being given to a select few (perhaps only to the teacher's favorites), are given arbitrarily, and are not perceived as linked to legitimate accomplishments, then the authority to give rewards is relatively meaningless. For example, if grades are viewed as arbitrary rewards not linked to genuine achievement, then the credibility of the teacher is undermined and reward authority is lost. Good and Brophy (1997) give some excellent guidelines for making teacher praise effective, and those guidelines can be extended to cover other types of rewards. The following are a selection of some of the guidelines.

A reward:
- Is given in recognition of noteworthy efforts;
- Provides information to the students about their competence and the value of their accomplishments;
- Rewards attainment of specific performance criteria;
- Shows spontaneity, variety, and other signs of credibility;
- Attributes success to effort and ability.

Another potential problem with reward authority relates to the ability to administer rewards desired by the group. Consider grades. There are many students in school who do not place high value on grades. Grades that are not valued or desired are not rewards, and, therefore, do not enhance reward authority. Some new teachers have a difficult time understanding this perception. They were always interested in good grades and would obey teacher and school directives in order to obtain them. In fact, some students ridicule those who work for grades. In this situation, a teacher who attempts to exercise authority and power through the reward of a grade will be frustrated.

One of the serious limitations of reward authority for teachers is that the rewards available for use in the classroom are frequently not those that are most important to students. For example, more prestige and status might be obtained from peers by challenging teacher authority than from following it. In addition, the social rewards of talking with friends or of having fun may be more desirable than the rewards administered by the teacher for attending to school tasks.

Coercive Authority

This is another type of authority linked to legitimate authority. It is the opposite of reward authority. Some positions, such as teaching, carry with them the authority to administer punishment. There are some individuals who enter teaching believing that the only way they can obtain respect and power is through intimidation or coercion. They are quick to remind students that failure to follow their demands will result in swift and sure punishment. Some teachers argue that, given the nature of contemporary society, this is the only type of power and authority respected by students. When individuals with this belief seek ways to improve their classroom management and discipline, they are interested in finding more powerful and effective punishments.

Coercive authority does have some short-term benefits. It usually puts an immediate stop to a behavior. This immediate benefit leads some teachers to conclude that coercive power is the best method for establishing authority in the classroom. However, coercive power has limited potential and undesirable side effects that can be detrimental to the creation of a positive learning climate and the development of self-control.

One such side effect is that a reliance on coercive power frequently creates power struggles between the teacher and students. Students attempt to counter teacher displays of authority by demonstrating that they cannot be intimidated. Some students will resort to passive resistance and other subtle ways of demonstrating power. More serious and destructive side effects are vandalism, assaults, anger, and truancy. The possible benefits of quickly stopping a behavior must be weighed against these other potential outcomes.

This is not intended to imply that coercive power should never be used. However, it should be used only as a last resort, when a student has lost control and it is imperative that a behavior be stopped quickly. Even in this extreme situation, it is likely to be ineffective unless the teacher has the respect of the student. Punishment has maximum impact on behavior when administered by someone who is respected and when the individual believes the punishment is just and fair. If the punishment is viewed as excessively harsh or arbitrary, a negative reaction will occur and the relationship between student and teacher will be harmed.

Expert Authority

When an individual is perceived by a group to be an expert or to have superior knowledge about a subject, the group will give that person authority or power. This is what is called "expert" authority. Because this type of power is earned and is based on respect, the individual possessing such power is in a good position to exercise effective leadership. Teachers who are effective classroom leaders are those who have obtained expert power. Students perceive the teacher as someone who is knowledgeable about the material being presented, possesses good teaching skills, and understands the needs of students. Surveys of student attitudes toward teachers highlight the importance of expert power. For example, the ability to explain and clarify content is high on the list of attributes that learners identify about teachers they like (Tanner, 1978).

Those who are experts often demonstrate several recognizable characteristics. They have confidence and poise when confronting an issue or problem, and their confidence gives confidence to others. In addition, the expert usually has enthusiasm for the topic or task. Because of their enthusiasm and confidence, experts demonstrate a high degree of task persistence and do not give up easily.

New teachers often have difficulty exercising expert power because they are uncertain about their skills and thus do not exhibit confidence and poise. They may have an initial enthusiasm, but it quickly diminishes if things do not go well. Their lack of confidence is also revealed by their hesitant behavior when confronting an unexpected event. Students note these behaviors and begin to lose confidence in the teacher. As a result, they are quick to question teacher authority.

How does one obtain expert power? A beginning point is the completion of a sound, well-balanced teacher preparation program. Teachers need to know their subject as well as the characteristics of learners and how to teach them. Being well prepared is also important. Teachers report that planning gives them immediate psychological rewards in terms of the reduction of uncertainty and an increase in their confidence level (Clark and Peterson, 1986). These feelings are then communicated to learners through the confidence and the certainty of the teacher. It is not surprising, therefore, that there does seem to be a direct connection between the quality of teacher planning and student achievement.

Referent Authority

Individuals who are liked and respected are also given authority. People are willing to follow someone who is perceived to be trustworthy, ethical, and concerned for the welfare of others. This type of authority is what is termed *referent*. Like expert authority, referent authority is earned rather than demanded. Those who aspire to leadership roles must develop referent authority. Even the attempts of experts to lead will be ignored if they are not perceived as ethical and trustworthy.

Referent power emphasizes the importance of teachers who like students and are interested in their welfare. Glasser (1969, 1986) emphasizes the need for caring teachers who create a warm and personal classroom where youngsters feel they belong and where their needs are being met.

Teachers who have negative feelings about learners will not act in ways that will increase their referent authority. Their lack of trust and respect will be communicated to the students in a variety of subtle ways and students will be less likely to trust them or to follow classroom rules and procedures. This is yet another place where you need to engage in self-reflection. What are your views of the nature of students? Do you believe they are inherently good or inherently bad? Do you believe that students are worthy of respect? Are you interested in teaching because of your interest in students? Your honest answers to these questions will help define your potential for developing referent authority in the classroom.

Referent authority is especially important at the secondary level. A common reason for misbehavior cited by high school students is that they did not perceive the teacher as respectful or caring. Their behavior is basically a way of retaliating by demonstrating little respect for the teacher.

A teacher can work to develop referent power in several ways. Simple things like learning the names of the students, providing genuine encouragement and praise, and avoiding sarcasm are important. Fairness in testing and grading is an essential element.

Tests and test items designed to "trick" students rather than to measure important learning outcomes results in a loss of respect.

In summary, the beginning point for developing authority and power in the classroom is for the teacher to demonstrate expertise and concern for the needs of students. Building your leadership around the concepts of expert and referent authority actually increases the legitimate authority of the teacher and increases the impact of reward and coercive authority. Being well prepared, demonstrating good teaching approaches, being sensitive to student needs, treating students with respect, demonstrating fairness, and consistency are important components in increasing referent and expert authority.

SHARING POWER THROUGH THE ESTABLISHMENT OF CLASSROOM RULES

Reasonable rules are an important part of any social situation. Whenever two or more people come together they must reach some agreement about appropriate behavior. The rules might be in the form of unwritten expectations assumed by both parties, or they may take a more concrete verbal or written form. Unwritten expectations, however, can lead to disagreement and conflict. This is especially true in classroom situations where there are many individuals with different expectations and understandings. Therefore, it is especially important for the teacher to spend considerable time at the beginning of the year establishing classroom rules and expectations. The way the teacher does this is an important component in developing a leadership style.

One of the first choices you will encounter at the beginning of a school year is that of establishing rules that will govern the social interaction in the classroom. One choice is to do this in an authoritarian way (Canter and Canter, 1976). This style is based on legitimate, reward, and coercive authority. You set the rules, communicate them to learners, and tell them what will happen if they follow the rules and what will happen if they do not. In essence, this style says to the students: "I am the boss. I expect you to follow rules, and if you do not, you will be punished. If you conform to my expectations, you will be rewarded."

This approach has some appeal because it does provide you with a sense of security and control. You can take time before entering the classroom to reflect on the rules that you think you need and you can plan how to communicate them clearly to students. In addition, the approach does not take much class time to accomplish and teacher authority can be communicated from the very beginning.

Studies have shown that this approach can increase the amount of work produced by students. Those who are successful in communicating to learners in a firm, but positive, manner that they mean business and will not tolerate disturbances find this approach useful in promoting on-task behavior. A potential problem, however, is that the authoritarian approach also seems to prompt student aggression toward the teacher (Mendler and Curwin, 1983).

Another option in establishing classroom rules is the democratic approach. This method involves shared decision making. It allows students a voice in establishing rules. This choice is based more on the exercise of referent, expert, and legitimate authority. There are some important educational benefits from using the democratic approach to rule setting.

The democratic approach has the advantage of giving students at least partial ownership of the rules, which in turn is more likely to develop a commitment to follow the rules. It also communicates to learners a respect for their needs and their ideas. In addition, the democratic approach to the establishment of classroom rules is more consistent with the democratic goals of education. There is some support from research that indicates that students in democratically oriented classrooms exhibit higher academic output and have more positive attitudes toward the teacher. Finally, the democratic approach provides increased opportunities for helping students learn essential elements of self-control.

The democratic approach does have some disadvantages. It is time-consuming and can cause teacher anxiety. Teachers worry: What if the class does not establish appropriate rules? You need to have some confidence in the motivation and judgment of the students. Most of them want a positive and productive classroom. If they believe that you trust them, they will take the task seriously. In addition, if there are a couple of rules that you simply must have in your classroom, announce them up front. Be open and tell them that, for you to be comfortable, you must have these rules. Students generally accept that as a part of the legitimate authority of the teacher. Inexperienced teachers sometimes lack confidence and are hesitant about using the democratic approach. The advantages, however, outweigh the problems. Implementing this approach does not mean that teachers abdicate responsibility.

Several basic steps can be followed when establishing classroom rules, regardless of the management style that you choose in establishing them. Those steps are rule specification, rule clarification, rule practice, and rule monitoring. Including these four steps can help ensure that behavioral expectations are clear and understood by all learners. These steps help prevent problems and communicate to students that you take the rules very seriously.

Rule Specification

Rule specification is the process of deciding on classroom rules. For the authoritarian teacher, rule specification is his or her responsibility. Rules are determined by the teacher and then shared with the students. In contrast, the democratic teacher shares the rule specification task with students. Mendler and Curwin (1983) recommend the social contract approach as a democratic rule specification method. A social contract is an agreement on a set of rules reached by group consensus. Three types of rules are included in the development of the social contract. The first type are the rules the teacher must have, the second type the rules the students have for each other, the third type are rules for the teacher. The social contract method of rule specification includes the following steps:

1. The teacher states the rules that must be included that are nonnegotiable.
2. Small groups of class members discuss and propose rules that they think are needed in order for them to work together productively.
3. All proposed rules are discussed and voted on by the entire class. Group consensus is preferred but if that is not possible, at least two-thirds of the class should agree on the rule before it is adopted.
4. Small groups discuss and propose rules for the teacher.
5. Rules for the teacher are discussed. If a rule is inappropriate or interferes with the authority of the teacher to conduct the classroom in an appropriate manner, the teacher can exercise veto power.
6. Possible consequences for all rules are then discussed. Either the teacher or the students may propose consequences for rule violation. The teacher must approve the consequences and has the right to veto any consequences that are dangerous or illegal.

Some teachers are uncomfortable with the idea of allowing students to set rules, concerned that students will establish unreasonable rules. However, experience with the procedure indicates that students usually take the process seriously and propose reasonable rules for the teacher. This procedure demonstrates that rules are for everyone. It also provides you with insight into student views of fairness and justice. Some of the behaviors they consider offensive may not have occurred to the teacher. For example, secondary students have established rules relating to teacher's respecting their privacy, letting the class out on time so that they have time to go to their locker or the next class on time, avoiding the use of "put-downs" or sarcasm, giving sufficient time to allow students to plan for the completion of time-consuming projects. Identifying these concerns at the beginning of the school year helps the teacher to avoid doing things that are likely to create student hostility. In addition, allowing students to specify rules for the teacher communicates to them that the teacher recognizes the value of rules and allows the teacher an opportunity to model the process of exercising self-control and accepting consequences when rules are violated.

Rule Clarification

The purpose of rule clarification is to make sure that all learners understand what a rule means and what constitutes appropriate and inappropriate behavior. An important component of rule clarification is to ensure that each rule is stated in a clear and concise manner. When possible, a rule should state what learners should do rather than what they should not do. For example, it is more productive to state that "we raise our hand before talking," rather than "we do not talk out of turn."

ACTIVITY 2-2   RULES FOR THE TEACHER

Allowing students the opportunity to establish rules for the teacher is not very common. Many teachers are quite nervous about doing so and believe that the authority of the teacher would be undermined if students are allowed this privilege. They are concerned that students would make rules that would make the job of teaching and managing the classroom more difficult.

What do you think?

1. What is your position on the issue?

2. What is your greatest fear about doing this in the classroom?

3. Do you think the age and the maturity of the students is a factor?

4. What types of rules do you think would be appropriate for students to develop for the teacher?

Each rule then should be then discussed and ambiguous terms removed or defined. Students should then identify acceptable and unacceptable examples of behavior for each rule. Taking time for rule clarification helps eliminate a common excuse for misbehavior, "I didn't understand."

Rule Practice

Rules, like anything else, require a certain amount of practice. Time should be taken to practice the rules. Rule practice is generally more important for young learners and for rules that might be vague or unfamiliar. For example, secondary students probably do not need to practice how to raise their hand if they want to make a contribution to the class discussion. However, they will need to practice certain safe practices in physical education, science, and some vocational classes.

A concluding step in rule practice might be for the students to take a short test on the rules. One junior high science teacher identifies, clarifies, and practices rules on the first day of school and gives a quiz on the rules on the second day. The quiz is kept short and simple so that all learners will pass all items. The teacher keeps these tests on file. Students who profess ignorance of the rules are then shown their test.

Rule Monitoring

Monitoring is an important component in making sure that the rules become meaningful and are followed. Sometimes teachers do not monitor rules very closely or

TABLE 2-1 **Establishing Teacher Leadership**

Task	Procedure for Accomplishing Task

1. Establishing Expert Authority
   1.1 In planning and organization
   1.2 Knowledge of subject
   1.3 Knowledge of teaching
   1.4 Awareness of needs of student
   1.5 Managing the classroom	

2. Establishing Referent Authority
   2.1 Communicating respect for students
   2.2 Creating positive classroom environment
   2.3 Communicating trust
   2.4 Implementing fairness
   2.5 Providing encouragement	

3. Establishing Rules and Procedures
   3.1 Rules that I Need:
   3.2 How will I:
       3.2.1 Determine rules
       3.2.2 Clarify rules
       3.2.3 Practice rules	

follow up rule violations with consequences. As a result, students choose to violate classroom rules because the probability of the teacher taking action is slight. The rules then become meaningless and respect for the teacher and the rules are lost. Teacher monitoring of the rules is especially critical during the first few weeks of the school year (Emmer et al., 1982). It is important that the teacher provide positive reinforcement and rewards when the rules are followed, as well as follow through with appropriate consequences when rules are violated.

SUMMARY

Establishing teacher leadership is one of the most important aspects of developing a classroom where problems are prevented and, when they do arise, learners are willing to follow the directives of the teacher. Leadership in the classroom is something that teachers must earn. It comes through the process of interacting with students over the course of the school year, not simply because of the position of "teacher." Many approaches suggested by various authorities for dealing with discipline problems in the classroom will be of limited usefulness if the teacher has not established a positive leadership style.

An important component for developing positive leadership is the way the teacher uses power and establishes authority. A teacher who approaches the classroom with confidence and enthusiasm and is well prepared develops expert authority. Demonstrating that you are a fair and trustworthy individual concerned about the students in your classroom develops referent authority. Referent and expert authority working together form a powerful foundation for teacher leadership.

The style you choose in establishing classroom rules also contributes to your leadership in the classroom. Although it may create some anxiety, the democratic approach is recommended because it does have some important benefits. A good method for implementing the democratic approach is the social contract method.

Once rules have been specified, it is important not to overlook the rule clarification and rule practice steps. These steps help prevent misunderstandings and communicate the importance of rules.

Finally, it is important that you are consistent in enforcing the rules for all students. You need to follow through on both rewards for appropriate behavior and consequences for inappropriate actions.

SUGGESTED APPLICATIONS

1. An understanding of your beliefs, attitudes, and values is important as you seek to become a classroom leader. Take a few minutes to perform a self-analysis. Why do you want to become a teacher? What do you find attractive about teaching? What are your beliefs regarding students? Do you believe that students are capable of learning self-control? How do you view the role of the teacher in managing the classroom? What do you worry about most as you consider managing the classroom?

2. Think back to when you were a student. Who were the teachers you respected the most and those you respected the least? How does each of these categories fit with the definitions of different types of authority? What specific things did teachers do to develop their expert and referent authority?

3. Develop a lesson plan outlining how you will go about establishing classroom rules, clarifying the rules, and practicing the rules. Identify any rules that are non-negotiable that you will require.

4. Brainstorm tasks or responsibilities that students can perform in your classroom. Share your ideas with other teachers and develop a list.

SUGGESTED READINGS

Boles, H. W. and Davenport, J. A. (1975). *Introduction to educational leadership.* New York: Harper & Row.

Canter, L. and Canter, M. (1976). *Assertive discipline: A take charge approach for today's educator.* Santa Monica, CA: Canter and Associates.

Clark, C. M. and Peterson, P. L. (1986). "Teacher's thought processes." In *Handbook of research and teaching,* 3rd Ed. M. C. Wittrock, (ed.). New York: Macmillan, pp. 255–296.

Cronbach, L. J. (1977). *Educational psychology.* New York: Harcourt, Brace, and Jovanovich.

Emmer, E., Evertson, C., Sanford, J., Clements, B. and Worsham, W. (1982). *Organizing and managing the junior high school classroom.* Austin, TX: Research and Development Center for Teacher Education, University of Texas.

French, J. R. P. and Raven, B. H. (1959). "The bases of social power." In *Studies in social power,* D. Cartwright (ed.) Ann Arbor: University of Michigan Press.

Glasser, W. (1986). *Control theory in the classroom.* New York: Harper & Row.

Glasser, W. (1969). *Schools without failure.* New York: Harper & Row.

Good, T. L. & Brophy, J. E. (1997). *Looking in classrooms* (7th Ed.). New York: Longman.

Hoover, R. L. & Kindsvetter, R. (1997). *Democratic discipline: Foundation and practice.* Columbus, OH: Merrill.

Kouzes, J. L. & Posner, B. Z. (1987). *The leadership challenge: How to get extraordinary things done in organizations.* San Francisco, CA: Jossey-Bass.

Mendler, A. N. and Curwin, R. L. (1983). *Taking charge in the classroom: A practical guide to effective discipline.* Reston, VA: Reston.

Render, G. F., Padilla, J. M. and Krank, H. M. (1988). *Self-esteem and assertive discipline: What educators need to know.* Paper presented at the annual meeting of the Association for Humanistic Education, Paducah, KY.

Rutter, M. (1983). "School effects on pupil progress: Research findings and policy implications." In *Handbook of Teaching and Policy.* L. Shulman and G. Sykes (eds.) New York: Longman.

Soar, R. S. and Soar, R. M. (1987). "Classroom climate." In *The international encyclopedia of teaching and teacher education.* M. J. Dunkin (ed.). New York: Pergamon.

Tanner, L. N. (1978). *Classroom Discipline for Effective Teaching and Learning.* New York: Holt, Rinehart & Winston.

Tauber, R. T. (1985). "Power bases: Their application to classroom and school management," *Journal of Education for Teaching* 11(2), 133–144.

3 Motivation and Discipline

Chapter Objectives

After reading this chapter you should be able to:

- List basic motivational factors
- Define the relationship between student needs and achievement motivation
- State how teacher expectations influence student motivation
- Explain how to use success to increase student motivation
- Define how to alter student perceptions of the difficulty of a task

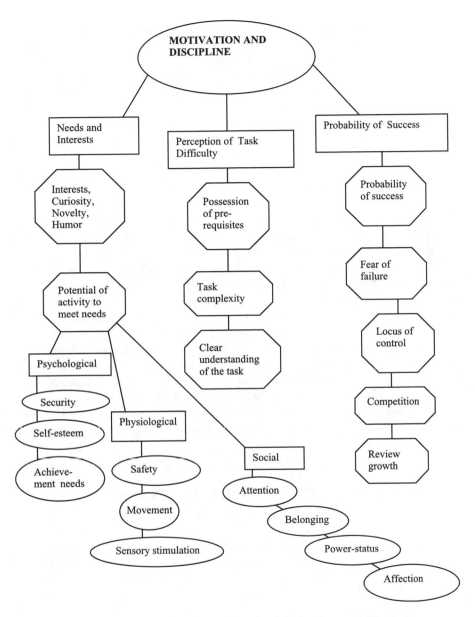

FIGURE 3-1   **Graphic Organizer for Motivation and Discipline**

What makes a student want to learn? Why do some students start work promptly and others do not? Why are some students interested in the content we teach and others are not? Why do some students have a great deal of task persistence while others give up quickly? What energizes and directs student actions? These are questions related to human motivation that are of great interest to teachers. Read the discipline scenario below with these questions in mind.

It is obvious that Richard is not energized and his actions are not directed toward learning. Richard has what most teachers would call "a motivation problem." Many teachers can identify a "Richard" in their class. Passive, unmotivated youngsters are often left alone because they are quiet and do not interfere with others. Other unmotivated students may be aggressive and disruptive. Regardless of the pattern, lack of motivation toward school tasks is a serious educational issue that will certainly lead to inappropriate behavior that must be responded to by the teacher. Motivation questions are some of the most important ones that need to be addressed as you seek to develop an environment that facilitates self-control.

A common teacher statement is that contemporary students do not seem to be as motivated as those in the past. What they really mean is that individuals do not seem motivated to perform those tasks required of them in school. There is really no such thing as an unmotivated person. Everyone is motivated to do something; it just may not be in the direction of school tasks. Slavin (1994) puts this in proper perspective when he notes that it is not your task to try and increase student motivation. Rather, it is your task to discover, initiate, and sustain students' motivation to learn. In other words, you need to know what is motivating to the students you are teaching and how to use that information to initiate, sustain, and direct it toward school tasks.

Addressing motivational questions may lead us in some uncomfortable directions. It may be discovered that what is termed "lack of motivation" is actually related

---

DISCIPLINE SCENARIO 3-1 **The Unmotivated Student**

Richard was not an especially troublesome student. He just sat and did not work. When assignments were given, he would daydream or play with objects on his desk. Sometimes he would put his head on his desk and close his eyes. When his work was turned in, the most the teacher could expect was to see his name scribbled at the top of the paper. No matter how hard the teacher tried, Richard just did not seem to have the least interest in learning.

What is your reaction?

1. How would you respond to Richard?

2. What might be some possible causes for Richard's lack of motivation?

3. Do you think this is a common problem?

ACTIVITY 3-1   WHAT MOTIVATES YOU?

Before continuing your reading, take time to reflect on your motivation. Answer the following questions and then see if you can identify principles of motivation that might be applied to others.

1. What are the things that interest or motivate you?

2. Where did you get that interest or motivation?

3. Think of a teacher that was successful in motivating you. Why was this teacher successful with you?

4. Think of a teacher who was unsuccessful in motivating you. Why were you not inspired to work?

5. From these reflections, what would be one or more statements you would make about motivation?

to poor teaching, an irrelevant curriculum, or a threatening classroom environment. While it may be popular to place the blame on the students for the apparent lack of motivation and label it "their problem," this is a simplistic view that interferes with the search for productive solutions.

All teachers dream of that eager class of cooperative students who find the subject fascinating. However, this is not a situation that happens merely by wishing it were so. In fact, your actions will have a major influence on the extent to which you approach this ideal. Achieving anything near this state requires a great deal of knowledge, effort, and planning. Unfortunately, motivation concerns must be addressed anew with each group of learners. What might be motivating for one group may be met with indifference by another. The motivational issue is complex, and there are no easy answers. However, research has helped uncover some of the variables that can be addressed. Understanding those variables and applying them to specific classroom problems can help you move toward making that elusive dream of a motivated and eager group of learners more likely.

MOTIVATIONAL VARIABLES

Motivation to learn includes a number of variables, such as personality, goal orientation, curiosity, past experiences, anxiety, needs and wants, self-concept, expectations and attributions of success and failure, and predictions of success or failure (Slavin, 1994). A framework for understanding how these variables interact is to begin by looking at a combination of two forces: the value of the goal to be achieved and the perceived probability of being successful in attaining it (Woolfolk, 1998). Remember that you need to consider these from the perspectives of the student, not yours. For example, you may place great value on learning the kings and queens of England. However, unless the students view that as a worthwhile goal, they will not be motivated to achieve it. In addition, you may have confidence in your ability to learn this sequence of people and therefore estimate a high probability of success in achieving this goal. Many students, especially those with a history of difficult school experiences, would make a low estimate of the probability of success. Because they believe that they have little chance for success, they would be less likely to attempt the task or would give up very quickly when faced with difficulty.

Another related variable that influences motivation is the perceived difficulty of the task. Although a goal might be perceived as one of value, and a person might believe that they can ultimately achieve success, motivation to begin the task can be diminished if it is believed that success would require too much effort. This is especially true as we consider alternative activities that might be used to accomplish the same goal. Individuals only have a limited amount of time and energy and we are interested in obtaining the greatest amount of satisfaction from the least amount of effort. The economic term *opportunity cost* is an accurate way of describing this state. When we choose one option, other options are eliminated. It is human nature to choose the option that appears to have the greatest potential benefit at the lowest possible cost. For example, popularity might be a very attractive goal for a student. However, if the student believes that popularity would be very difficult to achieve through academic accomplishments, a nonacademic route, such as being the class clown, might be the choice.

Think back to the description of Richard in Discipline Scenario 3-1. (Yes, Richard was a real student.) His apparent lack of motivation for academic tasks might have stemmed from a perception that the tasks were unimportant, uninteresting, or did not meet any of his needs. Perhaps, he was overwhelmed with the complexity of the tasks and thought they would require too much effort. He might have had a low estimate of the probability of success and therefore did not even try. In Richard's case, a conversation with him revealed that he was simply not interested in the work he was being asked to complete and did not think he needed to learn it. What would you do to try and direct Richard's motivation toward school tasks? The remaining sections of this chapter take each of the three motivational factors, discuss them, and provide suggestions for classroom applications.

VALUING LEARNING GOALS

One approach is to help the students clarify their understanding of the importance of learning and help them understand the importance of school tasks. This is what might be called "achievement motivation." Achievement motivation is the desire to accomplish a goal. Building achievement motivation requires that you obtain some knowledge of the needs and interests of the students you are teaching. Students will be more likely to engage in activities that they believe have the potential for fulfilling unmet needs or activities that are interesting to them.

Needs and Interests

There is a direct link between need fulfillment and motivation. Time and energy are geared toward those activities that appear to have potential for meeting needs or that are intrinsically interesting. There is also a connection between need fulfillment and discipline problems. Students who feel that their needs are being met in the classroom seldom cause discipline problems because interfering with something that is meeting a need is contrary to their self-interest. Glasser (1986) emphasizes this point in his description of a good school: "A good school could be defined as a place where almost all students believe that if they do some work, they will be able to satisfy their needs enough so that it makes sense to keep working (p. 15)." His contention is that many school problems stem from the false assumption that all students value what is taught and, therefore, the school does not need to take into account whether or not the experience is satisfying.

There are many ways that needs can be categorized. For our purposes, needs are divided into three groups: physiological, psychological, and social. Although they are discussed separately, in reality they are interrelated.

Physiological Needs
Physiological needs are fundamental needs that must be accommodated before any other needs can be addressed. If a student's physiological needs are not met, it is almost impossible for individuals to be motivated toward any activity other than the fulfillment of those unmet needs. These physiological needs are the need for food, rest, comfort, freedom from illness, movement, and stimulation of the senses. Although some of these needs may be beyond the teacher's control, understanding that these factors may cause discipline problems can help you search for the apparent lack of motivation in some of your students.

It is unfortunate, but the fact is that many youngsters come to school with inadequate nutrition. The popularity of junk food has contributed greatly to this problem, and it is not one that is confined to the impoverished. Not only is it difficult for malnourished youngsters to stay on-task, but, according to research, malnutrition plays an important role in behavior disorders and violence (Schauss, 1985). An understanding of the crucial role of this physiological need led to the establishment of free breakfast and lunch programs in schools. Also, nutritional therapy involving the use of vitamin and mineral supplements has been found to have significant positive effects on the behavior of some youngsters. Note, though, that only trained and licensed health specialists should do the testing and prescribing of treatment.

Teachers occasionally forget that students, especially younger ones, need to move and be mobile. It is physically impossible for some youngsters to sit still for extended periods of time. Unrealistic expectations or poorly planned schedules will surely give rise to discipline problems. For example, I observed a first-grade class in which the teacher expected students to stay in their seats doing a worksheet for 45 minutes. When the inevitable restlessness occurred, the teacher became upset and punished the class for violating the out-of-seat rule. While the rule governing movement around the classroom was reasonable, the expectation that young children could remain at their desks working on one task for 45 minutes was not. The problem was not with the students, but with the teacher's planning and organization.

In another school, primary grade children arrived by bus 30 minutes before the start of school. They were expected to sit quietly in the cafeteria until the start of school and then spend two to three hours working on academic tasks with little opportunity for physical movement or exercise. It was not surprising that many students demonstrated off-task behaviors during the latter part of the morning. Wise teachers provided opportunities for controlled movement and had much more satisfying and productive classrooms.

The comfort of learners is another aspect of the physiological dimension that needs to be considered. The advent of climate control and uniform lighting has led to the assumption that the comfort dimension has been met. However, other aspects of the classroom environment may cause discomfort and therefore interfere with learning. A typical problem involves the work area. Many teachers forget how uncomfortable it can be to sit in typical classroom furniture for an extended period of time. This is often a problem in secondary schools where there is less a tradition of allowing students to move around during lessons. Other problems that can cause discomfort relate to the type of classroom lighting, the density of students in the classroom, wobbly desks, or inadequate work areas. These conditions interfere with the students' ability to work on a task for any length of time. The resulting physical discomfort will demand relief. If not met, this relief will often take the form of disruptive behavior.

All individuals have a need for sensory stimulation so that the brain has something to process. In severe cases of sensory deprivation, individuals may begin to hallucinate. Sensory deprivation is a very painful experience. For example, when I sit in a physician's waiting room with nothing to do, I get a severe headache. Sensory deprivation leads to boredom, and there are few enemies of motivation more serious than boredom. Boredom demands sensory stimulation and too often that stimulation will take the form of behavior that you will find unacceptable.

Psychological Needs

All individuals have emotional and psychological needs. We all want to be accepted, loved, respected, feel significant and worthwhile, and feel psychologically secure. Glasser (1969) points out that the school is one of the few places where learners have an opportunity to feel significant and important. Teachers and schools that work hard helping learners feel significant and important discover that even the most difficult students can develop a commitment to school and an excitement about learning.

One of the major psychological needs is that of security, a need to feel safe. This includes helping students feel safe from physical and psychological danger. Unfortunately, physical safety has become a serious problem in some schools. Some secondary schools have had to install metal detectors and implement tight security measures in order to eliminate weapons from the school. In those schools where fear of physical harm is present, learning will be seriously hindered.

A more serious problem in many classrooms is the threat of psychological harm. This type of threat includes ridicule, verbal assaults, sarcasm, fear of failure, and a lack of respect. In some classrooms, every mistake is turned into a major failure and students are afraid to try something new or take risks. Psychological intimidation creates a level of anxiety that blocks learning. Students need to feel that they are entering a place where they will be physically and emotionally secure and where they are accepted as worthwhile. The difficulty is separating the individual from the behavior. Although some students behave in ways that are unacceptable, you still need to communicate to them that you still accept them as a worthwhile person that deserves to be treated with respect. Secondary students often indicate that lack of respect by the teacher is one of the major reasons for their misbehavior.

Self-esteem needs are critical psychological needs that must be taken into account. Self-esteem is the self-portrait that individuals have in their mind, a set of subjective beliefs about the value of self. Everyone has a need for a positive personal sense of identity, worth, adequacy, and competence. This self-portrait is learned in the "mirror of others." That is, the way others respond to us reveals what they think of us and therefore builds this subjective self-portrait. Because the teacher is an important "other," your response to each student is critical in helping students develop positive self-esteem.

Understanding the importance of the teacher in meeting the self-esteem needs of students underscores the importance of your expectations for students. Teachers are significant others for many students and your treatment of them can have a powerful impact. If your reaction to students communicates a low expectation of success or ability, then the student is likely to receive the message that they are less able than others. This will, in turn, influence their motivation and task persistence. A model developed by Good and Brophy (1997) indicates how the process works.

1. Through early experiences with a student the teacher forms expectations for the student's achievement and behavior.
2. The teacher behavior toward the student reflects these expectations.
3. This behavior sends a subtle message to the student concerning what the teacher expects of him or her.
4. When this behavior pattern persists over some length of time and the student does not seek to actively refute these expectations, then he or she begins to believe the expectations reflect an accurate view of his or her ability. This influences self-esteem, achievement motivation, and classroom conduct.

5. The behavior of the student then confirms and reinforces the original teacher expectations.
6. High expectation students are led to achieve at or near their potential, but low expectation students perform less well than they could have if they were treated differently.

The self-esteem of individuals serves as a guide to their behavior and their response to different situations. High self-esteem individuals tend to approach a task quite differently than low self-esteem individuals. High self-esteem individuals usually have more confidence and expectation of success and are willing to take more risks. Low self-esteem individuals demonstrate more anxiety, stress, and apathy when approaching a new task.

The importance of self-esteem in student behavior and achievement makes it critically important that you thoughtfully reflect on your expectations and the impact of your actions on students. Do you believe some students will misbehave? Do you believe that some either cannot or will not work to achieve success? What has influenced your perceptions of the students? Are the expectations realistic or are they based on factors such as ethnicity, gender, and social status? What might you do to determine if your expectations are influencing student self-esteem in a negative way?

Success experiences are another important component in building a positive image of self. It is through success, not failure, that a sense of adequacy and competence is developed. Unfortunately, some teachers seem to have the notion that failure is somehow "good" because it prepares students for the frustrations of life. The best way to prepare individuals for the difficulties they may experience in life is to provide them with a great deal of success and a strong self-image. Occasional failure can then be tolerated. You should be concerned with providing many success experiences, rather than many failures. You need to remember that everyone, especially those who are not successful in school, has self-esteem needs. If a student is unable to develop a sense of adequacy, competence, and power through productive behavior in school, other means of meeting this need will be pursued. Some of those means might involve behavior that you do not want.

Social Needs

The classroom is a social setting, and a considerable amount of student behavior can be explained as an effort by students to be accepted and belong to a significant group. An understanding of the social needs of students helps you understand the importance of the peer group. Peer group norms and sanctions counter to those held by the teacher can frustrate the best of intentions. Accommodating social needs in the classroom can prevent many problems.

Dreikurs (1968) considers the need to belong one of the most basic of human needs. This need becomes especially acute during adolescence. Adolescents spend a considerable amount of time worrying about acceptance and striving to become a part of the in group. When youngsters are frustrated in their attempts to belong through positive and constructive ways, they may develop what Dreikurs calls "mistaken goals," attention-getting, power, revenge, and withdrawal. Dreikurs emphasizes that everyone wants to receive attention and feel in control of events. If a person has difficulty getting attention through constructive approaches, then they turn to what Driekurs would call the "mistaken" goal of using unacceptable behavior to get attention. If a student feels powerless to control the events and the social climate of the classroom, the student may turn to the "mistaken" goal of gaining attention by challenging the authority of the teacher or by intimidating other students in the class. When students become totally frustrated and feel that everyone is opposed to them, they may turn to revenge as a goal: striving to make others feel as hurt and frustrated as they do. Other students experiencing these high levels of frustration may attempt to withdraw from the situation by trying to convince others that they simply cannot succeed.

A great deal of behavior that you feel is inappropriate in the classroom can be explained by understanding the goals that students might be pursuing. Are the students seeking attention? Do they feel powerless? Are they striking out to try and hurt someone in order to get revenge for their own feelings of hurt? Are they displaying inadequacies in order to convince others to leave them alone? Finding ways of helping students belong and be accepted as a part of a group can help students meet these goals in constructive ways.

Love and affection are powerful social needs that influence all individuals. Everyone needs to feel that someone cares. Unfortunately, changes in contemporary society often make it difficult for a student to feel loved. The mobility of society often separates youngsters from an extended family that can communicate a sense of love. The increase in one-parent families removes another source of love. The employment of both parents may leave them little energy to show the affection and love desired by an individual. These circumstances do not always result in a youngster feeling a need for love, but they can contribute to this need in many students.

It is very difficult for a teacher to meet the needs of youngsters for love and affection. The teacher cannot become a surrogate parent. However, this does not remove the need for the teacher to become aware of this powerful force and to try and accommodate it in the classroom. Communicating a sense of caring and affection for youngsters can pay tremendous dividends in fewer discipline problems and increased achievement.

It is important to note that youngsters interpret firm and fair discipline as a sign of caring, as a sign that someone cares enough to take an interest in their welfare and even tell them "no." Dreikurs (1968) asks the question: Whom do we discipline? He answers that we discipline those we love; the others we leave alone. It is because we care about someone and his or her ability to achieve a satisfying and productive life that we discipline.

This echoes the major purpose of discipline: We use it to help students learn self-control. Remember, however, that it is firm and fair discipline that keeps concern for the student at the forefront, not arbitrary and harsh discipline administered in order to meet the needs of the teacher.

Student Interests

All individuals have certain interests apart from those that might be seen as meeting personal needs. If these interests can be identified and classroom tasks structured so that the content is related to these interests, more than likely students will be motivated. For example, I once had great success increasing the reading ability of a group of young boys by relating the need for reading ability to prepare for taking a driver's license examination.

Understanding the "identification motive" can help us relate school to individual interests. People attempt to increase their similarity, or identification, with those they perceive to be important individuals in command of desirable resources, such as attractiveness, popularity, money, status, and power. The identification motive helps explain why youngsters seek to dress, talk, and act like popular musicians or athletes. These individuals are seen as having command of resources that are attractive to the students. Unfortunately, these identification models are not always those who have gained their status through intellectual achievement.

Things that are novel or different can also stimulate interest. The unusual or unexpected will attract interest for at least a short time. Remember, though, that the value of novelty in motivation is rather short-lived. The novelty will soon fade unless other interests and needs are included in the learning task.

ACCOMMODATING NEEDS AND INTERESTS IN THE CLASSROOM

Accommodating the needs and interests of students demands considerable time and effort on the part of the teacher. However, the rewards of doing so far outweigh the costs. Not only will discipline problems be prevented, but the classroom will be a more rewarding and exciting place to work. One of the advantages of teaching is that teachers can structure their own work environment to include excitement and novelty. Teachers who take advantage of this opportunity find themselves more satisfied with their job.

You should consider several factors when accommodating the physiological needs of the learners. First of all, the environment needs to be safe and comfortable. It is a reality that many youngsters start the school day with fear of physical assault. Students who fear assault either in school or on their way to and from school will have difficulty approaching school tasks. Completing schoolwork is relatively unimportant when compared to the need to survive.

Creating a safe school generally requires the cooperation of the entire community as well as the entire school. It sometimes takes a great deal of effort and extra work on the part of the school staff to identify and correct problem areas. The community may need to be made aware of problems that occur off school grounds and its assistance requested.

The class schedule should be examined to make sure that there is an appropriate balance of passive and active lesson components so that the need for movement can

ACTIVITY 3-2   SCHOOL VIOLENCE

School safety has become a serious concern for educators during the past decade. A number of articles have appeared in the news media concerning crime and violence in the schools.

1. How serious do you think the problem really is?

2. Why do you think there is a problem of violence in the schools?

3. What can be done to prevent violence in the schools?

4. Does the issue of violence in the schools frighten you as a future teacher?

5. What can you do to prepare yourself for a potentially violent confrontation?

---

be met. The environment needs to be checked to make sure that temperature and light are satisfactory in all parts of the classroom. Workspaces should be inspected to ensure that students are able to sit comfortably, work on a stable surface, and see the teaching stations.

You need to design the classroom environment so that there is some sensory stimulation and plan lessons with the need for sensory stimulation in mind. Bulletin boards can be used to stimulate the senses through pictures and artifacts and by posing unanswered questions. Thought-provoking displays or "centers," where individuals can touch and manipulate objects or conduct experiments, also provide stimulation. Changing from listening to responding or questioning and changing the configuration of the group from large to small are simple ways that the need for sensory stimulation can be met.

After the physiological needs are accommodated, the teacher then needs to consider how to meet the psychological needs. A major ingredient in creating a safe and productive psychological climate is the attitude of the teacher. Do you accept all of the youngsters in the class? Do you show respect for all learners, even those who are problems? Do you believe that all of the learners are capable of learning and hold high expectations for them? It is imperative that you create an environment that is psychologically safe and supportive in which students feel free to make mistakes and to experiment.

The need for love and affection can be accommodated in the classroom by listening nonjudgmentally to students, being aware of their accomplishments, both in and out of the classroom, remembering personal events such as birth dates, and by letting a disciplined student know that while you cannot accept inappropriate behavior, you are not rejecting him or her as a person.

Some students do not understand how to become a part of the group. They may not understand that their behavior actually interferes with their goal of gaining acceptance. In these cases you have a special responsibility to help students see the link between what they do and how others view them. Some individualized instruction and personal counseling might be needed in order for them to begin to understand how to behave in ways that will gain acceptance from others. Role-playing situations can be used to help the class understand how it feels to be left out and to help them learn how to make others feel that they belong.

Interests of the students need to be identified so that they can be integrated into the classroom curriculum. Administering an interest inventory and becoming personally interested in each student are important ways of finding out what is of interest for each student.

The identification motive can be taken into account in a variety of ways. First of all, the school should seek to accept, as much as possible, the different dress and grooming styles of youngsters. Dress and grooming standards should be related to those things that interfere with the learning process. School authorities that ignore the identification motive when seeking to enforce dress standards are unknowingly casting the school as a place out of touch with contemporary reality. Capricious and arbitrary standards of dress and grooming often communicate to students that the authorities are more concerned with the exercise of power than with the needs of learners. Some individuals will challenge standards just for the sake of proving their independence. It is unfortunate that so many schools waste a considerable amount of time trying to control individual behavior in ways that do not improve learning.

The initial attention of learners can be captured by beginning with something that is novel or unique, using humor, or by introducing lessons in unpredictable ways. The problem with these techniques is that learners may focus more on the introductory event than on the lesson. After capturing attention, something that is of perceived value must soon follow or attention will quickly fade.

ACTIVITY 3-3   USING NOVELTY AND HUMOR TO MOTIVATE

Novelty and humor can be used to stimulate interest. Take some time to reflect on a topic you plan to teach and then answer the following questions.

1. How might this subject have a direct relationship to some personal needs or interests of learners?

2. What are some novel facts or examples that might be appealing?

3. List some ways that you might use humor to capture attention.

4. Identify a strange event or puzzling situation that could be used to stimulate interest.

The use of unusual events or puzzling situations to challenge existing concepts or ideas is yet another way of capturing attention. Students are then motivated to look for a way to include the event or situation in their conceptual framework. Such a technique can have long-lasting effects. I once received a letter from a former student who enclosed a newspaper article containing information about an unusual event a full three years after it had been discussed in class.

ALTERING PERCEPTIONS OF REQUIRED EFFORT

Dealing with this component of motivation may be one of the most difficult tasks faced by a teacher. You need to view the task as the student views it and this can be very hard. You may have found the subject interesting and easy and may assume that all individuals view it in the same positive light. Remember that it is the perception of reality held by the student that is important, not the one held by the teacher. If the student believes that the task requires an effort not in line with the expected benefits, then there is little likelihood that he or she will be motivated.

Perceptions of task difficulty are related to several factors: an understanding of what the task requires, an understanding of prerequisites, views of task complexity, and estimates of task length. If the nature of the task is unclear, those students with a history of low achievement and low self-esteem will usually assume that the task requires too much effort. Even when the nature of the task is understood, individuals who do not believe they possess the necessary prerequisites may be unwilling to become involved. In addition, if the task is perceived as very complex or one that requires a long time to complete, motivation will be hindered.

Understanding these variables can help you structure the learning environment so that students are not overwhelmed by their perception of the effort required. This does not mean that the task should be perceived as not being difficult. Some effort and difficulty are required in order to offer a challenge to the student. The degree of perceived difficulty needs to be related to the educational background of students. Those with a history of educational success will tolerate, and even welcome, tasks that appear to require a great deal of effort. Those with a history of failure must be presented with tasks that appear to require minimal effort.

Several things can be done to help learners understand how much effort is required in a given task. A beginning step is to perform an informal task analysis. Break the task down into all of the subtasks and steps that are required for success. The basic question to be answered is: What does a person need to know or be able to do in order to perform this task? After brainstorming these subtasks, arrange them in a logical order. This provides a "map" of the route to successful completion. This map is very useful in communicating task complexity to learners.

The second step involves using the task analysis to diagnose the extent to which students have the necessary prerequisites or can already perform some parts of the task. This diagnosis need not be very complicated and can be based on the teacher's knowledge of learners' performance on previous assignments. This diagnosis helps match the student and the task at a correct level of difficulty. At this point, the teacher should have a clear understanding of the requirements for successful task completion and be able to match the learners' abilities to the task. This sets the stage for the third step, presenting the task to the class.

Perception of task difficulty is strongly influenced by the way the task is presented. Most college students can relate to this principle. Many professors take the first day of class to spell out the course requirements for the semester. This is often done quickly with a minimum of directions as to how each assignment is going to be accomplished. The immediate reaction of the students is usually anxiety and fear. They are fearful that they will not be able to complete what is demanded of them. After they have gone through this routine for all of their classes, they may feel completely overwhelmed. A few even drop out. However, because most have been successful learners, they will persevere and meet the challenge.

This approach will not work for students who have a history of school difficulty and already doubt their ability to succeed. You need to reduce task complexity and task length. Presenting learners with only one part of the task at a time can help. This is the point at which the task analysis becomes invaluable. The class is presented with a series of subtasks, each of which is perceived as being within the ability of students to accomplish. In some instances, it is worthwhile to mention the long-term goal so that students understand the relevance of each subtask to the whole.

Presenting students with very clear and precise objectives is another means of reducing the perceived difficulty of a task. Stating the objectives in clear terms helps lessen the uncertainty and ambiguity so that students can make a more accurate assessment of the effort required. If the teacher has already performed an informal diagnosis and a task analysis, then a clear objective stated at an appropriate level is likely to be an encouragement and lead to the perception that students can complete the task without an inordinate amount of effort.

A clear outline of the task and demonstrating or modeling its process is another helpful technique. When learners see another perform the task, and are presented with a clear outline of the procedure to be followed, they are more likely to arrive at a realistic assessment of the effort required.

Once the task has been presented and students have started working, they then need to be provided with encouragement and feedback. This feedback should be concrete and specific, including both affirmation of what is being done correctly and correction of those aspects that are being performed incorrectly. This informs learners that their effort is paying off and that progress is being made toward the objective.

INCREASING THE PROBABILITY OF SUCCESS

Few factors are more powerful in motivating people than success. Everyone has a need for achievement and a feeling of competence. Students who feel that they are in a situation where they are incompetent will not be motivated to continue working. This is similar to adults who believe that they are stuck in a job where there is no chance for advancement or success. These people, when possible, seek a better job, or, if stuck in their job, exert only a minimum amount of effort. Unfortunately, many students arrive at school each morning with the feeling that they cannot be successful and that failure is inevitable. Their response to school is similar to that of adults stuck in a "dead end" job. They exert only enough effort to get by and simply try to get through the day.

Fear of Failure

Few people will attempt to perform a task for which they believe that they have little opportunity for success. A great fear for many people is the fear of failure. Some anxiety about failure, if kept in perspective, can be motivating. However, when anxiety turns into an overpowering fear, learning is blocked.

Most of us seek to avoid situations in which the probability of failure is high. This is what occurs in some school settings. Students perceive little or no opportunity for success, so they emotionally and psychologically drop out. They see the situation as threatening and seek to avoid it. This avoidance may be accompanied by rationalizations that discredit the value and relevance of school or the learning task. If you are perceived to be the cause of the threat, efforts may be made to discredit you and make you feel like a failure. The anger and bitterness that accompany a situation in which a student perceives little opportunity for success often trigger aggressive and destructive behavior.

Motivating Through Competition

The importance of high expectations of success in motivating individuals prompts a reconsideration of the role of competition in the classroom. Many consider competition as a major motivational tool. Competition can serve to motivate individuals, but only for those who think they can win. A contest in which only one winner emerges is not likely to motivate a large group of students. Only a very few will believe that they have an opportunity for success and they will be the ones willing to spend time and energy on the task. Most of the class will sit back and watch them.

This principle helps explain the success of cooperative learning approaches. In cooperative learning approaches many individuals, not just one, can emerge as winners. Therefore, the estimation of the probability of success is significantly higher. In addition, the individual is encouraged because several people are working together toward the goal.

The Need for Achievement

Individuals must believe that they are achieving a higher level of competence in something that is important or relevant. Becoming more skilled in an area that is of no importance has little appeal for most people. Relevance or importance might be defined as something that is valued by society, something that is of importance to a significant other, or something that is related to an individual goal. If society places high status and respect on the acquisition of certain skills, if an individual feels that it is emotionally safe to try, and that there is a possibility of success, then he or she will be motivated. If the skill is something that a significant other has (the identification motive), or if a significant other may reward the individual for acquiring the skill, motivation is increased.

Locus of Control

Understanding locus of control is important when using success and achievement as a motivator. Locus of control refers to those factors to which an individual attributes success or failure. People with an internal locus of control attribute success to their own effort or ability. Those with an external locus of control attribute success to luck or chance factors beyond their control. The basic question is, Why did I succeed or fail?

Individuals with an internal locus of control tend to have higher task persistence and set higher levels of expected achievement, traits that a teacher desires (Fanelli, 1977). Success is reinforcing for this person because it confirms that his or her ability or effort paid off. On the other hand, individuals with an external locus of control do not believe that effort has much relationship to success, so there is little reason to exert effort. Success has less impact on the motivation of such people because it is attributed to chance rather than effort. In sum, in order for success to have the desired impact on behavior, individuals need to believe success is a product of their effort and ability, not luck.

Accommodating the Need to Achieve

The classroom is an excellent setting for helping individuals meet their need for achievement and success. However, schools are typically based on competitive goal structures that minimize opportunities to identify and celebrate success. In addition, the typical reward, the report card, is administered too seldom to really help a student see progress and achievement. It is also typical for students to view grades received as something "the teacher gave me" rather than something earned.

You need to find ways of visibly indicating short-term achievement growth. One way of doing this is to establish reference points at which achievement will be identified. Plotting or charting growth in achievement at these frequent reference points can help learners see the progress they have made. The more failure that an individual has experienced in the past, the greater the need to have visible and concrete displays of success.

Providing the student with the criteria that will be used in evaluating the learning can facilitate making a realistic assessment of the probability of success. Students who have a clear understanding of what they will need to do to in order to be successful will be more prone to try than those who are uncertain of what is required.

Teachers can inform students of the criteria for success by clearly delineating them in the objectives for the lesson or by providing examples of the finished product.

Teachers may need to adjust the objective for those learners who have a history of failure. Even when the criteria for success are clear and successful models are provided, they may still believe that the task is impossible. For example, one elementary teacher was experiencing difficulty with a group of boys who never seemed to learn the spelling words for the week. After several weeks of failure, the teacher asked the

TABLE 3-1   **Applying Motivation**

Motivational Variable	Classroom Application

1. Relating curriculum to student needs
  1.1 Physiological needs
      1.1.1 Comfort
      1.1.2 Lighting
      1.1.3 Sensory stimulation
      1.1.4 Movement
  1.2 Psychological needs
      1.2.1 Security needs
      1.2.2 Self-esteem
  1.3 Social needs
      1.3.1 Belonging
      1.3.2 Affection
  1.4 Building on student interests
      1.4.1 Identifying interests
      1.4.2 Using identification motive	

2. Altering perceptions of the amount of effort required	

3. Increasing the probability of student success
  3.1 Uses of competition
  3.2 Emphasizing effort
  3.3 Making progress visible	

4. Using humor and novelty
  4.1 Places to use humor
  4.2 Novelty
  4.3 Unusual events	

group how many words a week they thought they could learn how to spell. After a short discussion the boys agreed that they could easily learn three words. The teacher then gave this group a three-word spelling list rather than the usual twenty. At the end of the week nearly all of the boys had learned the three words. After a couple of weeks of success, the teacher then asked if they thought they could learn five words. When they replied that they thought they could, he provided them with five-word spelling lists. Over the course of the year the teacher began to add more words as the group continued to experience success. By the end of the year they were achieving at levels consistent with the rest of the class.

One important component in emphasizing success in the classroom is the attitude of the teacher. The desirable attitude is one that emphasizes success rather than failure. You need to stress the positive rather than the negative. One method for doing that is marking and highlighting what a student does right on a paper rather than what is wrong.

Taking a couple of minutes at the conclusion of a lesson to summarize, or have the class summarize, the important points of the lesson is yet another way of using success as a motivation. This summation emphasizes to students that they have learned something and are making progress.

It is important that the teacher constantly relate success to effort. Students need to believe that success does not result by chance factors but is a product of their own effort. Through testing procedures teachers often enforce the notion that success is merely the product of chance. Tests that include trick questions or those that are unrelated to important objectives communicate to the student that effort is not as important as is trying to guess what the teacher might ask. The test needs to be viewed as an assessment of what an individual has learned, not as a device to spread students out on a grading curve. Testing, when done properly, can be an important tool for helping individuals feel successful and therefore be motivated to work even harder.

SUMMARY

Motivation is an essential component in preventing discipline problems. Human beings are complex and have a variety of needs and interests. This obvious fact makes motivation a task requiring a great deal of knowledge, thought, and action. The successful teacher understands motivation and how it can be used to further the goals of the classroom. Three factors of motivation can be helpful as a teacher seeks to apply motivation theory in the classroom: the needs and interests of the individual, the perception of the difficulty of the task, and the probability of success. If the teacher can relate school tasks to the interests and the needs of the youngsters, reduce the perception of effort required to an acceptable level, and increase the probability of success, the resultant increased attention to school tasks and decrease of discipline problems will help make teaching a very rewarding career.

SUGGESTED APPLICATIONS

1. Interview several students and ask them the following questions:
   a. What are the things you like to do when given an opportunity?
   b. What are the things you do in school that you find interesting? Why?
   c. What are the things you like to do out of school?
   d. Do you think your teacher believes you are a good student? What makes you think that?
   e. What do you think could be done to make your school a better place to learn?

2. Observe in a classroom and list specific examples you see of a teacher using student interests or needs to motivate students. Identify ways that the lesson might be modified in order to relate it to student interests or needs.

3. Identify a segment of your subject area. Brainstorm ways you might use some of the motivational variables discussed in the chapter to increase student motivation to learn this content. You might begin by considering the types of things that you find interesting about the subject. Do you think students would be interested in those same things?

SUGGESTED READINGS

Dreikurs, R. (1968). *Psychology in the classroom,* 2nd Ed. New York: Harper & Row.

Fanelli, G. (1977). Locus of control. In *Motivation in education,* S. Ball, (ed.). New York: Academic Press, pp. 45–64.

Glasser, W. (1969). *Schools without failure.* New York: Harper & Row.

Glasser, W. (1986). *Control theory in the classroom.* New York: Harper & Row.

Good, T. and Brophy, J. (1997). *Looking in classrooms,* 7th Ed. New York: Longman.

Schauss, A. (1985). Research links nutrition to behavior disorders. *School Safety* (Winter), 20–28.

Slavin, R. E. (1994). *Educational psychology: Theory and practice,* 4th Ed. Boston: Allyn and Bacon.

Woolfolk, A. E. (1998). *Educational psychology,* 7th Ed. Boston: Allyn and Bacon.

4 Arranging the Physical Environment

Chapter Objectives

After reading this chapter you should be able to:

- State ways the physical environment impacts behavior
- List goals you should have for planning the classroom environment
- Define the action zone in the classroom
- State the advantages and disadvantages of different types of seating arrangement
- List elements of the spatial dimension that need to be considered
- Define what is meant by the ambiance of the classroom and identify factors involved in creating an ambiance
- State the impact of classroom density on student and teacher behavior

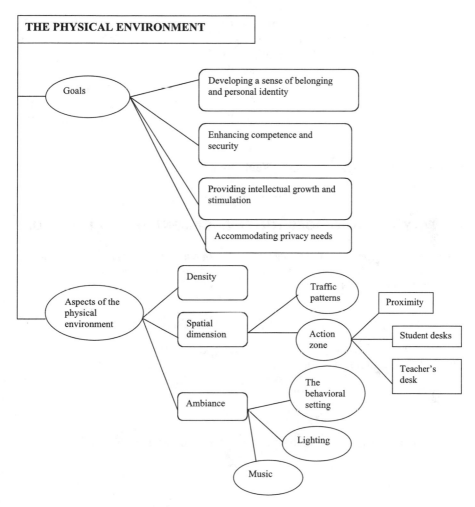

FIGURE 4-1　**Graphic Organizer for Arranging the Physical Environment**

The impact of the environment on behavior has been studied by scholars across several disciplines. Psychologists, sociologists, and architects are among those who have systematically studied the relationship between people and their physical surroundings. Their findings provide the basis for environments that are supportive of selected human activities. For example, shopping centers and stores are designed to support and encourage the buying behavior of customers. Similarly, workplaces in business and industry are designed to increase the productivity of employees.

The physical setting does more than just enhance or inhibit certain activities. The very design of the space sends a silent message to all that enter. Weinstein and David (1987) point out that created environments in schools have both direct and symbolic impacts on learners. The direct impact of the built environment is the manner in which certain activities are facilitated and others are inhibited. For example, a certain arrangement of furniture and equipment may enhance large-group instruction and inhibit small-group approaches. The symbolic impact is the manner in which the values and intentions of the teacher are communicated, excitement toward learning generated, status or respect given to different individuals and activities, and the feeling of comfort or threat that is present (Weinstein and Mignano, 1993).

ACTIVITY 4-1 HOW DOES THE ENVIRONMENT AFFECT BEHAVIOR?

Take a minute to reflect on the relationship between the environment and your behavior. Identify some settings where you feel comfortable. What is there about the setting that makes you feel comfortable?

What things about a setting attract you to it?

How do you feel when you are in settings that are cluttered or ugly?

What type of setting do you think is most appropriate for learning?

What do you think can be done to improve classroom environments so that problems are prevented and learning enhanced?

Becker (1981) studied the impact of the environment on behavior. He indicates that the proportion of behavioral variance attributable to the environment will vary according to the level of competence, health, intelligence, and ego strength of those using the space. The physical environment will less affect individuals with high feelings of competence and success than those with low feelings of success and competence. This emphasizes the importance of the physical environment when dealing with students who demonstrate persistent behavior problems. It is probable that the physical environment will be a more important consideration when trying to solve their problems.

The organization of the environment influences student perceptions of their place in the classroom, the sorts of activities considered appropriate, and how they are expected to behave. Although the impact of these perceptions may change over time, first impressions will have a lasting impact. These initial impressions can facilitate the establishment of a positive learning environment and help move students toward self-control, or they can interfere and make learning more difficult. It is therefore important for you to consider the impact of the environment you create on the behavior of your students. You need to consciously plan and create environments that facilitate your educational goals and desirable student behavior.

GOALS TO BE CONSIDERED WHEN PLANNING THE ENVIRONMENT

The systematic development of an environment conducive to learning begins with your goals and purposes. These goals and purposes should then be used as a framework for planning various dimensions of the environment. Weinstein and David (1987) identify a number of goals that are useful for this purpose: helping students develop a personal identity, encouraging feelings of competence, promoting intellectual growth and stimulation, providing a sense of security, and allowing for both privacy and social interaction.

Developing Personal Identity

The development of a personal identity is enhanced when classrooms are created where students feel they belong and where they have a sense of ownership. Students spend considerable time in a classroom during an academic year. It must be a place where they feel comfortable in order for it to be an environment that is conducive to learning. If it is also a place where they have a feeling of personal identity, the comfort level will be enhanced.

Feelings of ownership and personal identity are enhanced by allowing students to participate in decision making about the use of the space—the grouping of desks, room decorations, and organization and placement of learning centers. Allowing them the freedom to personalize their classroom helps students to develop a sense of belonging and pride.

Elementary classrooms, where the same group of students inhabits the same space all day, are usually easier to personalize than secondary classrooms that are shared by several groups of students. Some ways of helping students personalize the classroom is to allow them space on bulletin boards to display items of their choosing. Adding pets to the elementary classroom can also be very effective in helping to personalize the environment. Weinstein and Mignano (1993) suggest that you add things about yourself, your interests, and your hobbies to the classroom. This not only helps personalize the room but also communicates that the teacher is also a "real" person. What needs to be avoided is an environment that is cold, sterile, and devoid of interesting and personal objects.

Enhancing Competence and Security

One of the most fundamental functions of a space is to provide security. While many teachers see the need to provide for the physical comfort and security of students, they may forget the importance of psychological security (Weinstein and Mignano, 1993). Individuals thrust into an unfamiliar environment often feel threatened and insecure. Your goal should be to remove the threat and insecurity by helping students feel that they have some control over the environment.

The psychological security and comfort of the students can be addressed by making sure that the furnishings are appropriate for the size and the development levels of the students. Individuals of any size or stage of development cannot be expected to demonstrate much task persistence if they are sitting in an uncomfortable chair or writing on an unstable work surface. It is not uncommon to visit classrooms where some students are sitting in chairs that are an improper size and where work surfaces are inadequate for the tasks they are assigned. Reflect on your own experience. If you are assigned a task and you have inadequate workspace or inadequate tools to do the job, is your sense of competence enhanced? For example, as I attempt do-it-yourself projects, I often feel incompetent and frustrated because I lack the proper tools to do the job. Although overcoming barriers can be rewarding at times, most of us become extremely frustrated and even angry if there are too many of them.

Fortunately, recent attempts in school design are considering the fact that not all students are physically the same and that there is a need for flexible furnishings. However, there are other considerations. Do students have adequate surfaces to do writing when they are required to do so? Is there enough space for them to keep essential materials without them always falling on the floor? If you are asking students to perform experiments, do they have the necessary space and material to do it? If they are working in cooperative groups, can they easily communicate with each other?

For students to develop a sense of competence and security, the environment must be free of threat. The potential for physical harm should be a consideration in classes that involve unfamiliar or potentially dangerous equipment. Younger children might be fearful of unfamiliar equipment or animals that might be present. For example, I remember a high school science class where the teacher mentioned the potential danger of one of the acids being used in an experiment. As a result, one student became so nervous about handling the acid so that he was unable to conduct the experiment. As you look around your classroom, are there items that might generate fear? How might you discuss those items with the class so that their fears are minimized? You might want to establish some rules or routines so students clearly understand how to use the items safely.

Developing feelings of competence also requires that the classroom be a place where students have success and where success is celebrated. Teachers can structure the environment to celebrate success by making sure that bulletin boards and display areas include examples of successful work. This is relatively easy to accomplish in elementary schools, where students' work is often a prominent part of the classroom environment, but it can be more difficult in secondary schools. One high school teacher accomplished this task by displaying articles cut out of newspapers, recital programs, or other publications in which students in her class were named. She made a concerted effort to find something to display for every student in her homeroom. The effort paid off with student respect and affection and an almost total absence of discipline problems.

Promoting Intellectual Growth and Stimulation

Promoting the intellectual growth of students requires a rich and varied environment. This implies that the environment needs to be dynamic and changing rather than static. A classroom that is the same for the entire year or from year to year communicates stagnation and boredom, a symbolic statement inviting discipline problems. Bulletin boards and display areas should be changed and updated on a regular basis in order to promote intellectual stimulation and communicate that the classroom is a dynamic, changing, and exciting place. Although this is an aspect of the physical environment often overlooked by teachers, the long-term effects of an ever-changing environment are positive.

One caution is in order when discussing changing the environment. Changing the environment in order to promote cognitive growth and stimulation must be balanced with the need for a sense of security. Continuity and predictability in the environment enhance security. For example, most of us feel insecure if our workspace is changed dramatically. It takes a while to make the space our own and to feel comfortable in it. The same principle applies to the classroom. Massive changes in the organization of the space and seating assignments should be done infrequently. And, when making changes, it is best to involve students.

Another method for providing for stimulation in the classroom is that of periodically changing the classroom seating and grouping patterns. Studies indicate that teachers develop patterns of behavior so that they tend to spend a great deal of time in certain areas of the classroom and spend little time in other areas. As a result, the work of students in those areas where they spend little time does not get monitored as well and those students receive less attention. Changing the arrangement of seats from time to time so that different students sit in the area with high teacher contact does promote more at-task behavior and student satisfaction.

When planning your classroom environment, you should also consider arranging the room so that it is easy to quickly get to each student. This will allow you to move quickly to a student when assistance is needed or when you need to deal with a problem. This arrangement will make it easier for you to develop the habit of getting to all areas of the classroom during a lesson.

Accommodating Privacy Needs

Classrooms are generally organized to facilitate group activities and social interactions. They seldom consider individual needs for privacy. Although the typical classroom design makes it difficult to accommodate this need for privacy, privacy is a dimension that can have an important impact on learner behavior. Probansky and Fabian (1987) contend that a convincing case could be made that students use the strategies of withdrawal, fantasy, and acting-out for attaining privacy and isolation not normally permitted in classroom environments.

Weinstein and David (1987) also emphasize the importance of considering the privacy needs of students when designing a classroom environment. There are times when individuals like to be alone, away from the scrutiny of others. However, classrooms are characterized by a lack of privacy (Weinstein and Mignano, 1993). Students are constantly being observed by the teacher and by other students.

One way of accommodating the privacy need is to designate one corner of the classroom as a private work area. This area can be separated from the rest of the room by bookcases, file cabinets, or study carrels. Students move to that area to study or simply to be alone. Providing this type of retreat for students communicates that you are sensitive to their personal needs.

DIMENSIONS OF THE PHYSICAL ENVIRONMENT

There are several aspects of the physical environment that need to be considered. One important aspect is the spatial dimension—the size, shape, and organization of objects within the space. Another is the classroom ambiance, or the feeling that one has when entering the space. A third is the spatial density of students in the classroom.

The Spatial Dimension

The size and shape of the room, the location of doors and windows, and the circulation and traffic patterns combine to form the spatial dimension of a classroom. Although windows and doors cannot be moved and the size of the classroom cannot be changed, there are aspects of the spatial dimension that can be altered or controlled by the teacher. There are studies that indicate that many teachers are not very good at using classroom space effectively or in developing alternative spatial arrangements. For example, Smith (1987) found that more than 45 percent of all classroom activity took place in just one-twelfth of the classroom space. Teachers seem to get locked into a routine and do not consider optimal use of the space available to them. Teaching stations could be rotated to different areas of the room or different areas designated for different types of activities.

Seating arrangement deserves special attention. Weinstein (1979) found evidence of the impact of seating arrangements on student behavior. In a second-grade classroom, a teacher and a researcher worked together and identified a number of behavioral problems. In an attempt to solve the problems, the seating arrangements were then systematically changed. The result was a statistically significant decrease in the number of behavioral problems.

Furthermore, other studies found that the participation of high school and college students in classroom discussions was influenced by seating arrangement (Becker, 1981). Weinstein (1979) also discovered that seating position influenced student attitudes toward the class and toward the teacher. In summary, it appears that attending to seating arrangements can have an important payoff by influencing student behavior, classroom participation, and student attitudes.

Action Zone

A concept that pulls together the important dimensions of the seating arrangement is one that some researchers have labeled the *action zone* (Adams and Biddle, 1970). The action zone consists of the seats across the front of the classroom and down the center. Those students sitting in this action zone participate in the class more, attend to a task a greater length of time, have higher achievement, and have more positive attitudes toward the class. One explanation for these findings might be that the better students tend to choose these spots. There is some validity to this contention. Dykman and Reis (1979) found that the students who choose to sit on the periphery of the classroom generally feel more threatened and exhibit lower self-esteem than those who sit in the action zone. They suggest that students who choose to sit on the periphery want to distance themselves from the threat posed by the teacher.

However, there is some evidence that positive outcomes occur when students are assigned seats in the action zone. Dykman and Reis (1979) offer a partial explanation for this finding. Those learners with lower self-esteem, who feel less secure and more threatened by the teacher, tend to choose seats most distant from the teacher. As a consequence they get called on less frequently, are monitored less often, and are generally less involved in the class than those in the action zone. This neglect leads to increased failure, which in turn confirms their original feelings of self-doubt and fear. Moving such individuals into the action zone gets them involved, provides them with more opportunities for interaction with the teacher, and therefore begins to remove feelings of self-doubt and fear.

This information about the action zone can be used in several ways to arrange the physical environment. One application is to arrange the seating so those students with academic and behavioral difficulties are placed in the action zone. Moving students into this area will increase the amount of time they spend on-task, allow them to receive more constructive feedback, and result in higher feelings of competence and intellectual growth.

Because the action zone is defined in reference to the location of the teacher, the location of the action zone will depend on your location when instructing the class. You can change the location of the action zone by changing the teaching station. Teaching from different spots in the classroom will allow you to utilize the findings of the action zone without assigning or changing seats.

Some teachers prefer to allow students the opportunity, at least at the beginning of the year, to choose their own seats. This practice does have merit. Smith (1987) found in a study of achievement that gains were greater in classes where students were allowed to choose their own seats. The security and comfort of choosing one's location in the classroom may well create a positive climate in which students are more open to instruction. A variation of this is to allow students to initially choose their own seats. Those few students who experience difficulty might then be gradually and unobtrusively moved into the action zone.

Teacher Proximity

The concept of an action zone emphasizes the importance of teacher proximity to students. Other studies also indicate the importance of the teacher remaining as close to students as possible. For example, Weinstein (1979) found that grades decrease as a student is seated farther away from the teacher. In addition, student participation and positive student attitudes decline as the distance between the teacher and students increases (Smith, 1987). What could explain these findings? It may be that teachers have more difficulty monitoring the work of students who are seated farther away from them. This lack of monitoring does not provide students with the immediate feedback they might need to increase their understanding and therefore improve their grades. The distance factor may also contribute to a lack of teacher–student contact that could contribute to positive interpersonal interactions and feelings. Students do tend to stay on-task when the teacher is physically closer and this increased learning time could also translate into higher achievement and grades and therefore more positive feelings.

These findings emphasize that it is important for you to be as close as possible to the largest number of students for the greatest amount of time. How can this be accomplished? One technique would be to increase the number of students who are seated in the front of the class. Look at the physical dimensions of the classroom. If the space is rectangular, choose a primary teaching station on one of the long sides so that you will have more rows with fewer students. This will allow you closer contact with those students across the front and will reduce the space between you and those seated in the back row. Another technique would be to place your desk in a location that is near the largest number of students. Do not isolate the desk in some far corner of the classroom. One suggestion is to have a primary teaching station on one side of the classroom and the teacher's desk on the other. This increases your presence in two different areas of the classroom.

Another suggestion is to look at the traffic patterns of the ease of movement around the classroom. Arranging the traffic pattern so that you have easy movement around the classroom will facilitate your movement and increase the contact you have with all students.

Arranging Student Desks

Student desks are the most dominant features in the classroom. The discussion of the action zone and teacher proximity highlights the importance of giving desk arrangement considerable thought. The arrangement of the desks provides the major setting or "frame" that shapes teacher–student interaction and the behavior of students (Rosenfield, Lambert, and Black, 1985). Because different arrangements influence behavior in different ways, there is no best way to arrange desks. When arranging desks you should consider the teaching approach you use, the type of interaction you desire, student characteristics, and your ability to maintain classroom control.

The three basic seating arrangements most commonly used in classrooms are rows, clusters, and circular or semicircular patterns. There are advantages and disadvantages to each. When desks are arranged in rows all facing in one direction student interaction with each other is limited, listening is enhanced, and independent work is facilitated. Many teachers find that the row arrangement is easier for them to monitor and helps establish and maintain classroom control. Weinstein (1979) cites studies indicating that organizing desks that limited student-to-student interaction leads to higher on-task behavior, less off-task movement, and less disruptive talk. However, when participation in a discussion was used as a criterion, those seated in rows had higher incidents of withdrawal and more off-task verbal comments. If your teaching approach will be primarily direct instruction, you want students to work independently and you are concerned about your ability to promote on-task behavior, arrangement of desks in rows would be the best choice. This arrangement would require more movement and monitoring in order to keep students alert and focused.

Rosenfield, Lambert, and Black (1985) cite the advantages of the circular arrangement. In fifth- and sixth-grade classrooms, they found that a circular pattern increased student comments related to the content and that students had increased attending behavior. They also found higher incidents of out-of-turn responses by students seated in a circle. This may indicate more student spontaneity when they are arranged in this format. If your primary mode of teaching will be class discussion, you are not concerned about students speaking out-of-turn, you want to increase student attending and verbal participation, a circular pattern would be the best choice.

Students seated in cluster arrangements demonstrated more ordered turns while still maintaining a high percentage of on-task verbal behaviors. Clustered arrangements are most commonly used in cooperative learning. If your mode of instruction were to be cooperative learning, then clustering students into small groups would be the most appropriate choice.

Some authorities recommend that you begin the school year with desks in rows facing the major instructional areas and then move to other desk arrangements after you have established control of the classroom (Emmer et al., 1989). This prevents discipline problems during the critical beginning phases of the school year. This suggestion has a great deal of merit if you are insecure and are concerned about your ability to control the classroom. Once your confidence grows, you may use less traditional arrangements.

Student self-control is another factor to consider when arranging seating. Those students who have a high degree of self-control might be grouped into clusters for a large portion of the day. Such students are able to overcome the distractions of others seated near them and can resist the temptation to socialize at inappropriate times. However, those students who lack self-control should be arranged in rows so that the possibilities of social interaction are limited. As they develop self-control and learn to participate in discussions and cooperative learning groups, then the arrangement might be gradually changed to more of a circular or cluster arrangement.

Traffic Patterns

Traffic patterns in the classroom are very important. Students need to enter and exit the classroom quickly, they need to have easy access to materials, and they need to be able to move about without disturbing others. High traffic areas need to have plenty of space and be kept free of obstructions. Teacher movement is important in order to monitor student work and behavior. Therefore, the room arrangement should allow the teacher easy access to all learners. The best design would make it easy for the teacher to be at any student's desk within seconds. This arrangement facilitates movement around the room and helps keep the teacher in close proximity to the students.

The Teacher's Desk

The placement of the teacher's desk is important when considering the room arrangement. It not only has an impact on the traffic pattern; the placement affects a number of other dimensions of the classroom. It is a place you will use and is often a place to which the students will move on a frequent basis. The traditional place for the teacher's desk has been in front of the classroom. However, this location is often not the best. A better spot for the teacher's desk is in a less dominant and obtrusive spot, preferably in a corner or near the rear of the room (Weinstein, 1979).

The desk becomes the focal point of most of the activity in the classroom. Any activity at the desk is easily observable to everyone in the classroom. Placing the desk at the front of the room also makes it convenient as a teaching station. This prompts the bad habit of directing all activities from the desk and cuts down on the amount of movement of the teacher around the room. Teaching from behind the desk results in higher student off-task behavior and lower positive student attitudes toward the teacher (Smith, 1987).

Placing the teacher's desk in an unobtrusive spot also allows the teacher the opportunity to conduct conferences with students with some degree of privacy. The conference does not become a central focus of the class, and accommodates privacy needs of students. Students will feel more comfortable sharing feelings with the teacher, as the embarrassment that might accompany a conference is reduced. If the conference is related to discipline matters, the need to save face and demonstrate power in front of peers is eliminated.

Finally, placement near the rear of the room tends to promote higher student at-task behavior. Students tend to stay on-task if they are unaware of where the teacher is. In order to check on the location of the teacher, students must turn around. This behavior often indicates difficulty and allows the teacher the opportunity to move to the area and prevent problems from occurring.

Identifying Activity Boundaries

Another important aspect of the arrangement of physical space is the identification of space and boundaries for different types of activities. Identifying activity boundaries is more important in an elementary classroom where students inhabit the same space for many different types of activities. However, secondary teachers should also consider arranging space to allow for different activities such as independent study, group work, small-group discussion, use of technology, and so on.

Identifying boundaries for different activities helps to provide students with a sense of security and assists them in maintaining self-control. Clearly delineated boundaries serve as reminders of the types of behavior appropriate in different areas of the room and for different activities. Bookcases and file cabinets are especially useful for this purpose and can be used to change the shape of the physical environment, for example, to separate small-group work areas, learning centers, and independent work areas from large-group instruction. As indicated earlier, they can be used to separate an area to meet the privacy needs of students.

In addition, changing the shape of the classroom serves to promote sensory stimulation by making the room different from others. Students tend to get bored when every classroom is the same size, the same shape, and organized in rows facing in the same direction. Care should be taken, however, that boundaries do not interfere with the ability of the teacher to monitor quickly all areas of the classroom. The placement of visual barriers so that student behavior cannot be quickly and quietly observed creates a condition that invites misbehavior.

THE CLASSROOM AMBIANCE

Ambiance refers to the feelings that an individual gets when entering a place. An environment might communicate a feeling of excitement or a sense of quiet and peace.

Some environments are attractive and inviting, others ugly and forbidding. The ambiance of a place is created through orderliness, light, sound, texture, color, temperature, and odor. These elements can be combined in ways that are pleasant to create feelings of comfort, security, and warmth, or they may create a sense of insecurity, threat, and coldness.

ACTIVITY 4-2   I WAS HIRED TO TEACH, NOT DECORATE.

Some teachers complain about tasks such as putting up bulletin boards. Secondary teachers often consider the activity as suitable to the elementary level or frivolous. They contend that time is better spent preparing for teaching than trying to beautify the classroom. In addition, they point out that attractiveness and beauty exists in the mind of the beholder. They may create an environment they think is attractive that may be unattractive to students.

What do you think?

• Can teachers expend too much effort decorating a classroom? How much effort do you think is appropriate?

• How would you react to the contention that developing an attractive classroom is less appropriate for a secondary level teacher?

• What would you suggest for secondary teachers?

• What do students you teach or intend to teach regard as attractive and stimulating?

• At what point do you think that classroom decorations become a distraction rather than an enhancement to learning?

The ambiance of the classroom and classroom decorations have been the subject of debate. Some teachers argue that their role is not that of an interior decorator and that "beautiful" environments are not important. It is true that some teachers lose their sense of perspective and place too much emphasis on order and beauty at the expense of comfort and function. The basic issue, however, is not the creation of beautiful classrooms, but how the classroom influences those who must spend a considerable amount of time there. Recent studies have indicated that attractive environments do influence behavior in positive ways. It has been found that attractive environments increase task persistence and have a positive effect on group cohesion, class participation, and attendance. On the other hand individuals in "ugly environments report increased headaches, fatigue, discomfort, incidents of teacher control statements increased, and conflict among students increases" (Weinstein and Mignano, 1993).

These findings support the idea that it is important to spend time creating a pleasant classroom ambiance. There are benefits for teachers and students who spend a considerable part of each day in the space. The finding that the environment does exert a powerful influence on those who inhabit the space has been organized into the concept of "behavioral settings."

Behavioral Settings

Researchers in architecture and psychology who have conducted studies on the impact of the environment on behavior developed the concept of behavioral settings. The concept is widely used by architects as they design space. A behavioral setting is a place where the behaviors exhibited in the space remain relatively constant even though the occupants of the space may change (Weinstein, 1979). For example, churches or places of worship communicate to all that enter what is considered appropriate behavior. This is communicated through the arrangement of the seating, the lighting, stained glass, and the placement of symbols. Some behaviors are desirable in these settings and others are not. The ambiance that is created by combinations of light, color, temperature, and spatial organization defines a behavioral setting.

Because a classroom is a behavioral setting, it is important for teachers to ask, "What types of behaviors do I want the students to exhibit?" Do I want to excite students or calm them down? Do I want to encourage or discourage social interaction? Once teachers are clear about the answers to such questions, they can consider how the environment needs to be changed in order to create the setting that will elicit the desired behaviors. Teachers who design very informal classrooms should not be surprised when students behave informally. Similarly, teachers who design very stiff and formal classrooms should not expect their students to demonstrate spontaneity.

Teachers who wish to create behavioral settings where creativity is promoted can use bright colors, a variety of objects to provide sensory stimulation, and bulletin boards that pose problems rather than give information. Teachers concerned with decreasing student activity can use softer colors, plan bulletin boards that are decorative rather than provocative, soften the lighting, and have a very orderly room arrangement. These dimensions are aspects of the room environment that can be manipulated to create the desired ambiance or behavioral setting.

Softening the Environment

Softer environments can be created by having flexible lighting, carpets on the floor, decorations on the walls, and live plants. Studies of high school and college students indicate better attendance, more student participation, and higher student evaluations of the teacher in rooms where the environment was classified as soft. Unfortunately, many classrooms are very cold and "hard" environments. They are painted the same color, have relatively harsh lighting and are generally unappealing. In recent years the importance of the environment has been recognized and more classrooms are being built that do include carpeting and flexible lighting. If you find yourself in a classroom that is cold and hard, there are several things you can do to soften it. Consider adding some live plants at strategic locations, add one or two wall hangings, place a lamp in a corner of the room where the overhead light can be turned off, and cover some part of the floor with a small rug. All of these little touches will serve to make the room softer and more appealing to students. You may be surprised at the impact such changes have on student behavior.

Background Music

Another feature of classroom ambiance is sound. Sound has long been used outside of education to influence behavior. Stores often play music designed to lift spirits and increase buying, and elevators have soft music designed to comfort and lower anxiety. You might consider the use of background music in your classroom at appropriate times. For example, background music might be used when students are working independently or to help mask interfering noise when students are working in groups. A problem with music is that not everyone enjoys the same type of music. Music that might be stimulating to one individual might be irritating to another. However, a background of soft music can provide sensory stimulation and mask intruding sounds.

Generally, the goal of the teacher in creating a classroom ambiance and behavioral setting should be the creation of an environment that is businesslike, yet warm and stimulating. Students should get the feeling that the classroom is a good place to be and one where learning is important. They should also sense that learning in this room is going to be stimulating and exciting.

CLASSROOM DENSITY

The density of individuals in a space is another important aspect of the physical environment that influences behavior. Density refers to the numbers of individuals who occupy a given space. A major concern of teachers is that too many classrooms are overcrowded. Most will indicate that it just seems more difficult to teach and manage the classroom when it is overcrowded. Although the impact of increased density on student achievement is an item that is under debate, there have been some studies on the impact of density on behavior. Students in crowded classrooms demonstrate less attentive behavior and more aggression and deviant behavior (Probansky and Fabian, 1987). For some students withdrawal and reluctance to participate is a common behavior in crowded classrooms (Weinstein, 1979).

How much density is too much is influenced by cultural norms. Individuals from certain cultures are able to tolerate a large number of people in a given space without classifying it as crowded, whereas individuals with a different cultural background would find the same density excessively crowded. The important concern is not the actual number of learners but, rather, their perceptions of whether or not they are crowded.

TABLE 4-1 **The Physical Environment**

	Yes	No
• High traffic areas are free of congestion		
• Placement of student desks communicates the desired interaction pattern and teaching approach		
• Teacher's desk is in an unobtrusive area		
• High traffic areas are free of obstruction		
• The teacher can gain easy access to all students		
• Students can clearly see instructional stations		
• Frequently used material is accessible		
• The equipment and furnishings are appropriate for the age of the students		
• Room arrangement allows for some privacy		
• The classroom ambiance creates a pleasant yet businesslike environment		
• There is sensory stimulation		
• There is evidence of personalizing and softening the environment		
• The classroom is attractive and creates a good, comfortable, and secure feeling		
• There are definite areas and boundaries for different activities		

One study found that those students who performed poorly in a classroom with relatively high density were those who classified the room as crowded (Weinstein, 1979).

Several factors explain the impact of density on student and teacher behavior. High-density classrooms decrease the amount of privacy for students and increase opportunities for social interaction. These two factors may then result in anxiety and interpersonal conflict. High-density classrooms also create competition for the attention of the teacher. Students who have high attention needs may feel they have to misbehave in order to attract attention. The loss of opportunities to interact with the teacher may also be a factor influencing student achievement in high-density classrooms.

Lowering the density of individuals in a given space may not always be desirable. Placing more individuals into a smaller space will increase the interaction among individuals. Therefore, higher densities are desirable when the task to be completed requires communication and cooperation among students. Activities such as cooperative learning and small-group work are then enhanced.

While it may be difficult for you to change the density of students in your classroom, you need to realize that too many students in a given space will lead to problems. Increased aggression and anxiety are a couple of indicators that students may feel crowded and that someone is invading their "personal space." These problems may not be related to your skill as a teacher but are simply artifacts of the situation. If you find yourself in this situation you may want to consider if there are ways that you can create feelings of decreased density. Perhaps you can move some objects, such as file cabinets or your desk, from the room in order to reduce the feeling of crowdedness. You may need to sacrifice small-group work areas in order to spread out student desks so that they do not feel crowded.

SUMMARY

The physical environment of a classroom does influence student behavior. The design of the classroom makes some activities possible and eliminates others. In addition, the environment sends symbolic messages to all that enter about the values and the intentions of the teacher. Teachers who wish to minimize problems are well advised to consider the messages their classroom environment sends to students and how it facilitates the outcomes they desire.

In order to design productive environments, teachers should plan environments that help students develop personal identity, encourage feelings of competence and security, promote intellectual stimulation and growth, and allow for privacy when it is desired. Attending to the spatial dimension of the classroom, which includes the way seats are arranged, the proximity of the teacher to the students, the movement of the teacher around the space, and the ambiance of the room, helps teachers accomplish these goals. The concept of behavioral settings is useful when teachers begin consideration of the classroom plan. Creating a behavioral setting that is consistent with teacher expectations requires that teachers consider the goals and expectations they have for the classroom. Clearly delineating these goals and expectations can then be used to plan an environment where desired behaviors can occur.

SUGGESTED APPLICATIONS

1. Analyze a classroom in your school. What is the ambiance of the room? What is there about the classroom that creates the ambiance? How does the arrangement of the room facilitate the attainment of educational objectives? How does it interfere with the attainment of educational objectives?

2. Visit several classrooms and note the extent to which the rooms are organized to meet the goals of developing a personal identity, encouraging competence and security, providing for intellectual stimulation and growth, and allowing for privacy. Suggest changes that would help create a more supportive environment.

3. Observe in a classroom and keep track of the location of students who are called on to participate in the classroom discussion. Where are these students located in the classroom? How does this pattern compare with the action zone that was described in the chapter?

4. Take an existing classroom and develop a plan. Justify the decisions you make in designing the plan.

SUGGESTED READINGS

Adams, R. L. and Biddle, B. J. (1970). *Realities of teaching: Explorations with videotape.* New York: Holt, Rinehart & Winston.

Becker, F. (1981). *Workspace: Creating environments in organizations.* New York: Praeger.

Dykman, B. and Reis, H. (1979). Personality correlates of classroom seating position. *Journal of Educational Psychology* 71(3), 346–354.

Emmer, E., Evertson, C., Sanford, J., Clements, B., and Worsham, M. (1989). *Classroom management for secondary teachers,* 2nd Ed. Englewood Cliffs, NJ: Prentice-Hall.

Probansky, H. and Fabian, A. (1987). Development of place identity in the child. In Weinstein, C. and David, T., (eds), *Spaces for children.* New York: Plenum, pp. 21–40.

Rosenfield, P., Lambert, N., and Black, A. (1985). Desk arrangements effects on pupil classroom behavior. *Journal of Educational Psychology.* 77, 1, 101–108.

Smith, H. (1987). Nonverbal communication. In Dunkin, M., ed., *The international encyclopedia of teaching and teacher education.* New York: Pergamon, 466–477.

Weinstein, C. (1979). The physical environment of the school: A review of the research. *Review of Educational Research* 49(4), 577–610.

Weinstein, C. and David, T., eds. (1987). *Spaces for children: The built environment and child development.* New York: Plenum.

Weinstein, C. S. and Mignano, A. J. Jr. (1993). *Elementary classroom management.* New York: McGraw Hill.

5 Preventing Problems Through Time Management

Chapter Objectives

After reading this chapter you should be able to:

- Define different concepts of classroom time and their importance in teaching
- Identify factors that influence time allocation decisions
- State the importance of maximizing classroom time focusing on lesson objectives
- List classroom tasks and activities for which you will need routines
- Identify ways of making lesson pacing decisions
- State the importance of giving clear directions
- List steps that can be taken to improve teacher monitoring of student work

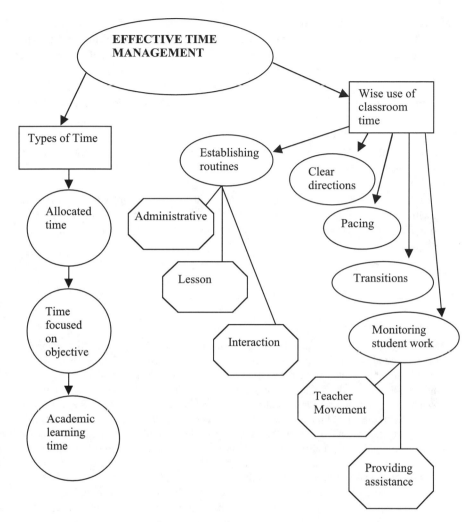

FIGURE 5-1   **Graphic Organizer for Preventing Problems Through Time Management**

Teachers never seem to have enough time. Most teachers complain that there is simply not enough time in the day to complete all of the tasks that need to get done. In recent years policymakers have proposed extending the academic year to include more school days so that more material can be covered. This may not seem like a problem to you as you anticipate an academic year of approximately 180 days of 6 hours a day. The beginning teacher worries about filling up this amount of time.

However, it does not take long to discover that there are many ways that time is lost during the school day. There are numerous routine tasks such as taking roll, making announcements, returning work, distributing materials, and collecting work that takes time away from teaching. Then there are the unplanned interruptions and special events such as assemblies that reduce the time available for instruction. Careful planning of time is extremely important in helping students achieve success. This is labeled "opportunity to learn." The concept of opportunity to learn indicates that student achievement is directly related to the amount of time spent or the opportunity to learn the content presented to them (Good and Brophy, 1997). Berliner and Biddle (1995) argue that the opportunity to learn is the most important predictor of student achievement

Chapter 3 indicated that an important element of motivation was providing students with success. This provides support for the importance of providing the students with sufficient time to learn. Students' motivation will increase if they believe they can achieve success.

DISCIPLINE SCENARIO 5-1

Members of the class were noisily filing into the room as the bell rang. Most seemed unconcerned about the bell and continued socializing with friends. The teacher asked the students to be seated so that she could take attendance. Several students complied while continuing to talk. The teacher began taking attendance and occasionally inquired about the presence of a particular student. Once attendance was completed, the required form was completed and posted near the door to be picked up by the attendance monitor and taken to the main office. At this point, the teacher announced the return of homework papers and began calling out names and moving about the room to return the papers. Afterward, the teacher began asking for silence. Initial calls were unheard because of the conversation level. Gradually the class began to quiet down. At this point the teacher began to admonish class members for the high noise level. The students were then told to open their books to page 100. Several groans and two inquiries concerning forgotten books greeted this. A third youngster wanted to know if a pencil would be required. A general undercurrent of murmuring and discussion began to swell up in the room. Ten minutes of the class period had now elapsed, and the frustration and anger of the teacher were beginning to show.

What is your reaction?

1. Do you think this is a common event?

2. Do you think this could have been prevented?

3. What do you think is the problem in this situation?

4. What would you do differently?

Time management is not only important in facilitating achievement, it is important in the prevention of discipline problems. Successful teachers often indicate that they keep students so busy that they do not have time to misbehave. There is a great deal of wisdom to this approach. However, we must remember that "busy work" with little meaning or relevance will not suffice.

Take a couple of minutes to review Discipline Scenario 5-1. See if you can identify places where this teacher could improve time management.

Is this scenario realistic? The answer is yes! A large portion of every class day and instructional period is spent on tasks unrelated to learning. In the typical classroom several minutes each day are wasted because of inefficient time management. For example, if you are able to claim only 5 minutes more each day for instruction, this would add 15 hours of instructional time for the year (the equivalent of adding 18 more class periods to a secondary class that meets for 50 minutes a day or almost three days for the typical elementary class)! It is a safe prediction that those students receiving the equivalent of 15 additional hours of instruction will learn more.

This chapter outlines some of the methods a teacher can use for managing class time and promoting on-task behavior. The discussion covers using time productively, giving directions, pacing classroom activities, establishing classroom procedures and routines, monitoring student work, managing transitions, and responding to inappropriate behavior.

UNDERSTANDING DIFFERENT TYPES OF TIME

Effective time management that keeps students on-task is a key element in preventing problems and enhancing student achievement. Individuals with nothing to do become bored and search for some sort of sensory stimulation. Unfortunately, the stimulation they seek will probably be something you do not desire.

Decisions about time management begin during the planning stage and continue through the conclusion of a lesson. There are at least three different definitions of time. Understanding these different definitions can help you do a better job of making decisions about time management.

Time Allocation Decisions

One type of time that needs to be considered in improving time management in the classroom is "allocated time." This refers to the actual time that the teacher allocates for teaching a skill or a concept. Considerable evidence indicates that the time allocated for a given subject in the curriculum or for a given concept varies greatly among teachers (Good and Brophy, 1997). For example, one elementary school teacher may allocate 30 minutes a day for reading instruction, whereas another teacher at the same grade level in the same school may allocate 90 minutes to reading instruction. Secondary school teachers also show great variation in the amount of time they allocate their content area. Science teachers vary considerably in the amount of time they spend in the lab and how much they spend in direct instruction. English teachers differ in the amount of time they spend on writing and literature or on different types of literature, social studies teachers differ in the amount of time they spend on different topics, and math teachers vary in the amount of time they spend on different concepts.

Although one would expect some variation among teachers in the allocation of time because of the ability level of the students, the skill of the teacher, and the interests of the students, the wide variation observed in many classes is extensive. In fact, time allocation decisions are more often made according to teacher interest and preference than student needs and abilities. Teachers who like reading teach more reading; teachers who dislike science or social studies allocate little time to those subjects. An English teacher who feels comfortable with and likes a particular work by Shakespeare will allocate more time to that work than to others. A social studies teacher who is fascinated with one historical era will spend considerable time on that era and may skip others. Good and Brophy report that those teachers who enjoy mathematics spent over 50 percent more time teaching math than those who did not.

It is natural for an individual to spend more time on something that is enjoyable, and teachers are certainly no exception to this rule. However, you must remember that school is for the student, not for you. You have a professional and ethical obligation to teach those subjects and concepts that are important for the future well-being of the students. Many adults end up ill-prepared for a future class or assignment because of teachers who ignored important segments of the curriculum. To ignore a subject, such as science in an elementary classroom or significant lab experiences in a secondary classroom, can have a profound effect on the future success of the student. In addition, omitting some aspects of the curriculum in the classroom may actually deprive some students of the opportunity for success. In recent years considerable attention has been devoted to the idea of multiple intelligences (Gardner, 1993). Gardner proposes that there are at least seven types of intelligence. The success of students in school can be dramatically changed if they are allowed to achieve success in their area of strength (Woolfolk, 1998).

Teachers faced with decisions about how to allocate time need to address several questions. First, *What do learners need to know?* The decision about how much time to spend on different topics should be related to educational needs and objectives rather than the personal interests of the teacher. If a given group of learners is deficient in some necessary skill, time should be allocated to teaching that skill. The future needs of the youngsters should also be considered so that their development in a given subject is not hindered.

Second, *How much time will be required for this group of students to achieve success and a sense of competence?* Covering topics too quickly creates a sense of frustration and will lower future motivation. Students need to develop a growing sense of competence and mastery, and the amount of time needed to meet these needs will vary from student to student.

Third, *Am I allocating so much time to this subject that students will become bored and lose interest in the topic altogether?* Too much time can be just as deadly as too little. While students need to master the subject, they should not be drilled to the point where they lose interest.

Finally, *Am I providing a balanced curriculum?* Time should be allocated to all of those areas that the students need to learn. This question addresses the ethical and professional concerns of whether teachers are meeting district and state requirements and are doing so in a fair and responsible manner. Providing a balance will also increase the probability that all learners can find some place to achieve success.

Time Spent Focused on the Lesson Objective

Once the time allocation decisions are made, the focus should then shift to how time is actually spent in the classroom. A guiding principle is to spend a maximum amount of the allocated time focusing on the instructional objectives. This concept is sometimes referred to as "engaged time." Engaged time is often used to indicate the amount of time students actually spend during the class period working. However, time related to the objective is a little more precise and useful than just engaged time. Engaged time might include the time the students were working, but it was not spent working on material related to the objective. For example, some teachers, in an attempt to keep the students busy, assign a number of tasks for the students to complete. Some of these tasks are merely busywork and do not contribute to the achievement of the lesson objectives. Therefore, the students are engaged or working, but they are not spending the time focused on the objectives. It is not merely the engaged time that is important, but the amount of time that is spent working on the objective that makes the difference.

The amount of time focused on the objective is determined by subtracting from the allocated time the amount of classroom time students spend doing tasks unrelated to the objective for the lesson (such as the routine duties of taking attendance, returning papers, distributing materials). For example, a teacher may allocate 45 minutes for teaching a given concept. However, 5 minutes are spent taking attendance, 2 minutes for announcements, 3 minutes to return papers, 3 minutes to distribute materials, 3 minutes to handle discipline problems, and 4 minutes to clean up at the end of the period. The result is that 20 minutes have been spent on tasks unrelated to the objective so that the actual time spent focusing on the objective was only 25 minutes.

You can begin to maximize the amount of time spent focusing on the objective by considering all those places where time might be spent performing tasks that are not directly related to the lesson objective. Some tasks, such as taking attendance, are necessary. You need to find ways of accomplishing them quickly and efficiently. Others, such as taking time during class to return work can be eliminated altogether by using alternative methods.

Maximizing Academic Learning Time

A third aspect of time usage is maximizing the academic learning time of each student. Academic learning time is a step beyond the amount of time spent focusing on the objective and is the most important aspect of time management. Academic learning time is the amount of time the student is working on the objective with success. For example, Johnny may spend 30 minutes of the allocated time actually working on tasks that are related to the objective. However, at the conclusion of the lesson, he does all of the work incorrectly. Johnny has had 0 minutes of academic learning time. On the other hand, Jose spent only 15 minutes of the allocated time actually focusing on the objective. However, he successfully completed the assignment. Provided that this was an assignment he could not do at the beginning of the class, his academic learning time would total 15 minutes.

Academic learning time is time that translates into success and achievement gains for students. It provides them with a growing sense of competence and a realization that time spent working will have a payoff. This translates into increased motivation. Therefore, it is not just allocating more time or keeping the students busy that is key to successful time management. It is keeping them working with a high level of success.

ACTIVITY 5-1   KEEP THEM BUSY AT ALL TIMES

Ms. Tao believes that students should be kept busy the entire time they are in class regardless of what they are doing. She prepares a number of tasks and assignments for students to complete when they finish daily assignments. This work is of a general nature and often includes practice of previously learned material. For the most part, this procedure works very well. However, Ms. Tao does have a couple of concerns. It seems that fewer and fewer students are completing their assigned work. In addition, she states that she must constantly patrol the classroom in order to keep students on-task. She attributes this poor work pattern to short attention spans and the need for students to be constantly entertained. "Students can't seem to stay on-task for more than a couple of minutes at a time. I think it is because they are used to watching television. And being entertained all the time."

What do you think?

   1. Do you agree with Ms. Tao's analysis?

   2. What parts of her plan have merit?

   3. What alternative hypotheses might explain their behavior?

   4. What would you recommend that Ms. Tao try to get more students to complete their work and yet prevent misbehavior at the end of the class time?

Increasing the academic learning time for all students is an important part of the link between good teaching and the prevention of discipline problems. Teachers interested in maximizing academic learning time need to ask the basic question, What is preventing students from achieving success on this lesson? Those barriers directly related to teacher behavior need to be eliminated. These include teaching at a level that is too difficult or too easy for the academic level of the students, providing unclear instruction and confused directions, not identifying and correcting student misunderstanding and learning difficulties, or maintaining an inappropriate lesson pace. To overcome these potential problems, you need to stay active and alert during the entire lesson. You must also keep students alert by constantly checking for student understanding. When students are working independently, you need to actively monitor student work in order to provide individual assistance and give corrective feedback quickly.

Consideration of these three aspects of time is the beginning point for making good time management decisions. Teachers who consider how they are allocating the time spend most of the time focusing on activities relevant to the objectives, and try to ensure maximum student success in order to eliminate the boredom and frustration that are at the root of many discipline problems. The following section focuses on those areas related to the productive use of time in the classroom.

Establishing Classroom Routines

Emmer, Evertson and Anderson (1980) conducted a series of research studies that emphasized the importance of establishing clear classroom rules and routines. They observed a number of teachers during the first of the year and kept detailed records of their observations. As a result of observations during the rest of the year, they labeled the teachers as either effective or ineffective managers. When they then reviewed their records from the first of the year they noticed some important patterns. Those who became effective managers took the first couple of weeks of the school year to establish classroom rules and routines and systematically taught them to the class. In Chapter 2 attention was directed to the establishment of rules. In this chapter attention will be focused on the establishment of routines.

Much time is lost in handling routine chores. Such tasks as taking attendance, distributing materials, making announcements, and collecting work are central to the role of the teacher. Other problems, such as students who come to class without proper materials, with broken pencils, and requests for special privileges, occur less frequently but are just as predictable. Success in handling these interruptions is basic to effective time management. These concerns should be considered before the school year begins and appropriate routines developed for handling them in a quick and efficient manner.

Identifying Predictable and Recurring Events

The first step in developing routines that help you avoid wasting time is to identify those recurring and predictable events that occur in the normal course of a day. This is a basic management principle regardless of the setting. A good manager, whether in the classroom or the business office, will anticipate routine events and will establish a well-defined procedure for handling them. These events can then be handled automatically without much thought. This helps simplify a complex environment and allows the manager the opportunity to focus energy and attention on the exceptions. This is important for your well being. If you have to devote all of your attention to events that occur during the day, you will become mentally and physically fatigued.

Weinstein and Mignano (1993) suggest three different categories for routines. One category relates to the types of predictable events related to the nonacademic events that are necessary for running the classroom. The second category is those predictable events related to learning during a lesson. The third category of routines are those that related to guiding the interactions between individuals in the classroom.

You need to develop classroom routines that are simple, easily understood, and quickly performed for each of these major areas. The routines should then be taught to the class as they are needed. There needs to be a special emphasis on teaching these routines during the first few weeks of the school year. Students need to know what is expected and how to perform these tasks efficiently. While some new teachers balk at spending time during the beginning of the year for teaching these routines, the time will be well spent by avoiding considerable amounts of wasted time during the rest of the school year.

Establishing Routines

The routines established will vary according to the grade level of the students, their ability to exercise self-control, and the goals of the teacher. Kindergarten classes will require different routines than would upper elementary classrooms. Secondary school classrooms would require even different ones. However, in general, some tasks and events are predictable across grade levels and students.

Administrative Routines

Routines for this category include all of those administrative duties that are required of teachers but are not a part of the academic program. These include entering the classroom, recording attendance, transitions from one subject of class to another, getting materials, sharpening pencils, leaving the room, and participating in various drills.

An especially important time is the beginning of the class period or the school day. It is important to get the students engaged in learning activities as soon as possible. Several routines may be needed: entering the room, taking attendance, collecting homework, making announcements, getting a lunch count, and checking previous absences, Other related routines might be needed for handling tardy students and making sure that each student has the required materials.

Whenever possible, students should perform these tasks. This accomplishes two purposes. It gives responsibility to the students and frees the teacher to monitor activities and to start the lesson promptly. One suggestion for getting the day started quickly, while attending to the administrative duties, is to have an opening activity written on the board. This might be in the form of review questions, an open-ended question related to the objective for the day, an answer sheet for correcting homework,

ACTIVITY 5-2   GIVE THE STUDENTS RESPONSIBILITY

Ms. Epstein believes in giving students responsibility. In addition, she likes to reinforce those students who have been following the rules. She does not assign certain students tasks but chooses students to pass out materials, collect papers, and perform other classroom tasks based on their behavior at that time. By the time she chooses students and they do what is required, several minutes of class time have elapsed. In addition, those students not chosen get upset and complain that they never get a chance. Handling their complaints also wastes additional time and sometimes creates a discipline problem.

What do you think?

1. What is positive about Ms. Epstein's approach?

2. Why do you think she has these problems?

3. What do you suggest as a solution to her problems?

---

or a fun activity such as a puzzle or riddle. Students are taught to enter the room, get settled, and immediately begin working on the activity. Students with assigned responsibilities, such as taking attendance, quickly attend to these responsibilities. This helps engage student attention at the beginning and helps eliminate the excessive socialization that often delays the start of class.

Another troublesome area where you need to consider a routine is when students need to leave the room. This may include going to the restroom, the library, the nurse, or for special programs. Pencil sharpening and coming to class without needed materials are other problem areas faced on a frequent basis. Many teachers designate only a certain time for pencil sharpening and keep several pencils sharpened for those who need them. It is a good idea to keep several short, undesirable pencils sharpened to prevent students from deliberately swapping for better ones.

Secondary teachers often have difficulties with students coming to class without appropriate materials. One secondary teacher established a "rental" procedure. Students who came without the appropriate material could "rent" the material for the class period. For older students the rent consisted of an exchange of the material for the student's drivers' license. Since this was a valuable commodity that few secondary students wanted to be without, students seldom came to class without the proper material.

Lesson Routines

There are a number of events you need to consider relating to running a lesson. These include collecting homework, making up missed assignments, turning in late assignments, returning corrected papers, distributing materials, and rewarding students who completed their work. You also need to develop a procedure for how papers are to be headed, the margins, and the proper writing instrument to use.

In managing student work, the teacher needs to consider how assignments will be made. Many teachers write assignments on an overhead projector or on the chalkboard before the beginning of class. Others place written assignments in student folders or notebooks. It is helpful to post long-term assignments on a designated bulletin board so that students are constantly reminded of due dates. Do not rely on oral explanations of assignments. Oral assignments are easily, and conveniently, forgotten. When making an assignment for seatwork, you should provide the instructions along with an example of what is to be done. This can be included on the paper or on the overhead projector so that it is visible for all students. This simple procedure saves an amazing amount of time by eliminating the several minutes of delay when students claim that they don't know what to do.

It is especially important that homework assignments include clear directions. This helps parents to understand the assignment, assist their children, and hold them accountable for doing the work. Few things are more frustrating for a parent than trying to help a child with schoolwork and not being able to understand the assignment. Such a situation can seriously erode the credibility of the teacher in the eyes of the parent.

Another important part of managing the lesson is establishing a procedure for students to follow when they have completed the assignment. Teachers often instruct students to read a book, complete unfinished work, move to a learning center, or engage in acceptable free-time activities. The type of routine will vary with the type of the class and the preferences of the teacher. The important point is to make sure that when students finish their assignments, they do not become bored or begin bothering other students.

Classrooms are generally materials-rich environments. Books, papers, reference works, audiovisual equipment, art supplies, lab equipment, and special machines are found in most classrooms. The constant use and distribution of supplies can be a source of wasted time. Materials and equipment should be ready before the students begin a lesson. They should be stored in a location that is easily accessible so that they can be returned efficiently. Procedures are also necessary for passing out needed materials quickly with a minimum of movement and disruption. Students should know when they are free to obtain needed material and how they are to behave when doing so.

Those teachers who have special equipment in their classrooms should remember that careful instruction is needed before allowing students to use the equipment. Not doing so is to invite legal charges of negligence should a student be injured. Careful supervision of objects such as paper cutters and audiovisual equipment is an absolute must. Not only does the teacher need to ensure that students have been instructed in their use, but the equipment also needs to be inspected to make sure it is in proper working order and that all safety guards are in place.

Interaction Routines

There are a couple of items that you need to consider when establishing routines that control the interaction in the classroom. Probably the most common one is a procedure for being recognized and contributing to the discussion. The most common procedure is that of raising a hand. With some classes this might not be necessary, because the students have enough maturity to take turns.

One area that you need to consider is how the students request assistance from the teacher. Do you want students coming to your desk to request assistance or will you go to them? It is usually best to keep the students in their seats and for you to go to their desks to provide assistance. This raises another question: How will they get your attention? Students generally raise their hands to request help. However, when students are sitting with their hands in the air, they are not working. This also provides them an opportunity to carry on a conversation with those around them. Some teachers have solved this problem by using a sign system. Students request help by placing a help card or some other symbol on their desk. They then skip to the next problem or task and keep working until the teacher arrives.

Another important interaction procedure is needed for getting the attention of the class. This frequently happens when students have been working in groups and you need to get everyone's attention. Most teachers use some sort of a signal, such as blinking lights, to signal that they now need everyone to stop talking and pay attention.

Students talking to each other is another area in which you need to develop procedures. When are students allowed to talk with each other? How are they to be informed if the talk is getting too loud? These routines will be based on your preferences and comfort level. Some teachers try to prohibit nearly all talk between students. This is probably unrealistic because students are social and want to interact with each other. It is most realistic to decide on those times when you will allow them to talk with each other and establish a routine to govern their interactions.

You may want to use the checklist in Table 5-1 and begin to establish routines for the items on the list. You may want to add some items that you need or you might want to delete items that do not fit your circumstances. If you do not yet have a classroom, you may discuss the procedures with experienced teachers to find out the routines they use.

Teaching Routines

Once you have developed your routines, you will need to teach them to the class. You need to do this as they are needed. There are a number of them that you will need to teach during the first couple of weeks of class. New routines can be added as new situations arise.

Routines are learned like anything else, through explanation, modeling, practice, and reinforcement. When introducing the routines to the class, you should identify the problem, state the rationale for the procedure, teach it step by step, have

TABLE 5-1   **Establishing Routines**

Areas where routines are needed	My routine
Administrative routines	
Entering classroom	
Attendance	
Making announcements	
Fire/Disaster Drills	
Tardy	
Coming to class without material	
Movement while in classroom	
Pencil sharpening	
Getting a drink	
Going to restroom	
Leaving the room	
Use of equipment	
Class dismissal	
Lesson routines	
Collecting assignments	
Make-up assignments	
Returning work	
Materials distribution	
Proper form for papers (heading, margin, etc.)	
Student movement (transitions)	
When assigned work completed	
Students assisting each other	
Interaction routines	
Participating in discussion	
Requesting assistance from the teacher	
Working in groups	
Student talk during class (when, how)	
Using centers, stations, etc.	
Getting total class attention	
Quieting class when talk too loud	

students demonstrate the procedure, and then have the class practice it. The practice should continue until you are certain that everyone understands how it is to be performed.

It is unrealistic to expect to teach a procedure during the first day or two of the class and have it followed perfectly for the rest of the year. Those who do follow the routines should be given occasional reinforcement; if the class begins to ignore the routine or become lax in its application, you will need to remind students of the routine and have them practice it again. These two actions signal that the routines are important and that students are expected to follow them. Establishing routines for recurring and predictable events, insisting on compliance, and monitoring students during the school year can result in more learning time, more positive relations between class members and the teacher, more teacher energy for dealing with the exceptions or the serious problems, and fewer behavioral problems.

PACING CLASSROOM ACTIVITIES

One of the most important elements of time management is the pace of activities during the lesson. The obvious result of any activity that proceeds too slowly is boredom. However, deciding on an appropriate pace for classroom activities is difficult. Because classrooms are composed of individuals with diverse backgrounds and abilities, some students may grasp a concept or master a skill very quickly while others struggle. Many teachers find themselves in a bit of an ethical dilemma. They want to make sure that all students have an opportunity to learn and are reluctant to move too quickly. However, moving at a pace so that all students succeed runs the risk of losing the attention of those who quickly master the material.

Another problem in making pacing decisions is that some teachers are unaware of the pace of the classroom. Some teachers seem to have an intuitive feel for moving at a rate appropriate for students, whereas others are nearly always moving too rapidly or too slowly. It is probable that those teachers who do seem to make appropriate pacing decisions do so with the aid of something more than mere intuition. Teachers tend to form "reference groups." The reference group is a group of individual students that provides cues to the teacher regarding boredom or frustration. Although many teachers are unable to consciously identify particular students whom they observe for cues, this reference group often exists. Think of the times you are in front of a group. Do you not judge the pace and clarity of your presentation by observing the behavior of the listeners?

The influence of the reference group in pacing works like this. Ms. Garcia is teaching a difficult concept. As the concept is being taught, she is also attending to the nonverbal behaviors of the class. She observes the puzzled expression on the face of a high achieving student and interprets this expression to mean that the student is lost. Because this is a high achieving student, she infers that the difficulty must be in the pace of the instruction and not with the concentration of the student. Her action is to slow the pace and reteach some portion of her lesson. Later on, Ms. Garcia notes an expression of boredom on the face of another student. This student is an academically able student so she interprets this to mean that the pace is too slow and needs to be accelerated. Later, during another lesson, Ms. Garcia sees a puzzled expression on the face of another student. This time the student is one who often has difficulty. She interprets this to be due to the lack of attending behavior on the part of the student and not something that is symptomatic of widespread student misunderstanding. Therefore, she does nothing to alter the pace of the lesson.

The basic point is that you need to be aware of the students you are using for a reference group and the interpretation you place on their actions. The problem is that many nonverbal behaviors are ambiguous and open to several interpretations. Teachers who are successful in managing a classroom and in establishing an appropriate pace are those who check their inferences and become more skilled at reading and interpreting the nonverbal behavior of a reliable reference group. Unsuccessful teachers attend to the wrong students or misinterpret student behavior.

Make sure that your reference group is composed of students who are most helpful for making pacing decisions. For example, if the teacher selects those students who are usually at the top of the class as the reference group, the pace may be too fast. Most of the students will get lost and fail. However, if the teacher chooses the slowest students in the class as the reference group, the pace may be too slow for most of the class. Boredom and behavior problems may then result. A good suggestion is to choose students at about the 25th percentile for the reference group. This means that the pace will be appropriate for 75 percent of the class. Although this pace may still be a bit slow for the more able learners, it will keep the lesson moving at a moderate pace and provide for the success of most of the students.

Establishing a reference group at the 25th percentile does not mean that you ignore the bottom quarter of the class. You may choose to reteach these students as a group or arrange for peer tutors to assist them. The point is that neither the slowest nor the fastest students should be the indicators for pacing decisions.

PROVIDING CLEAR DIRECTIONS

Much time is lost in getting students to work after a task is assigned. A major contributor to lost time at this point is unclear or poor teacher directions. Students who do not understand the directions will ask for clarification or begin doing the task incorrectly. In both cases, you have to stop the flow of classroom activity to repeat directions or to assist a large number of students.

You can implement several measures to increase the clarity of directions. One basic step is to write the directions and have another teacher read them and suggest clarifications. Written directions also prompt teachers to be more concise in their direction-giving behavior. Another method is to give oral directions and then randomly choose a couple of students to explain in their own words what they are to do. The students should be able to state the task clearly. If they cannot, this provides you with the opportunity to identify missed points or misunderstandings.

MANAGING TRANSITIONS

Transitions between lessons or between activities are another major source of wasted time. There are approximately 30 major transitions each day in a typical elementary classroom (Doyle, 1986). Although secondary school teachers may have fewer transitions, the average number, counting the transitions between classes, is still in the range of 12 to 15.

Transition times provide students with opportunities to talk, move about the room, and engage in other nontask behaviors. Therefore, it is not surprising that many discipline problems occur during transition times. Once students become off-task, they are likely to stay off-task for some time. Getting them back on-task then leads to confrontations and power struggles between the teacher and the students. It is important that these transitions be handled quickly and smoothly with a minimum of disruption.

You can minimize wasted time and the problems that occur during transitions by planning for them in much the same way you plan lessons. You should outline the steps of the transition carefully, give clear directions to the students, and make sure that all students understand where they are to go and what they are expected to do. Transitions that occur frequently should be developed into routines and practiced.

Another part of the teacher responsibility in providing for a smooth transition is to make sure that all material is ready and at hand before the lesson begins. Trouble will almost certainly occur if the teacher has to make the class wait until the material is located or prepared for distribution. Posting daily schedules and notifications of any changes in the daily routine are also useful in preparing students for transitions. When they understand what is going to be happening and when time limits are established for activities, students develop a sense of security. Transitions then tend to be smoother and less disruptive. Students do get accustomed to a schedule, and when an unusual break occurs, they may waste considerable time complaining that it is not yet time to change.

MONITORING STUDENT WORK

Research has shown that elementary school students spend nearly half their time working independently on seatwork or independent work activities (Jones and Jones, 1986). Although the amount of independent work in secondary schools may be somewhat less, it is still a significant portion of the school day. In order to facilitate success and increase the academic learning time of each student, you need to actively monitor the progress of each student.

Monitoring should be done continuously and systematically so that all parts of the room and all students are included. Some teachers stay in one spot, often at the teacher's desk, or have a tendency to check only one part of the room. There are several important reasons why you should try to avoid this. Having students who need assistance come to you creates problems. First of all, many students who need assistance will not actively seek it. Second, when students get out of their seats, the potential for mischief increases, and those students lined up at the your desk are not engaged in academic learning time. Students gathered around your desk also prevent you from actively monitoring the classroom for any behavior problems or off-task behavior. Because student misbehavior decreases with the increased physical proximity of the teacher, you should try to stay close to students. This cannot be done if you are seated at your desk.

Two basic components need to be considered when systematically monitoring student work: teacher movement around the class and provision of assistance to those who need help.

Teacher Movement

You need to develop the habit of moving around the classroom. Some teachers develop the poor habits of checking only certain parts of the classroom and interacting with only a few students. Because it is important to monitor all learners, it is helpful to develop a systematic plan for moving around the room.

One procedure that is useful is to try and check the work of every student within the first five minutes of assigning independent work. Once the assignment is given and directions reviewed, you should immediately start moving around the classroom, checking to make sure that all students are working. At this point you should not stop to provide in-depth assistance to those who request it. A reminder, a quick hint, or a promise to return in a minute or two is all that should be done at this point. If many students seem confused, you might need to stop the class and review the assignment. Positive reinforcement should be given to those who have promptly started to work on the task.

After making this initial pass through the room, you can now return to those who need more assistance. Make sure however, that you do not ignore those students that do not request additional assistance. Some students may think they are doing the work correctly when they are not; others may be reluctant or embarrassed to request assistance. Checking student work and providing positive comments as well as corrective feedback are important parts of monitoring. You should have a movement plan in mind that will place you next to every student in the room a minimum of one or two times during the independent study portion of the lesson.

It may be productive to have someone observe you and plot your movement patterns. This can be very revealing and can help you identify bad habits that you have developed or help you target specific areas of the classroom that are being neglected.

Providing Assistance

One of the most important components of effective monitoring is providing assistance to those who need help. Those students who need help, yet must wait an extended period of time before receiving assistance, are wasting their time waiting for you. In addition, it is convenient for students who are waiting to talk with neighbors. Disruptive talk with neighbors constitutes abut 80 percent of the discipline problems in a typical classroom (Edwards, 1997). Therefore, an effective technique for providing fast and efficient help needs to be developed.

It is important for you to have interactions with as many students as possible. You need to give as much feedback as possible to the maximum number of students. Therefore, spending an extended period of time interacting with a few students decreases the impact of effective monitoring. For example, suppose that you have assigned a 20-minute independent study task. If you spend an average of four minutes with each student who requests assistance, no more than five students can receive feedback.

Jones (1987) studied this aspect of the classroom and discovered that teachers did spend an average of about five minutes per student when providing assistance. He concluded that effective assistance could be provided more quickly, so he developed and tested a procedure he called the "praise–prompt–leave" procedure. This procedure, with some modification, is as follows:

1. Arrange student seating so that you can easily and quickly get to the desk of each student in the classroom.
2. Provide models, charts, or displays of the directions and the assignment so students can seek clarification independently.
3. Provide for a signal system to indicate those who need assistance.
4. When you arrive at a student's desk, use the following procedure. First, quickly identify and praise something the student has done correctly. Then give a brief and concrete prompt about the next step, a quick correction about what the student is doing incorrectly, or simply tell the student what to do next. Then quickly leave the student and move on to assist someone else. In a couple of minutes check back to see if the prompt or suggestion helped the student. If not, give another concrete prompt and quickly move on. The total process of providing assistance to a student should take no more than 60–90 seconds.

Some teachers have difficulty with the suggestion about moving on quickly. Moving quickly from student to student, however, not only maximizes contact with the students but helps make them independent learners. Some students have learned the benefits of playing dumb. If you can be convinced that the student is hopelessly lost you may end up doing most of the work. Some students are simply insecure and demand teacher assistance even when it is not needed, and some just want attention.

They are getting attention by constantly seeking assistance. You do not want to reinforce this behavior. By monitoring the work of all students and providing reinforcement for those who are doing the work, you demonstrate to the student that the appropriate way to get attention is by working.

SUMMARY

Time management is one of the more important aspects of your managerial responsibilities. Not only does proper time management prevent discipline problems, it facilitates student achievement. A considerable amount of time is spent on nonacademic tasks during the typical school day. Capturing this time and using it to teach the content can actually add several days to the academic calendar. One dimension of classroom time that is of special importance is academic learning time. It is not enough to merely keep students busy. Your goal should be to maximize the amount of time all of the students will be working on the objectives with success.

Another important component of managing time is to plan procedures and routines for predictable, recurring events. If time has to be taken to deal with each of these events, a considerable number of minutes can be lost. Planning routines for these events, teaching them to students, and monitoring the application of these routines during the year make the task of teaching considerably easier. Time is also lost in inappropriate pacing of lessons. Lessons paced too rapidly will result in confusion and lost time reteaching; lessons paced too slowly will cause boredom and misbehavior. Establishing a reference group of students to monitor during the lesson is a useful way to make pacing decisions.

Much misbehavior occurs during the transition time between lessons or activities. It is important that teachers plan for transitions so that they are done quickly and efficiently. Keeping students focused on learning and not allowing them an opportunity to misbehave are important aspects of problem prevention. Managing transitions requires well-planned routines and constant attention. Many teachers spend more time providing assistance to students than is necessary. As a result, they are unable to monitor and provide assistance to the maximum number of students. Some students learn quickly that by playing dumb they can get the teacher to do a significant amount of work for them. Learning how to provide assistance quickly and then move away from the students helps teachers solve this perplexing problem.

SUGGESTED ACTIVITIES

1. Observe in a classroom and use a second hand or a stopwatch to keep track of the time spent on tasks that are not related to the objective. Compare this time to the total class time allocated for the lesson. Identify those places where time could be saved.

2. Visit two or more classrooms where the same content is being taught. Compare the amount of time allocated for the different topics and activities in the class. Ask the teachers to provide you with their rationale for their time-allocation decisions. Note differences between allocations and the actual time spent focused on the objectives during the class.

3. Plot the movements of a teacher around a classroom during independent work time. Identify those places where the teacher spends the most time and the least time. Which students seem to get the most contact? Are there students who get no contact? Is there a pattern to the movement?

4. Plan for your first day of class. Develop a set of routines that you think you will need for the first day. Plan on how you will teach these routines. Decide on the materials that you think you will need and begin developing a list. It might be helpful for you to develop your own checklist of things you will need to get ready for that first day.

SUGGESTED READINGS

Berliner, D. and Biddle, B. (1995). *The manufactured crisis: Myth, fraud, and the attack on America's public schools.* New York: Addison-Wesley.

Doyle, W. (1986). Classroom organization and management. In Wittrock, M., (ed.). *Handbook of research on teaching.* New York: Macmillan.

Edwards, C. H. (1997). *Classroom management and discipline,* 2nd Ed. Columbus, OH: Merrill/Prentice-Hall.

Gardner, H. (1993). *Multiple intelligences: The theory in practice.* New York: Basic Books.

Good, T. and Brophy, J. (1997). *Looking in classrooms,* 7th Ed. New York: Addison-Wesley.

Jones, F. (1987). *Positive classroom discipline.* New York: McGraw Hill.

Jones, V. and Jones, L. (1986). *Comprehensive classroom management,* 2nd Ed. Boston: Allyn and Bacon.

Woolfolk, A. E. (1998). *Educational psychology,* 7th Ed. Boston: Allyn and Bacon.

6 Preventing Problems Through Lesson Management

Chapter Objectives

After reading this chapter you should be able to:

- Identify the relationship between lesson management and prevention of behavior problems
- Define aspects of teacher clarity that interfere with effective teaching
- Describe lesson smoothness and how it can be accomplished
- Give examples of "withitness"
- Identify teacher behaviors that impede lesson momentum

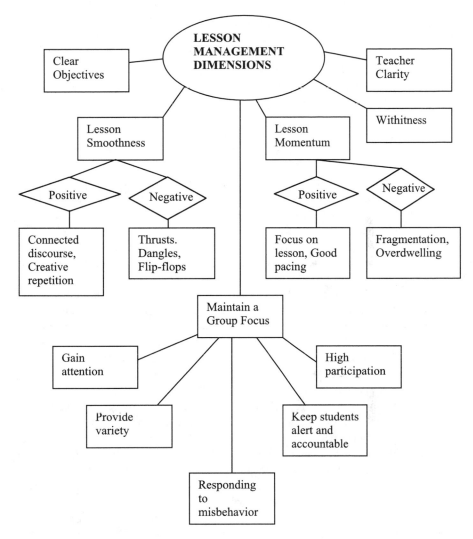

FIGURE 6-1   **Graphic Organizer for Preventing Problems Through Lesson Management**

Teachers are responsible for two major tasks in the classroom: instructing and maintaining order. Beginning teachers are often told to plan and deliver exciting lessons as a means of preventing misbehavior. There is much wisdom in this advice. Well-planned and well-executed lessons not only help students achieve a sense of satisfaction from their work but also promote prompt cooperation. Planning and delivering effective lessons, however, are complex tasks. Several basic and generic components must be considered regardless of the philosophy of the teacher, the content of the lesson, or the teaching strategy. These components include gaining student attention, presenting content, distributing materials, keeping students involved, monitoring student progress, and concluding the lesson.

Doyle (1986) identifies several characteristics of classrooms that make managing them difficult. He points out that classrooms are multidimensional, simultaneous, unpredictable environments that have a sense of immediacy and are very public. The casual observer is often unaware of the difficulty of managing a classroom with these characteristics. When handled by a skilled teacher the task seems much easier than it is.

The multidimensional characteristic is based on the fact that classrooms have a large number of participants, events, and tasks. In addition, any one event can have multiple consequences. Classrooms are reciprocal places in which the behavior of the teacher influences learners and the behavior of learners influences the teacher. The behavior of any one student can affect other students and the behavior of the teacher. Understanding and managing the dynamics of this multidimensional environment is no easy task.

Classrooms also have the characteristics of simultaneity and unpredictability. Many things happen at once in a classroom. Teachers not only deliver lesson content; they keep track of time, monitor student understanding, decide if additional instruction is required, attend to the pace of the lesson, and scan the class for misbehavior.

Different groups of students might be working on different tasks at the same time. The teacher needs to keep track of these activities and provide assistance to all students when it is needed.

The classroom is extremely unpredictable. You never know how a group of students will react to a lesson. An activity that was successful with a group of students the first period may be met with apathy during fourth period. You never know what questions students might ask. Right in the middle of an engaging lesson the principal makes an announcement over the loudspeaker or someone trips the fire alarm. Students are often looking for any excuse to be distracted or to try to get you off the track. This unpredictability can extract a heavy toll on teachers.

Immediacy is yet another dimension that makes classroom management difficult. The rapid pace of activities does not allow you much time for reflection. When a problem occurs, you cannot say, "Hold it until I look up a solution!" It must be dealt with immediately. Teachers must deal with a great number of these immediate concerns during a given day. Gump (1967) and Jackson (1968) estimate that an elementary school teacher has more than 500 exchanges with individual students during a single day. Each one of these exchanges requires an immediate response.

As if this were not enough complexity, classrooms are public places where your responses and actions are observed by all of the students. They see all of your mistakes and they are constantly interpreting your every move. All students will evaluate your management and teaching skills. Before very long they will know all of your mannerisms and habits. In addition, the public nature of the classroom provides a ready audience for anyone who desires attention and decides that misbehavior is the easiest way to obtain it.

Taken in combination, the factors of multidimensionality, simultaneity, unpredictability, immediacy, and publicness make the management task a considerable one. The research of Minnick (1983) clearly identified the relationship between lesson management and discipline problems. In a study of an inner-city junior high school with serious discipline problems, Minnick found that teachers with a high incidence of discipline problems did a poor job of planning activities, had little variety in their lessons, infrequently communicated to students the importance of the lesson, rarely had students discuss or evaluate what they had learned, and did a poor job of monitoring student work.

Over two decades ago Kounin (1970) and his associates conducted impressive studies on the relationship between discipline and management. They began their research by focusing on discipline problems. Like many new teachers they wanted to learn how successful teachers responded to incidents of deviant behavior and how their responses influenced the subsequent behavior of the student disciplined and the others in the classroom. After some observations, Kounin became convinced that they were looking at the wrong variable. He became convinced that the differences between successful and unsuccessful teachers was related more to how they managed the class in order to prevent problems rather than in the way they responded when problems did occur. As a result, he developed a number of management concepts that

---

DISCIPLINE SCENARIO 6-1 **Classroom Complexity**

Janis Lam has always believed that exciting lessons prevent discipline problems. However, she has changed her mind. During the first weeks of her first teaching experience she worked hard every night to plan interesting lessons that required a lot of student involvement. However, it seemed as if that was the wrong thing to do. The students got too noisy and spent their time talking and joking around. Finally, the class became totally out of control. They were not accomplishing anything, Ms. Lam was spending most of her time trying to keep them under control, and she finished every day totally exhausted. "Boring, lock-step lessons in which all students are doing the same thing at the same time and all stay in their own seat and quietly follow directions seem to be the only ways students know how to behave. I now understand why so many teachers use this approach."

What is your reaction?

1. Do you agree with Ms. Lam's analysis of the problem?

2. What do you think could have been causing her difficulties?

3. How would you try to prevent this problem from occurring in your classroom?

are especially helpful in presenting lessons so that misbehavior is prevented. Looking at the concepts developed by Kounin as well as the findings of research on teaching effectiveness will be the focus of this chapter.

THE DIMENSIONS OF LESSON MANAGEMENT

Attending to several generic skills or concepts relating to lesson management can enhance your success regardless of your philosophy or method of instruction. One basic concept that emerges from numerous studies indicates that you need to be engaged in "active teaching" (Good and Brophy, 1997). Being active means that you spend most of your time instructing students or monitoring their progress and providing feedback. A review of the characteristics of classrooms as outlined by Doyle would seem to reinforce this concept of active teaching. Managing an environment that is multidimensional, immediate, public, and unpredictable requires a teacher who is involved and active to keep a diverse group of students moving in the desired direction. The following concepts will help teachers manage lessons so that desired outcomes are attained and problems are minimized.

Clear Objectives

A beginning step to effective lesson management is the specification of clear objectives and goals for the lesson. Clarity about your goals helps you identify those activities and approaches that are most likely to bring about student success. Further, it helps you focus on the main points of the lesson and keeps you from wandering off the topic and confusing students. When students are clear about the goals and objectives of the lesson, their motivation is enhanced. They are better able to understand the logic of the lesson and the reasons for the various activities.

These clear goals and objectives should reflect what students should learn or be able to do as a result of the lesson and not what the teacher intends to do. Some teachers tend to define goals and objectives in terms of their own behavior. For example, a teacher might have as an objective for a lesson a discussion of the similar themes in literature. The teacher then proceeds to lecture the class on literary themes. The basic question is: What should the students be able to do as a result of this particular lesson? Will they be able to identify similar themes from literature? When teachers begin to consider what they want students to know or be able to do, they often discover that the activities they have designed and the time they have allocated are inappropriate.

Clear objectives serve yet another purpose. In fast-moving and unpredictable environments, teachers must make quick decisions. Some criteria should be established to enable them to make such decisions. A clear sense of purpose or clear goals can assist the teacher in making management decisions that are more likely to keep the group on track and moving in the right direction. A lack of clarity often results in a lesson without cohesion and in student confusion.

Clear goals and objectives benefit students. They help students understand the purposes of the activities and the content that is being covered. Clarity of purpose enhances student motivation and helps students make time and effort choices. In addition, clear goals become a framework or advance organizer for the material that is being presented. Such a framework helps students organize and understand the material with greater comprehension and clarity. This increased understanding facilitates student achievement and creates a climate of success.

Teacher Clarity

One of the most important variables in implementing and managing successful lessons is teacher clarity. Substantial verbal communication goes on in a typical classroom. The clarity of that communication has a profound effect on lesson success. Teacher messages that are confusing, garbled, or unclear will result in student confusion and frustration. Although it is easy to determine that a message is unclear, it is much more difficult to identify specifically what makes it unclear. Clarity involves a number of teacher behaviors and is made more difficult by the fact that it is a combination of what the teacher does and says and how students interpret the message (Gephart, Strother, and Duckett, 1981).

Vague and ambiguous terms interfere with lesson clarity. These include approximations (*about, almost*), ambiguous designations (*somehow, somewhere, someone*), bluffing (*everyone knows, it's a long story*), indeterminate quantification (*a bunch, a lot, a few*), and statements of probability (*frequently, generally, often*). While these terms cannot be eliminated entirely, their repeated use during a lesson signals lack of teacher knowledge and precision.

Another enemy of clarity is the presence of "mazes." Mazes are best compared to a winding path, including blind alleys, that one must navigate in order to get to the central point. When teachers are clear about their goals and careful about their communication style, they can avoid leading students into mazes out of which they may never emerge. Mazes often involve statements that lack logic or semantic sense. Mazes are frequently created when giving verbal directions. Directions are not presented clearly and concisely and too many are given at the same time. As a result, students are unsure of what to do. This confusion becomes a fertile ground for misbehavior.

"Withitness"

One of the basic concepts that emerged from the research of Kounin is the concept of "withitness." The "with-it" teacher, according to Kounin, is one who is aware of what is happening in different parts of the classroom. Such teachers are the ones that, when working with a small group in one part of the room, are aware of the behavior of students in other parts of the room. Their awareness of student behavior allows them to respond quickly when potential problems arise. Teachers with withitness are those that students describe as "having eyes in the back of their heads."

One dimension of the response of the with-it teacher is the ability to identify misbehaving students correctly. This is known as being on target. Teachers who lack withitness often identify the wrong student as the one misbehaving. In addition, correct timing enhances withitness. The with-it teacher promptly identifies unacceptable behavior and stops the behavior before it has a chance to spread to other students or become a serious problem.

Because it is one of those talents that is primarily acquired with experience, withitness is difficult to teach beginning teachers. However, withitness can be enhanced if you have planned well before you get in front of the class. Having a good plan allows you the opportunity to focus on students rather than on worrying about what you need to do next.

Overlapping

Overlapping is another Kounin concept for successful classroom managers. Overlapping refers to your ability to handle more than one task at a time. Once again, this concept is consistent with Doyle's description of the multidimensional and simultaneous classroom. A teacher skilled in overlapping is able to present lesson content to students, monitor comprehension, unobtrusively remove an object from an off-task student, make a decision about lesson pace, and respond to student questions all at the same time. In addition, they may need to handle unpredictable intrusions, such as an inquiry from the office, without missing a beat. Teachers who lack the skill of overlapping simply get lost in the maze of events and lose control of the direction of the lesson. They have trouble getting much accomplished and find themselves frustrated at the end of each day.

An element of overlapping not included in Kounin's description but that also seems important is an ability to know which events need to be handled immediately and which ones can be ignored. Many beginning teachers make the mistake of focusing on unimportant events. Those that need attention are overlooked while attention is directed to minor incidents. In a comparison of successful and unsuccessful teachers, researchers noted that successful teachers make rapid judgments during teaching, group events into larger units in order to deal with them effectively, and are able to discriminate among the events in terms of their immediate and long-term significance (Clark and Peterson, 1986).

Some people just seem to have trouble in the classroom because they do not have the characteristic of overlapping. They seem to be able to focus on only one thing at a time. They understandably have trouble in the simultaneous and fast-moving environment of the typical classroom. Overlapping, like withitness, would seem to be a difficult skill to teach. Research studies (Clark and Peterson, 1986) indicate that it might be a skill acquired through experience. However, for experience to be beneficial, teachers must develop a schema, or frame of reference, related to classroom teaching and learning that helps them select cues to attend to, understand the meaning of the cues, and make an appropriate decision. It is probable that a well-developed and context-appropriate schema is what makes teaching look so easy when demonstrated by an outstanding teacher. Student teachers often become painfully aware of this phenomenon when they take over the class of just such a teacher. The act of teaching and managing suddenly becomes much more difficult than it looked during observations.

Another action that you can take to help with overlapping is to simplify the complex classroom environment. This is what Clark and Peterson refer to when they identify the ability to group events together. In addition, having well-established routines will help simplify the environment and make it easier to overlap.

Lesson Momentum

Those of us who are sports fans frequently hear announcers state that one team now has the momentum. They mean that this team now has control of the game and things are going its way. In the classroom we want the momentum to be on the side of learning and not on the side of off-task behavior. Lesson momentum involves keeping the lesson moving forward at a steady and appropriate pace. In a class with good lesson momentum, students move ahead at a relatively brisk pace and stay on-task with no breaks in the flow of the lesson. Although unpredictable events, such as an announcement over the loudspeaker, will break the lesson momentum, teachers are the major offenders in slowing down lessons and breaking the momentum. Kounin identified two teacher behaviors that break lesson momentum: lesson fragmentation and overdwelling.

Fragmentation
Fragmentation, identified by Kounin as the major problem in maintaining lesson momentum, occurs in several ways. One way is breaking a lesson into several unnecessary steps when the task could be quickly accomplished in one or two steps. As a result, students spend time waiting rather than maintaining their focus on the lesson and lesson objectives. A good example of lesson fragmentation is some of the earlier forms of programmed learning. Some of these programs broke the content into such small steps that the person completing the program failed to see the whole picture and how the pieces fit together to make the whole. Another commonly observed example of fragmentation is when a teacher asks one student to come to the front and solve a problem while the rest of the class sits and watches. This often produces boredom and provides an opportunity for students to focus their attention on something other than the lesson.

Overdwelling
Overdwelling, another enemy of lesson momentum, occurs when you spend too much time in needless repetition or elaboration of instructions. While it is true that some repetition is important for learning to occur and you do need to make sure that students understand instructions, too much time spent doing this will bring lesson momentum

to a standstill. Teachers have a tendency to talk too much. This is particularly evident when giving directions. Some teachers deliver their directions in a rambling discourse that confuses the most dedicated student. You need to be concise in your lesson presentations and learn to give clear directions.

Another form of overdwelling occurs when you spend an inordinate amount of time on a minor or insignificant part of a task rather than emphasizing the main ideas. Because students may fail to see the relevance of what is being discussed, their motivation decreases. In addition, students lose sight of the lesson objectives and attend, instead, to insignificant content. They then become confused and angry when they fail to achieve success.

Lesson Smoothness

Lesson smoothness, another concept developed by Kounin, is also concerned with the flow of the lesson. Not only does a lesson need to move forward at an appropriate pace but also parts of the lesson need to be thematically related so that one part of the lesson flows smoothly into the next. Two dimensions of lesson management that contribute to lesson smoothness are connected discourse and creative repetition. Factors that detract from lesson smoothness are thrusts, dangles and truncations, and flip-flops.

Connected Discourse

Connected discourse refers to the logic or connectedness of teacher talk. The parts of the lesson should be thematically connected so that there is a logical flow and the lesson makes sense. Some teachers have developed the bad habit of starting a lesson and then going off on a tangent. They then return to the topic of the lesson for awhile and then go off on another tangent. This causes confusion as students try to sort out the point that the teacher is trying to make. Although connected discourse is not one of the factors of lesson smoothness identified by Kounin, it has been identified as an important variable in research on teacher clarity and fits nicely with the concept.

Detailed planning can increase lesson smoothness. Trying to teach "off-the cuff" or without giving much thought to the flow of major points almost always results in a loss of smoothness. Clear objectives specified before the class begins help keep you focused on the main points of the lesson and help eliminate fruitless digressions. When doing your planning you should evaluate your plan for a logical flow of concepts and activities. Do the pieces fit together to make a whole? Does it make sense, and is it likely that a student following that sequence would learn the material presented?

Creative Repetition

A certain amount of repetition is necessary for learning to occur; telling students once is seldom enough. However, merely repeating the same thing over and over

ACTIVITY 6-1 CATCHING THE TEACHABLE MOMENT

Bill Brundidge believes that the key to effective teaching is finding the "teachable moment." He believes that very complete plans make the lesson too rigid and therefore the teacher misses teachable moments. He prefers to identify a topic and then let the discussion be free-flowing. As the discussion progresses, he picks up on ideas that interest the students and they become the focus of the day.

During a typical day several of his students are actually involved in the discussion. About five of them appear to be working on assignments for other classes and two or three have their heads down on their desks. Bill does not consider this inappropriate because no one is actively disturbing the discussion.

What do you think?

1. Do you agree with Bill's approach to teaching? Why or why not?

2. Does planning interfere with catching the "teachable moment"?

3. Would you agree with Bill's assessment that he does not have a discipline problem?

4. What would your recommendations be?

---

is not effective. Instead, try to think of creative ways of repeating previous points. Rather than merely repeating the same idea or concept, effective teachers try to find a new application, a new problem, or a new way of illustrating the main points of the lesson.

Creative repetition at key points in the lesson helps make the structure of the lesson clear and provides the redundancy necessary to promote learning. Presenting internal summaries at key points in a lesson is another way of providing repetition. Like connected discourse, creative repetition is not one of Kounin's concepts, but has emerged out of the research on teacher clarity.

Thrusts

One other way that teachers interfere with lesson smoothness is by bringing in statements or questions for which the class is not ready. These abrupt statements are called "thrusts." An example of a thrust is a direction given to students to pass out books or papers in the midst of a lesson. Although this material is required for the lesson, giving the direction during the lesson thrusts the interfering activity to the forefront and interferes with lesson smoothness. Thrusts are often evidence of a poor sense of timing. Teachers who are guilty of thrusts do not consider when it is best to give directions or attend to routine tasks.

Dangles and Truncations

Dangles and truncations are breaks in the lesson flow. They occur when a teacher leaves an activity in midstream. For example, as you are teaching a lesson you suddenly remember something that must be done and you stop the lesson before the objective has been reached and switch to the other activity. That would be a truncation. If, however, the alternate activity only took a few minutes and you now switch back to the initial activity, it would be called a dangle. Dangles and truncations interfere with student concentration and feelings of achievement. Lessons are not properly brought to a close and the smoothness and logic of the lesson are destroyed. Truncations often occur when you forget to watch the clock. Suddenly you realize that time is almost up so you abruptly stop the activity without providing closure.

Flip-Flops

In some respect, flip-flops are like dangles. They occur when you stop one activity, begin a second activity, and then return to the first activity. Flip-flops often occur when teachers plan lessons and make decisions poorly. For example, an elementary reading teacher might plan a lesson in which the students begin by reading a story. Then they do a worksheet and then return to reading the story. A secondary modern language teacher might begin with practice speaking, then introduce new vocabulary, and then return to more practice speaking. Some beginning teachers introduce flip-flops when they realize that they don't have enough material to last the entire period. They then try to fill the time by adding some filler activity in the middle of the lesson. Unfortunately, many students never return to the original focus and those that do may have difficulty understanding the purpose of the lesson.

Group Focus

Maintaining a focus on the group is another area identified by Kounin as important when managing a lesson. Teaching is an activity involving groups of students rather than individuals. Although this fact seems obvious, teachers often have trouble because they focus on individuals rather than on the entire group. The ability to keep the entire group focused and on-task is an important aspect of successful teaching. There are several dimensions of group focus: gaining student attention, providing a variety of tasks and avoiding satiation, keeping individuals in the group alert and accountable, gaining the active participation of the students, and responding to misbehavior.

Gaining Student Attention

Gaining and keeping student attention throughout the lesson is a central element of effective group management. Some teachers think that if they have students' attention at the beginning the task is accomplished. A variety of alternatives are available to help gain students' attention at the beginning of the lesson; some are helpful to maintain attention, and others facilitate a successful lesson conclusion and build motivation for future lessons (Wlodkowski, 1978).

Gaining student attention at the beginning of the lesson can be accomplished by appealing to the sense of curiosity and by starting the lesson with something novel or unique. Relating the lesson to student needs and developing a positive attitude toward the subject are also important. Maintaining student attention throughout the lesson is enhanced by making the experience an enjoyable and challenging one. Sensory stimulation can help maintain attention if the students have been engaged in one activity for some time and are likely to become bored. Ending the lesson with an emphasis on what the student has learned and positive reinforcement can establish the foundation for gaining attention the next time the subject is taught. Students need to end the class feeling good about the subject and their efforts. Those who believe that their efforts will have a payoff and that their need for achievement is being satisfied will begin to develop an intrinsic interest in the topic and exercise more self-control.

Providing Variety and Avoiding Satiation

Having a variety of tasks in a lesson provides sensory stimulation. For example, students should not be expected to listen or read for an entire period. Kounin identified this as one of the crucial lesson management variables. Variety helps to avoid satiation. Satiation refers to the state when someone is well past the point of being tired of the activity. When students are satiated, they become restless, make more errors in their work, and start seeking an escape.

Several techniques can help provide for variety during a lesson. One is changing the group configuration from large- to small-group or to independent study. Changing the mode of delivery is another approach. Students can listen for a short time, watch a film, read a short selection, and then have a discussion. Rotating teacher input activities with student production activities is yet another way of providing variety. One high school modern language teacher I once worked with had a rule of thumb that was very effective. Her rule was that students should not be asked to perform any one activity for more than 15 minutes. This meant that she had at least three different tasks. She might have dictation for 15 minutes, reading for 15 minutes, and writing for 15 minutes during any one period. Boredom and satiation were seldom problems in her classes.

Keeping the Group Alert and Accountable

Throughout a lesson you need to make sure that all students are kept alert. This can be accomplished by holding the students in suspense so that they never know when they might be called on to respond to a teacher question or perform a task. Group alerting techniques, such as having all students signify their agreement or disagreement with a statement or question by holding up their hands, are useful in keeping students on their toes. If students believe that you have started a lesson during which there is little probability that they will be called on to respond, their attention will wander and their involvement in the lesson will decrease.

Keeping students accountable means letting them know that they will need to use what is taught in some manner. A good example of accountability can be observed in

ACTIVITY 6-2   KEEPING THE CLASS ALERT AND ACCOUNTABLE

Plan a lesson in your subject and at a grade level of your choice. Imagine that you are making a presentation to the entire class. Consider how you would present this topic to a group of students and keep them alert and accountable.

- What specific things would you do during the lesson to keep students alert?

- How would you gain their attention?

- What would you do to provide variety?

- How would you ask questions of students? Would you randomly call on them?

- How might you use creative repetition?

- How would you inform the students that they would be accountable for the material?

- What specific tasks would you have the students do to have them apply the material?

---

college classrooms. For example, my students often ask, "Will this be on the test?" This is their way of determining accountability. They want to know whether or not they will be required to do something with what is being presented. What happens if I say, "No, you don't need to learn this?" Pencils go down and their attention begins to wander.

Testing students is not the only way, or even the best way, of making them accountable. You should try to have students use the material you present in class. This can be done by having them do things such as summarizing the material to a partner, doing a worksheet related to the topic, applying the material to a new situation, writing a reaction paper, or taking a short quiz. When students know that they will be required to demonstrate their understanding, their attending behavior shows a marked increase.

Gaining Active Participation and Involvement

As Doyle (1986) points out, for an activity to succeed, a sufficient number of students must cooperate with the teacher and participate in the lesson. Individuals who are not involved will seek some diversion. More often than not, this diversion will be destructive to the progress of the lesson. Regaining the attention of those students who have wandered off the task is difficult. It is better to keep the entire group focused throughout.

As you conduct lessons, you need to be alert for opportunities for involving students. They should not be expected to sit passively for more than a few minutes at a time. The basic goal is to get a high percentage of involvement during every stage of the lesson. To do this, students might be asked to complete an outline as you are going through the lesson. They might be required to signal their agreement or disagreement with certain statements. Another technique is to space problems throughout the lesson so that they have to do something immediately with the material. Well-designed cooperative learning groups are an excellent way of facilitating the active involvement of a large percentage of learners.

Kounin divided work involvement or active participation into two types: work involvement during recitation or whole group instruction and work involvement while doing seatwork. His research indicated that withitness, lesson smoothness, lesson momentum, group alerting, and accountability were all positively associated with maintaining high levels of active participation and involvement in lessons involving recitation or whole group instruction. Lesson variety was most strongly associated with a high level of work involvement during seatwork (Dunkin and Biddle, 1974). Applying these group management concepts to the various parts of the lesson can be helpful in maintaining high levels of group participation in the lesson and in delivering the types of lessons during which misbehavior is prevented.

Responding to Misbehavior

Responding to misbehavior is the major focus of the later chapters of this book. However, it does need to be mentioned in relationship to lesson management. Unfortunately, some teachers spend a considerable amount of their instructional time responding to discipline problems. In these situations, lesson smoothness and momentum are destroyed, student attention is diverted from the lesson to the misbehavior, and participation and cooperation drop to unacceptable levels.

A major principle you need to consider when responding to misbehavior during a lesson is to try and respond in a manner that keeps the attention of the class on the lesson content rather than diverted to the misbehavior. If possible you need to try and respond in an unobtrusive manner that gains the attention of the offending student but does not attract the attention of others. This is not always possible because there is some misbehavior that is so intrusive or serious that you need to stop the lesson in order to gain control. However, some teachers are guilty of responding to each minor incident in such an obtrusive manner that the attention of all students is focused on the misbehavior. Instead, the teacher should respond as quietly and as unobtrusively as possible.

In choosing how to respond you need to assess how disruptive the behavior is to others and how likely it is to spread. If it is not attracting the attention of other students and it is not likely to spread beyond the one student, you need to respond in a very unobtrusive manner. However, if the behavior is attracting the attention of others, you need to act quickly before the problem spreads. This is one of the aspects of withitness, discussed earlier in this chapter. Later chapters will provide you with some concrete suggestions on choosing an appropriate response.

TABLE 6-1 **Lesson Management**

Management Dimension	Response
Objectives:	
Are they clear?	
Do the objectives provide focus?	
Clarity:	
Have I avoided ambiguous terms?	
Does my plan have a logical flow?	
Withitness:	
How will I monitor all parts of the classroom?	
Lesson Momentum:	
How will I keep the lesson moving at a good pace?	
What will I do if students try to get me off on a tangent?	
Is my lesson coherent and not fragmented?	
Am I giving clear directions and not overdwelling?	
Lesson Smoothness:	
Is my input connected and does it follow a logical sequence?	
How can I use creative repetition?	
Have I avoided thrusts, dangles, and flip-flops?	
Group Focus:	
How will I gain initial attention?	
What strategies will I use to keep all students alert?	
What will I do to hold all students accountable for learning?	
How have I provided for variety during the lesson?	
How will I respond to misbehavior?	

SUMMARY

Lesson management is one of the primary tasks of teachers. Those who can manage a lesson with skill prevent problems and help students move toward the goal of self-control. Outstanding teachers often make the task appear simple. In fact, managing a classroom takes considerable skill and knowledge. Classrooms are multidimensional, simultaneous, unpredictable, public places where teachers must act immediately. These aspects of the environment make classroom management difficult.

A beginning step for successful management is to develop clear goals and objectives so your decisions keep the lesson moving in a positive direction. Teacher clarity is important so that confusion is avoided and students remain focused on the task. The work of Kounin identified "withitness," overlapping, lesson momentum, and lesson smoothness as important variables in lesson management. Teachers must be aware of what is happening in the classroom at all times, be able to handle more than one task at a time, and keep the lesson moving at a good pace with a logical flow of activities and events.

Maintaining the attention of a large number of the group members is necessary if the lesson is to be successful. This can be facilitated by gaining student attention at the beginning of the lesson, maintaining it during a lesson, and reinforcing the learning at the end. Adding variety to the lesson, keeping students alert and accountable, and maximizing work involvement are also important dimensions of lesson management.

Finally, your response to misbehavior is another important dimension. Teachers may, by their responses, cause more disruption than the misbehavior. Therefore, you should attempt to respond in ways that keep student attention on the lesson rather than on the behavior. When the behavior appears to be one that might spread, quick action is required in order to prevent the spread and to keep the maximum number of students focused on the lesson.

SUGGESTED APPLICATIONS

1. "Withitness" is an important aspect of classroom management. Brainstorm with a group of individuals those things that indicate teacher withitness and what teachers can do to develop this important skill.

2. Observe a lesson from beginning to end. Identify how the teacher tries to keep momentum and smoothness in the lesson and those things that interfere with smoothness and momentum. Note examples of the multidimensional, simultaneous nature of the classroom.

3. Tape-record a lesson. Listen to the tape and identify instances when there seems to be a lack of clarity. Suggest ways that clarity could be improved.

4. Meet with a group of individuals and brainstorm techniques that can be used to keep students alert and accountable during the course of a lesson.

SUGGESTED READINGS

Clark, C. and Peterson, P. (1986). Teachers' thought processes. In *Handbook of research on teaching,* 3rd Ed. M. C. Wittrock, (ed.). New York: Macmillan, 255–296.

Doyle, W. (1986). Classroom management and organization. In *Handbook of research on teaching,* 3rd Ed. M. C. Wittrock, (ed.). New York: Macmillan, 392–431.

Dunkin, M. and Biddle, B. (1974). *The study of teaching.* New York: Holt, Rinehart & Winston.

Gephardt, W., Strother, D., and Duckett, W. (1981). Practical applications of research. *Phi Delta Kappa,* 3(3),

Good, T. L. and Brophy, J. E. (1997). *Looking in classrooms,* 7th Ed. New York: Longman.

Gump, P. (1967). The classroom behavior setting: Its nature and relation to student behavior, final report. *ERIC Document Reproduction Services No. 015515.* Washington, DC: U.S. Office of Education, Bureau of Research.

Jackson, P. (1968). *Life in classrooms.* New York: Holt, Rinehart & Winston.

Kounin, J. (1970). *Discipline and group management in classrooms.* New York: Holt, Rinehart & Winston.

Minnick, D., ed. (1983). Student disruption: Classroom chaos linked to teacher practices. *Research and Development Center for Teacher Education Review* 1, 2–3.

Wlodkowski, R. (1978). *Discipline and motivation: A genuine partnership.* Washington, DC: National Education Association.

PART TWO

Responding to Problems

7 Responding to Inappropriate Behavior

Chapter Objectives

After reading this chapter you should be able to:

- Identify criteria to use when evaluating a classroom discipline plan
- Define basic principles to be used when choosing a response to inappropriate behavior
- State questions that you can use when developing a discipline plan
- Define three categories of responses that can be used when selecting a response to inappropriate behavior
- Describe the basic components of assertive discipline

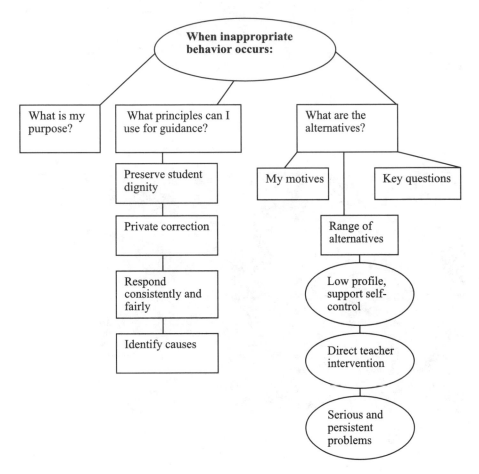

FIGURE 7-1   **Graphic Organizer for Responding to Inappropriate Behavior**

Your first concern as a teacher is to prevent discipline problems. However, as Kohn (1996) notes, no degree of skill on the part of the teacher can prevent all problems. Any time that there are a significant number of people together for any length of time we can expect problems. Even the best teachers have to respond to inappropriate behavior, they just have fewer problems that require a response. Everyone makes mistakes and everyone misbehaves on occasion, even teachers. Mistakes and problems are an important part of life and responding to problems is an important part of being a teacher. However, the manner and style that you use in responding to problems will influence whether or not the students learn from their mistakes and grow toward increased self-control. Inappropriate behaviors can be used as important learning experiences or they can turn into major confrontations in which the relationship between the teacher and the student is harmed and the probability of significant learning decreased.

There is no shortage of suggestions about what to do when problems do arise in the classroom, and most of the suggestions have been useful for some teachers. However, what works for one teacher in a specific situation may not work for another in a different situation. There are simply no easy solutions. If there were, lack of discipline would not be one of the major problems cited by teachers. You must become a decision maker who can evaluate the situation, understand the unique combinations of the students you are teaching, weigh alternatives, and choose a response that is consistent with your needs and those of the students. This requires that you have some knowledge of alternative responses and some criteria to use in making a choice. As we move into the section of the book that focuses on responding to inappropriate behavior, a number of alternative responses will be presented and some criteria suggested for helping you make choices.

THE PURPOSE OF DISCIPLINE

The focus of this book is that the purpose of discipline is to help students grow toward increased self-control. We want students to have satisfying and productive lives. This is simply not possible if one does not have self-control. However, self-control is not something that is innate. It is learned. Self-control is learned as we grow and experience the consequences of our actions. It is the role of the teacher to help students understand and reflect on their actions and the consequences of those actions. The major point is that the welfare of the student is preeminent in selecting how to respond to inappropriate behavior. When viewed in this context, the occurrence of inappropriate behavior is not something that is totally negative, something to be avoided at all costs. Rather, we need to view the occurrence of inappropriate behavior as an opportunity to help students learn some of the most important lessons in life.

The basic question that you should constantly ask yourself as you respond to problems is, "Will my response help move the student in the direction of increased self-control?" This question should take priority over concerns such as maintaining quiet classrooms or covering the content of the lesson. This does not imply that covering the content is unimportant. It means that there are times when content coverage needs to be given a lower priority when choosing a response. There are responses that will stop a behavior so that you can continue with the lesson but that do not help the students learn self-control. In the long run, not learning self-control will mean that less content is covered and it will take more time and effort to maintain an orderly classroom.

Keeping the purpose of self-control at the forefront also helps you evaluate the effectiveness of your discipline program. If students are not demonstrating increased self-control as the academic year progresses, you need to seriously question whether your approach is working. This does not mean that you should always expect immediate and dramatic change. Growth and learning can be a slow process. Some students who have not developed much self-control are not likely to demonstrate much improvement in a week or even in a month. In fact, they may be so used to getting their own self-centered desires met that their behavior gets worse before it gets better. Nor does it mean that there will even be progress toward this goal. There will be good days and bad. However, over several months, there should be some evidence that the class is progressing toward increased self-control.

SOME PRINCIPLES TO CONSIDER WHEN CHOOSING A RESPONSE

As you begin to consider your response to inappropriate behavior you need to consider why you might choose a particular response. You might choose a response because you think it will communicate to students that they had better not mess with you. Or, you may choose a response because it will allow you to get revenge for any hurt or embarrassment that the student might have caused. Unfortunately, these reasons seem to dominate the reasoning of some teachers. There are some principles that you can keep in mind that will assist you in choosing responses that are more likely

---

DISCIPLINE SCENARIO 7-1   **What Is Hector's Problem?**

Hector is generally a likable student but one who has had a difficult life. He is a hard worker and tries hard but has trouble achieving success. He is a large boy and is bigger than most of the other students in the classroom. His family is in the lower socioeconomic range and Hector does not have any money. On occasion, he has not even had money for lunch. His family has moved frequently so that he has been in several different schools in different parts of the country. He does not have any close friends in the classroom. Hector becomes easily frustrated. When this happens he becomes very aggressive and disruptive. He has challenged other students to fights and has called the teacher names.

How would you respond?

1. What do you think might be the cause of his behavior?

2. What might be some immediate things you could do to try and prevent his eruptions?

3. What would be your motives when you respond to his outbursts?

4. What immediate response might you make when he loses his temper?

5. What might be some long-range responses that would address the causes of his behavior?

to promote a healthy classroom environment where students are learning and growing toward increased self control.

The Dignity of Students Should Be Preserved When Responding to Their Behavior

When individuals believe that their dignity is being challenged, the tendency is to strike back. Rather than stopping a behavior, a response that does not respect the student is likely to lead to more serious problems. Docking (1987) points out that students often see maliciousness as a way of restoring their self-dignity when confronted by situations in which they feel that they are not being treated as persons. Misbehavior is often a symbolic rejection of authority (Docking, 1987). A significant percentage of secondary students state that this is precisely why they misbehave. They believe that the teacher is not respecting them as a person and is assaulting their self-respect and dignity.

It is hard to solve a problem unless there is a positive relationship between the teacher and the student (Kohn, 1996). Students need to trust you, know that you respect them, and that you have their best interests at heart. This will not occur if you have humiliated or demeaned students. When you do so, you lose the respect of the students and establish the basis for a power struggle. This casts teachers and students as adversaries. Little can be accomplished in helping students move toward improved self-control and more desired behavior if these conditions are present in the classroom.

Private Correction Is Preferable to Public Correction

This principle is an outgrowth of the first one. Preserving the dignity of the student is easier when the correction is private. Public correction has several potential dangers. Not only does public correction have the strong potential for public humiliation; it focuses attention on the inappropriate behavior. Students who have high attention needs have learned that it is often easier to get attention by misbehaving. For example, an especially difficult student once stated, "Everyone in school knows me because I'm always in trouble. But, what do you get for being good?" He clearly saw that there was a payoff for his inappropriate behavior. As much as possible, we want to avoid giving public attention to inappropriate behavior.

In addition, public correction can make the situation more difficult for the teacher. Many of us have observed the situation in which a teacher corrects a student in public. The student then refuses to change. The teacher is now on the spot. The student has engaged the teacher in a challenge and all of the class is watching to see how the teacher will respond. The typical response of the teacher is to escalate the conflict by trying to get tougher. What originally started as a minor incident has now become a major confrontation that is played out in front of an audience.

Responding in private helps remove the audience. The need for a student to save face and prove something to peers is removed. The problem can be dealt with in a quiet manner that preserves the dignity of the student and maintains the credibility of the teacher.

Not all problems can be dealt with in private. There are times when the situation requires that the teacher respond in a public manner. For example, if inappropriate behavior is disrupting a lesson and interfering with your ability to teach, you may need to respond in order to stop the behavior. When you do need to respond publicly, you need to ask yourself, "How can I deal with this as unobtrusively and unemotionally as possible?" If you can keep public correction to a minimum, you will find that it is more effective when you must use it.

Respond to Incidents of Misbehavior Consistently and Fairly

Implicit in this statement is the assumption that you need to respond to incidents of misbehavior. Few problems will disappear if you just pretend that they do not exist. Some well-meaning authorities counsel teachers to ignore misbehavior because the withholding of attention deprives the student of reinforcement and the behavior will soon cease. This will work if the teacher is the only source of reinforcement for the student. However, this is rarely true in the classroom. Other students are also providing reinforcement for behavior in the classroom. Simply withholding teacher reinforcement is likely to have little impact if other students are providing attention and reinforcement.

It is important to understand what responding consistently means. Responding consistently to misbehavior means that you respond to all incidents of misbehavior and each day. If something is against the rule on one day, it is against the rule every day. Your enforcement of the rules is not dependent on your daily mood. Those classes characterized by students' constant testing of the rules are usually those in which the teacher has inconsistently enforced the rules. Students need to know what is unacceptable in your classroom and should be able to predict that if they engage in those behaviors, there will be a consequence. This does not necessarily mean that as a teacher you promote mindless conformity or that you have to respond to each student and each incident in exactly the same way.

Fairness means that you follow through with consequences regardless of who is misbehaving. Teachers have a tendency to overlook the misbehavior of a star student and to be excessively harsh when responding to a student for whom they have little affection. This uneven treatment leads to resentment. You need to make sure that if cute little Sarah misbehaves, she will experience a consequence just as surely as will Barbara, the perennial problem.

Identify the Causes of Misbehavior

This requires an attitude of inquiry on your part. You need to seek answers to questions concerning why the individual might be behaving in a certain way. Kohn (1996) notes that the adult's role in an unpleasant situation begins with the need to diagnose what has happened and why. Attempts to correct behavior often fail because the underlying reasons causing the behavior are ignored. This failure to identify causes almost always results in a recurring pattern of behavior. It is probable that persistent misbehavior signals some deeper, more fundamental problems either with the organization and climate of the classroom or some personal problems being experienced by the student. Merely responding to the surface behavior may temporarily stop the behavior but it will not solve the problem. You can be sure that misbehavior will recur and might even take a more serious form.

It has been my experience that persistent misbehavior is often a desperate call for help. The student understands that he or she is in serious difficulty and knows no other way to signal the need for help. Understanding this can help you respond to the student in ways that not only eliminate the problem but also result in great professional and personal rewards.

Being willing to search for the causes of misbehavior requires a professionally and personally secure teacher. You must be willing to consider the possibility that your actions might be causing the problem. We have discovered from research that teachers do not readily recognize that they might be a causal factor of student misbehavior (Brophy and Rohrkemper, 1981). It is sometimes difficult to look beyond the surface problem and raise questions about our own practice. However, that might be exactly what is required in order to find a solution (Kohn, 1996). We need to make sure that the students are not blamed for all problems. Misbehavior, for example, could be a signal of student anxiety and fear of failure because the lesson is

---

ACTIVITY 7-1   APPLYING THE BASIC PRINCIPLES

Everyone makes mistakes and everyone has been disciplined. Think about a time when you were disciplined and respond to the following questions.

My experience:

1. What was the problem?

2. How did the teacher (or parent) respond to the problem?

3. Which of the principles of discipline were followed?

4. Which of the principles were not followed?

5. What was the outcome? How did you feel or respond?

6. What advice would you give that person that could lead to a more productive response?

not at the appropriate level of difficulty. Perhaps the student is bored, lacks an understanding of the importance or relevance of the topic, or perhaps the lesson pacing is inappropriate. Probing for the causes of the misbehavior might lead the teacher to professional improvement that can prevent future problems.

Some misbehavior merely reflects youthful exuberance and enthusiasm. If this is identified as the reason for the behavior, it should not treated as a major offense requiring stiff penalties. Occasional, minor infractions may be nothing more than uncontrolled enthusiasm. We certainly do not want to reduce student enthusiasm; we just need to help them learn how to demonstrate it in appropriate ways.

CHOOSING A RESPONSE TO MISBEHAVIOR

With these principles in mind, you are now ready to consider how to respond to incidents of misbehavior. Some teachers have difficulty in choosing a response because they are unaware of the options and therefore rely on a limited number of responses that soon lose their effectiveness. New and inexperienced teachers sometimes overreact to relatively minor incidents, or don't respond at all because of uncertainty about how to respond. Being an effective classroom manager involves knowing a range of alternative actions and when to implement them. Randomly choosing responses or following an impulse is usually ineffective.

Choosing a Response Best for You

One of the things that makes discipline so difficult is the personal dimension. We have different personalities and different interpersonal skills. Each group of students is different and has a different set of group dynamics. What might work for you in one setting might not work for another teacher in another classroom.

Students bring their previous experiences with them to the classroom. Advanced placement students who have high expectations of success and an academic orientation will respond to teacher correction somewhat differently than will learners with a history of school failure. Teachers discover that they have to change their methods according to the types of students in the classroom. Not all students arrive at your classroom door enthusiastic and positive. They may come from home environments that are less than helpful and positive. They may be used to getting their way through power and intimidation. Although we can not do anything about their background, we should not use it as an excuse to give up. We can respond in ways that will help them grow and learn some valuable lessons that will be important to them for the rest of their lives.

Students come to school with different cultural and social values concerning the importance of school and appropriate behavior in the school environment. You must understand that you probably will not be teaching students who are like you. There is a tremendous diversity contained in many classrooms. This diversity will not only include ethnicity but socioeconomic status, religion, gender, and learning disabilities.

One of my professors used to regularly remind us, "In the public schools, we teach *all* of the students from *all* of the families." We must get used to the fact that students will not be just like us.

As you search for approaches that will be most comfortable for you and most appropriate for the students you teach you need to ask yourself some questions. The following are some that can help you choose responses that will be most effective.

1. *What are your values and beliefs about the nature of learners and your role as a teacher?* The attitudes and beliefs that you hold toward learners will have an important impact on the way you choose to respond to incidents of misbehavior. A key issue is whether you view learners as basically good or basically bad. If you believe, for example, that learners are not capable or trustworthy, then your response to a discipline problem is likely to be one that is heavy on teacher power and low on student choice. If, on the other hand, you believe that students should be given a great deal of freedom because they can be trusted to make appropriate choices, then approaches to discipline are likely to be indirect ones that de-emphasize teacher control.

A rather prevalent belief among many teachers and parents in our society is that individuals should do what is good and right with no expectation of a reward or reinforcement. As a result, few reinforcers are used and much negative attention is directed toward the inappropriate behavior. Individuals who have this belief are often reluctant to use approaches that emphasize positive reinforcement for expected behavior. To them, providing frequent reinforcers is viewed as unethical.

Your view of the learning process will also affect your choice of an approach. Teachers who view the learning process as hard work that takes place in a strict, nononsense environment will define discipline problems differently and will respond to incidents of misbehavior differently than those who consider learning as a process of activity and exploration that requires freedom and choice.

Your role as a teacher is yet another topic that needs consideration. If the role of the teacher is defined as one of primarily communicating content and subject matter, and the social and emotional needs of learners are not your concern, then little effort will be directed toward helping students deal with these problems or move toward increased self-control. This is sometimes the situation with secondary school teachers. They have chosen teaching because of their love of the subject. Their concern is to teaching English or history. They do not want to be bothered with the emotional concerns of students and see them as the responsibility of school counselors. Slee (1995) points out that reducing discipline to the status of what we do to generate student compliance and organizational harmony limits the potential for a successful intervention that will lead to successful learning. You need to realize that the emotional and social needs of the students will affect your classroom. Students do not leave their personal lives at the classroom door. Nor can it be expected that school counselors can solve their problems. If you respond to problems based on a definition of the role of a teacher as that of covering prescribed content, you will probably be disappointed in the results.

ACTIVITY 7-2   WHAT IS YOUR PHILOSOPHY?

A beginning point in developing a discipline plan is an awareness of your values and beliefs about the nature of the students and the nature of the learning process. In order for your plan to be effective, it must be consistent with your beliefs and understanding. Take a few minutes to reflect on your views. For this to be effective you need to be open and honest with yourself.

What I Believe:

1. What are your views and beliefs about students? Do you think they are inherently good or inherently bad? Do you think they are interested in school or do they view it as merely something they must endure?

2. What do you think your role is as a teacher? Should you be expected to deal with emotional problems? What is your role relative to discipline?

3. How do you believe that people learn self-control?

4. What do your views imply in terms of the types of responses you would choose when misbehavior occurs?

5. What do you think is the best way to establish control in the classroom?

——————

2. *What is the maturity level of the students I am teaching?* Some responses to misbehavior require more maturity on the part of the learners. It is unrealistic to think that responses that are effective for very young children will also be effective for older children. Some approaches require considerable abstract reasoning and that the student be able to take the perspective of another. Very young children have not reached the developmental level where they are capable of abstract reasoning or adopting another perspective. Approaches based on these assumptions are not likely to be successful.

It is important to realize, however, that age alone is not a reliable indicator of emotional and moral maturity. There are some individuals at the secondary school level who have not yet attained the moral maturity to understand the function of law and accept the notion of social and moral responsibility. These students need to be assisted in their emotional and moral growth if they are to move toward the self-control required of a responsible citizen.

3. *What are the cultural backgrounds and the values of the learners I am teaching?* Teachers often overlook the influence of culture on behavior. Individuals often believe that others view the world as they view it. This causes problems for a teacher who comes from one subculture who is teaching students from another subculture. Students may have a different view of the role of school and what constitutes appropriate behavior and may interpret teacher responses very differently. For example, some cultural groups teach their children that proper behavior in school is to sit quietly and listen. Other students from other cultural groups arrive at school with a tradition that emphasizes sharing and joint performance (Au, 1980). These different cultural perspectives need to be taken into account when you define appropriate and inappropriate behavior.

Nonverbal communication is an area where different cultures attach different meanings to behavior. Some subcultures do not encourage touching behavior and others do. A teacher uncomfortable touching individuals may be viewed as cold and uncaring by students who come from a "contact" subculture.

The teacher who wishes to be successful in developing an effective discipline plan must consider the cultural expectations and norms of the group being taught. This can be accomplished by discussing the culture with members and simply observing the students.

4. *What is the previous school history of the learners in the classroom?* Answering this question requires a high level of professionalism and care. Knowing the background of a student can help you search for the reasons behind certain behaviors. If you can find the causes for the behavior then you can seek to eliminate them. However, it is easy for a teacher to develop lower expectations and find excuses for students who have a history of problems and failures. These lowered expectations can then influence your behavior so that the student learning opportunities are lost. The professional teacher needs to learn to use records in an appropriate and professional manner.

When you have a student who appears to have some difficult problems, search the record and look for events or patterns of behavior that might help you understand the student. Has the student had some illnesses in the past? It might be that that period of illness caused some significant gaps in learning so that the student is unable to achieve success. Does the student have a history of moving from school to school? He or she might feel afraid and lonely. Was the student retained? They might have poor self-esteem and perceive themselves as failures. In summary, the records of students need to be used for diagnostic, not labeling, purposes.

5. *What type of support can you expect from the parents?* The support of parents is extremely important in developing and implementing an effective discipline plan. You need to solicit support from parents actively and make them allies, not adversaries. Remember that you are dealing with the parents' most valued possession, their child. Nearly all parents want their children to be successful and most parents are more than willing to help. However, some parents do not know what they can do to support you and are initially fearful and defensive when contacted by a teacher. Unfortunately, this is because all some parents have ever heard from the teacher is bad news. They rarely are contacted about something good. Because many of us take the failures of our children personally, we tend to become defensive when someone else criticizes them.

ACTIVITY 7-3   INVOLVING PARENTS

Parent involvement can be a critical component in dealing with discipline and in creating a positive learning environment. However, working with parents is an area in which new teachers are often uncertain and fearful. You need to consider how you can involve parents. Take a few minutes to think about how you might involve parents.

What Can I Do?

1. How will you inform parents of your rules and expectations?

2. Some parents have only heard from a teacher when there is something wrong. You need to get good messages to parents. How will you send good messages to parents? How can you involve them in your classroom in positive activities?

3. How will you communicate with parents when there is a problem?

4. What will you do if you get a hostile reaction from a parent?

You need to make efforts to have positive contacts with parents. Keep them informed and seek avenues for getting them involved in the school program. It is much easier to deal with someone you know. If you do have a difficult parent you need to keep the administrator or counselor informed and involved. You may need to remember that you have a responsibility to all students in your classroom. One individual cannot be allowed to interfere with the learning of others simply because the parent refuses to cooperate. In more serious situations, outside agencies and resources may offer some needed resources to assist parents.

6. *How much time and effort will the response require?* Some responses require more investment of time than do others. Some approaches may require a meeting or a counseling session with the student. There are situations in the classroom when this time is simply not available. When this occurs, you need to choose, at least temporarily, a less desirable approach. Some approaches, such as behavior modification, require a large investment of out-of-class time to develop the reinforcement plan and considerable in-class time to implement it. An elementary teacher with a class of 30 students or a secondary teacher with several different preparations simply does not have the time to implement behavior modification plans for several students. Keep in mind that you may have to respond one way in the interest of time. However, you must find long-term solutions or you will continue to deal with the behavior over the course of the academic year.

7. *What resources will the response require?* Some approaches to discipline require specific materials or space. For example, time-out requires that you have some class space where you can put the student. Removing the student from the classroom requires that he or she has some place to go where he or she will be supervised. Are these resources available to you? Do you have enough space in the classroom? Do you have something you can use as reinforcers? Is there a time-out area in the school where students are to be sent? These factors must be considered when you consider the responses available to you. They may involve preplanning and cooperation with others, such as the school principal, to make sure that the time and the space are available to make the plan work.

8. *What support can I expect from the school administration?* Canter and Canter (1976) declare that you have a right to expect support from the school administration. You do need to accept that you have this right and that the administration needs to be supportive of teacher efforts to develop a positive classroom climate. However, this does not mean that you abdicate your responsibilities as a teacher and send all problems to the office. In addition, some administrators, like some teachers, are uncertain of appropriate ways of responding to the discipline problems that land in their office. As a teacher you may have to take an active role in obtaining administrative support. This can be accomplished by meeting with the administrator and explaining your plan and your expectations. This discussion needs to include the conditions under which a student will be referred to the administrator and what the administrator will do when a student does come to the office. Sending a student to the office should be a last resort, tried only when other efforts have failed.

Keeping these few questions in mind will help you search for responses to inappropriate behavior that have a higher probability of success. When selecting responses to inappropriate behavior you also need to consider your reasons for choices. Research by Brophy (1985) found that the motives of teachers are related to the type of responses that they choose.

Teacher Motives When Responding to Misbehavior

Brophy identified seven motives that guide the responses that teachers make to discipline problems. The following is a discussion of those seven motives.

1. *Survival or personal authority.* This motive indicates that the teacher is merely trying to make it through the day or trying to maintain personal authority and power. Teachers with this motive often view students as a threat and interpret misbehavior as a direct challenge to their authority. About 12 percent of the teachers in Brophy's study cited this as a primary motive for responding to misbehavior.

Consider how a person who has these motives would be likely to respond to classroom incidents. They are likely to feel threatened and be angry. Their response is not based on student feelings and needs but is based on meeting teacher needs for survival and security. We would not predict responses that respect the dignity of the students or address the causes of the behavior. Long-term solutions would generally not be considered. Attempts to obtain immediate compliance through direct threats and an exercise of teacher power would be the most likely scenario. Scolding, blaming, and threatening would be probable responses. Teachers who cite this as a primary motive seem to lack successful strategies for dealing with misbehavior (Brophy, 1985).

2. *Time on-task or an instructional concern.* The motive here is to increase the time the students are working toward the accomplishment of lesson objectives. The major concern is to get through the lesson and cover the content. About 24 percent of the teachers responded that this is a primary motive when responding to misbehavior.

Individuals with this motive are not likely to consider the causes of the behavior. Their response tends to be more impersonal and places the needs of the students second to content coverage. Individual conferences and counseling would not be chosen because they would take too much time.

3. *Group safety or continuity.* The motive of these teachers is to keep the classroom moving in an orderly fashion, not letting anything interfere with the learning and the welfare of the larger group. Individuals could not be allowed to interfere with the smooth operation of the class. About 61 percent of the teachers responded that this was a primary motive when responding to problems.

The focus of these teachers is not on the individual but on the group. They are more likely to focus on prevention measures and more long-term changes in behavior. The methods used often focus on group appeals and group sanctions to get the student to comply.

4. *Concerns about the student.* Individuals who cite this as a motive for their response indicate that they place the needs of the students first. Their motive is to help students solve problems and develop more positive behaviors. About 46 percent of the teachers cited this as a primary motive.

Teachers with this motive are focused on the needs of the individual student. They are clearly concerned with teaching students self-control. They are more likely to choose a response that they consider most appropriate for this particular student. The dignity of the student is a major concern. Individual counseling and guidance are often the choices. A long-term change in the behavior of the student is the goal.

5. *Future life.* Teachers choosing this as a motive cite a concern about future learning or success of the student. They are concerned that individuals who are not corrected will fail, drop out, or have difficulty with authorities. About 12 percent of the teachers chose this as a primary motive for their response.

These teachers are clearly concerned about teaching students coping skills and self-control that will assist them throughout their life. Immediate compliance is not the goal. They are willing to sacrifice short-term benefits, such as content coverage, in order to help the student develop changed attitudes and behavior. A primary goal is to establish positive relationships with the student. Once again, counseling, discussing behavior and consequences, and personal attention to the student are likely to be choices.

6. *School rules.* Individuals choosing this as a motive simply state that the reason they respond as they do is because the behavior is a violation of a school rule.

Therefore, they had no choice but to respond. About 11 percent of the teachers cited this as a primary concern in their response.

These teachers have a "law-and-order" orientation. Their primary concern seems to be for students to learn to comply with the law. There is usually no attempt to develop interpersonal communication with students. In fact, developing strong relationships with students might be discouraged because then the rules could not be applied objectively. These teachers tend to respond to students in a very impersonal way. There is no personal feeling or involvement. In addition, these teachers usually do not accept any responsibility. It is up to the student to follow the rules and there is no excuse.

7. *Anger or irritation.* Individuals who cite this as a motive indicate that they dislike the student or are personally angry with him or her. About 11 percent cited this as a basic motive for their response.

The responses of individuals with this motive are often those of blaming, threatening, and scolding. Some teachers actually respond in ways designed to seek revenge or hurt the student. There is a tendency when dealing with students who have been hurtful to decide that the student has done something bad so something bad needs to be done in return (Kohn, 1996). Teachers with this motive are not in a position to help students learn self-control because they are not exercising self-control. Confrontations and power struggles are the usual results when anger and irritation are the motives.

Helping students learn how to exercise self-control is clearly related to a personal concern about the welfare of students. Students are not easily deceived about the concern that a teacher has for them. Your priorities will be identified quickly and your motives for disciplining students uncovered. When your motives are perceived to be related to your own concern for power and authority, you can expect that students will challenge that power and try to make you feel insecure.

Certain conditions must be met if students are to respect teacher authority. You must have a good reason for disciplining a student, must be fair in your demands, and must communicate concern for the student as a person. Attempts by the teacher to exercise authority will be rejected unless the students believe that the teacher is exercising authority on suitable grounds and in a suitable manner (Docking, 1987). It is imperative that your motives for responding to discipline problems place concern for students as a high priority. This does not mean that motives such as time-on-task and group continuity are unimportant. You certainly do want to keep the focus on important objectives and maintain a healthy group climate. However, these are best accomplished when you have clearly communicated to students that it is their welfare that guides your actions.

Developing a Range of Alternatives

In order to choose productive responses, you must be aware of the alternatives. An important component of successfully responding to problems is being aware of alternative responses and choosing the response most appropriate for the student and the situation. One of the most productive activities that you can do is to begin developing a list of alternative responses that you can use when problems occur.

One way of thinking about alternatives is to organize them into categories. These categories can be arranged according to their degree of intrusiveness. The first category can be those responses that require minimal effort and are relatively unobtrusive. As you progress through the categories they require more teacher effort and are more intrusive. Responses to minor problems can be chosen from the first categories with the responses to more serious problems in the latter categories. As a general rule you should try the unobtrusive and less severe measures first. You should select a response that will have the least disruptive impact on the flow of the lesson. This might mean responding rather unobtrusively at the time and then returning to deal with the problem in more depth when time permits.

I have developed three categories that can be helpful to you as you begin to develop your range of alternative responses. Each of these three categories will be dealt with in depth in a later chapter. The three categories are low profile approaches that support self-control, direct teacher intervention, and responses for serious and persistent misbehavior.

Low Profile Approaches That Support Self-Control

This category includes two basic kinds of responses: positive responses that are intended to support incidents of appropriate behavior and teacher responses directed toward minor offenses. The responses grouped in this category allow students considerable freedom and choice. Your intent is to communicate in an unobtrusive way that there is a problem. The student is then given the opportunity to exercise self-control. By allowing the student the freedom to choose to exercise self-control and then reinforcing this choice, you create a positive environment that helps him or her discover satisfaction in proper behavior.

The specific actions grouped under this category are relatively low profile and simple ones that require a minimal amount of teacher effort. In fact, response might be not to intervene at all and allow the student to experience the natural consequences of the act.

Direct Teacher Intervention

Problems that do interfere with the ability of other students to learn and teachers to teach, and students who lack self-control, require more direct teacher intervention. The responses group in this category are those that require more overt and specific action by the teacher. This action may be as simple as a firm command or a rule reminder or involve more complex actions such as a teacher–student conference. If the misbehavior is a relatively persistent one, you may need to develop a behavior modification plan. This requires considerably more time and skill but can prove to be very worthwhile in stopping a behavior and putting the student back on the road toward self-control.

Responses for Serious and Persistent Misbehavior

The responses in this category should be chosen only if the problem is very serious and after other less severe and obtrusive measures have been tried. The responses in this category place a great deal of the responsibility and power in the hands of the teacher. Student choice is limited. In addition, because these responses are more severe and include more teacher power, they are more likely to be accompanied by student anger and resistance. However, there is a time when these actions need to be implemented. When you use one of these responses, it is important that the student be made aware that it is a consequence of his or her behavior and something he or she earned, not something that the teacher is doing to get revenge. Establishing this link between behavior and consequence is very important because it keeps a lot of the responsibility with the student rather than placing total responsibility on the teacher. When possible, the intervention should relate to the nature of the offense. For example, if the offense is one that results in a waste of time, then the student makes up the wasted time. If the behavior results in the destruction of property, then restitution needs to be made.

Specific actions that might be grouped under this category include isolation, loss of a privilege, removal from class, or remaining after school. These actions should be implemented with care and used infrequently. If used as a response to minor offenses or used too frequently, they lose their potency.

The majority of the misbehaviors that occur in the classroom can be successfully handled by the suggestions given in these three categories. However, there may be some serious incidents of misbehavior for which nothing seems to work. Those problems may require the involvement of individuals other than the classroom teacher: the principal, the school counselor, or even outside agencies.

SUMMARY

Teachers often experience difficulty because they do not know how to respond to problems that occur in the classroom. They often rely on one or two methods that they have experienced or that they have observed. Such methods are often applied without much thought and they soon lose their effectiveness. Some teachers overlook problems because of their uncertainty about how to respond or may respond in an overly harsh manner that harms the relationship between the student and the teacher.

Discipline, like other aspects of teaching, works best when it is the result of thought and planning and is personalized to fit the needs of the students and the values of the teacher. It is unlikely that the same approach will work for all students regardless of the context and their prior experience. An important part of personalizing discipline is for you to recognize your values and the motives that guide your responses to problems. An understanding of your values and your motives can help you avoid responding in ways that might make the situation worse rather than better.

Another variable that needs to be considered when choosing a response is the maturity level and the cultural backgrounds of the students you are teaching. You should not assume that they will be like you and will respond as you did when you were a student.

Finally, when you are choosing a response, you need to keep in mind some basic principles. You should remember to respect the dignity of the students, respond in a consistent and fair manner, identify the causes of the misbehavior, and keep in mind that your purpose is to help the students to learn self-control and accept responsibility.

SUGGESTED APPLICATIONS

1. Begin developing your range of alternative responses. Begin with the three categories suggested in this chapter. Interview teachers and ask them about their responses. Group their responses in one of the categories.

2. Interview some students at the grade level of choice regarding their views of discipline. What do they think are the common misbehaviors that occur in the classroom? Why do they think they occur and what do they think effective teachers do when confronted with discipline problems?

3. Observe in several classrooms. Note the types of misbehavior and the responses that teachers make to them. What percentage of the behaviors would you classify as minor and what percentage as serious? Which teachers seem to have the most positive results? What do you think accounts for their success?

SUGGESTED READINGS

Au, K. (1980). Participation structures in a reading lesson with Hawaiian children: Analysis of a culturally appropriate instructional event. *Anthropology and Education Quarterly* 11(2), 91–115.

Brophy, J. (1985). "Teachers' expectations, motives and goals for working with problem students." In *Research on Motivation in Education,* Vol. 2. *The Classroom Milieu,* Ames, C. and Ames, R. (eds.). New York, Academic Press.

Brophy, J. and Rohrkemper, M. (1981). The influence of problem ownership on teacher perceptions. *Journal of Educational Psychology,* 73(3), 295–311.

Canter, L. and Canter, M. (1976). *Assertive Discipline: A Take Charge Approach for Today's Education.* Santa Monica, CA: Canter and Associates.

Docking, J. W. (1987). *Control and discipline in schools: Perspectives and approaches,* 2nd Ed. London: Harper and Row.

Kohn, A. (1996). *Beyond discipline: From compliance to community.* Alexandria, VA: Association for Supervision and Curriculum Development.

Slee, R. (1995). *Changing theories and practices of discipline.* Washington, DC: Falmer Press.

CHAPTER

8 Responding to Minor Problems and Supporting Self-Control

Chapter Objectives

After reading this chapter you should be able to:

- Define a number of low profile actions that can be taken when responding to problems
- Identify appropriate times for using low profile responses
- State the importance of teacher modeling in assisting students in learning self-control
- Define elements of good communication that will assist teachers in dealing with inappropriate behavior
- Define group dynamics and the roles that students might assume

135

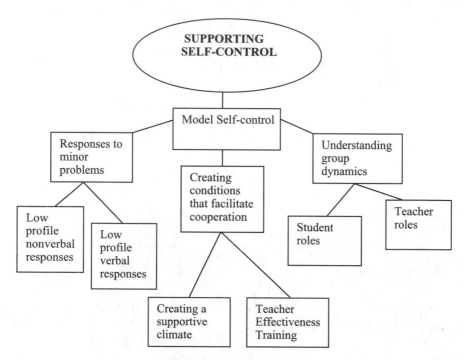

FIGURE 8-1   **Graphic Organizer for Responding to Minor Problems and Supporting Self-Control**

An important step in moving students toward the goal of self-control is how you respond to their behavior. Randomly choosing a response to student behavior is not sufficient. You must consider the nature of the behavior, the student, the situation, and the probable reaction. Your responses can create embarrassment, guilt, anger, and even hostility. When these emotions occur, students are not likely to exercise self-control. Instead, it is probable that they will exhibit even more disruptive behavior. On the other hand, a well-chosen response can lessen the probability of future difficulties. For example, many teachers who seem to have few discipline problems often have difficulty articulating their "secret formula" for dealing with problems. In fact, other teachers who try to follow their suggestions often fail to see any improvement. The secret is not in any single response. The secret is in knowing how to respond in a given situation. Successful teachers seem to have developed this insight.

This chapter will begin the process of helping you develop a range of alternatives for dealing with inappropriate behavior. It begins by presenting a number of low profile approaches. Low profile approaches are those that involve rather unobtrusive teacher behavior. The intent is to stop the inappropriate behavior while avoiding focusing attention on it. Low profile approaches are best used for minor

---

DISCIPLINE SCENARIO 8-1 **Dealing with Billy**

Before she started the school year, Billy's previous teacher informed Ms. Johnson that he was a problem student. She stated that Billy was the instigator of many disturbances. During the first week of school, several students seated around Billy are talking loudly and laughing. Ms. Johnson decides that she wants to send an early message to Billy and to the class that she will not tolerate disturbances. In addition, she wants to stop the behavior before it spreads. She thinks that Billy is the cause of the disturbance so he is singled out for attention.

> *"Billy, I do not tolerate that type of behavior in this class. If you want to have another difficult year, then just keep it up. I want you to leave the room and go to the office. I will deal with you later."*
>
> *"But, Ms. Johnson, I wasn't doing anything. I was looking for a pencil so that I could do the assignment."*
>
> *"I'll not tolerate back talk from you. Leave the room!"*

Billy glares at the teacher and then slowly gathers his belongings and moves toward the door. The rest of the class sits in stunned silence.

What is your reaction?

1. Was Ms. Johnson's response appropriate and fair? Did it demonstrate a concern for the students?

2. Do you think this action will have the desired effect?

3. What would you do instead?

---

behavior problems. They are also useful for students who have demonstrated some self-control.

The advantages of low profile approaches are that they are generally easy to use, do not require a lot of teacher effort, maintain respect for the student, and help prevent power struggles between the teacher and the students. The responses in this category keep the responsibility for correcting the problem with learners, providing them with an opportunity to correct the problems. This allows the student an opportunity to practice self-control. Unless the problem is a serious one to begin with, your first response should be from this category. If they do not work, then you can move to more direct teacher responses.

The final part of the chapter addresses some classroom conditions that can facilitate the use of low profile responses and facilitate self-control. Attention is given to gaining student cooperation through communication and understanding how group dynamics influence student behavior.

MODELING SELF-CONTROL

Before we begin a discussion of specific teacher actions, it is once again time to get personal. In order for students to learn self-control, they must be involved with a responsible adult who demonstrates self-control. Unfortunately, the permissive society in which we live does not seem to provide or value those who exhibit this virtue. Instead, many elements of the culture seem to imply that individuals should be primarily concerned with their own wants and needs and should live for the present rather than the future. Many of our social problems, such as drug and alcohol abuse, can be directly related to the unwillingness or inability of individuals to exercise self-control. You, the teacher, are a significant other to many of the students you teach. Whether or not you like the role, you may have the awesome responsibility of being one of a very few responsible adults in the life of a student. You cannot expect your students to grow toward self-control and the acceptance of responsibility unless you possess those traits.

Let me provide you with an example. A number of years ago when I was teaching in a public school, we were required to attend some staff development meetings. I began to notice that those teachers who complained about being required to attend, sat in the back of the room doing other work, and slipped out as soon as attendance was taken, were the same teachers who complained that students did not know how to behave in school! It is not surprising that some teachers who complain of a lack of self-control in students are individuals who have trouble exercising self-control. They are unable to control their emotions, are self-centered, tend to take the path of least resistance, and come to class unprepared.

An uncomfortable first step you need to take is one of introspection. What messages are being sent by your own behavior? How do you respond when things do not go well? To whom do you attribute problems that occur? Do you take responsibility, or is it always the students, the parents, or the system that is at fault? Do you admit mistakes? What do you do when you make a mistake in front of the class? Do you see each incident of misbehavior as a challenge to your authority that cannot be tolerated? Are you fearful that others will think you professionally incompetent if they see students in your class misbehave? When a student does misbehave, what motives guide your response? The answers to these questions may go a long way toward revealing why students in your classroom may or may not be making progress toward self-control.

LOW PROFILE RESPONSES

The majority of misbehavior in the classroom is what might be called "minor." It is estimated that about 80 percent of the behavior problems are students talking without permission or generally "goofing off," including daydreaming or being out of their seats (Charles, 1992). Teacher responses to these relatively minor problems

TABLE 8-1 **A Selection of Low Profile Responses**

Nonverbal Responses

    Facial Expressions

    Eye Contact

    Gestures

    Proximity Control

    Removing Distraction

    Waiting for Compliance

Low Profile Verbal Responses

    Using the Student's Name in the Context of the Lesson

    Redirecting the Student Activity

    A Quiet Word

    Rule Reminder

    Reinforcing Appropriate Behavior

should be of a low profile nature that allows the students an opportunity to self-correct their behavior and practice self-control. Unfortunately, teacher responses to these incidents often tend to disrupt the entire class and focus a great deal of attention on the misbehavior. Teacher overreaction to minor problems often results in student embarrassment or unwanted attention. The student now has a need to "save face." He or she engages the teacher in a power struggle and a minor problem now becomes a major one.

Therefore, it is important for you to develop a number of low profile responses to minor problems. Your purpose in using low profile techniques is to communicate to the student that you are aware of their misbehavior and you are giving them an opportunity to self-correct. The following are some low profile techniques that teachers can use in responding to minor problems of misbehavior.

Nonverbal Responses

It has been estimated that as much as 65 percent of the meaning of a message is communicated nonverbally (Borisoff and Victor, 1998). There are a wide variety of nonverbal signals that can be used to stop a behavior. You can probably remember a teacher whose facial expression could strike fear in the hearts of the misbehaving student. Nonverbal signals can be extremely effective. One study (Weinstein and Mignano, 1993) found that nonverbal signals stopped misbehavior 79 percent of the time. Nonverbal signals offer the advantage dealing with misbehavior in a way that does not attract the attention of others in the classroom. In fact, it is often possible that the only individual who is aware of the signal is the misbehaving student.

Charles (1992) contends that about 90 percent of discipline is body language. Body language and other nonverbal signals, such as posture, facial expressions, gestures, and eye contact, can go far in helping teachers deal with discipline problems. A major difficulty that you may encounter when attempting to use nonverbal communication is the fact that nonverbal communication is often communication from an unaware sender to a very aware audience (Borisoff and Victor, 1998). We are often not conscious of our nonverbal behavior but the students are very aware. They are constantly interpreting not only our words but our actions. In fact, because the nonverbal signals tend to be more spontaneous, they are often trusted more than the words. When in front of a group of students, what does your body posture communicate? Does it communicate confidence, poise, and security? Does your eye contact communicate uncertainty and anxiety? Do you make eye contact with students or do your eyes seem to be focused somewhere in the heavens? What messages do your facial expressions communicate?

You may need to increase your awareness of your nonverbal behavior as it may be communicating messages to students that you would not care to send. You may need to learn how to use nonverbal communication to emphasize the messages you do want to send. Videotape recorders can be very helpful in helping you become more aware. If that is not sufficient, you may need to consider some coaching by someone who does know nonverbal communication.

An important part of the nonverbal message is your body posture. The way you stand and walk can communicate messages about your confidence and poise. When a problem occurs, how do you react? Does your body slump in resignation? Does your walk signal uncertainty? When responding to a problem, you need to have an erect and confident carriage to your body. Students will interpret your body posture to mean that you are not intimidated and you are confident that you can handle the problem. Simply standing up, placing your hands on your hips, and moving or leaning toward the problem area communicate to students that you mean business.

Facial Expressions

All of us use facial expressions as an important part of the messages we receive. In fact, expressions are often trusted more than words. We can communicate our feelings to students very effectively using facial expressions. If someone is not behaving, a stern unsmiling face with lips drawn tight, accompanied by an unwavering look and creased forehead, communicates disapproval. Some people use facial expressions very naturally and easily. Others have difficulty. If you have difficulty using facial expressions, you may need to get a friend to help you practice.

Eye Contact

Eye contact has long been recognized as a powerful means of communicating. Sometimes all that is needed to stop a behavior is eye contact. When someone is misbehaving, catching his or her eye and maintaining eye contact while you continue to perform another task is often enough. When you do make eye contact, keep your gaze steady and continue your gaze until well past the time that the student has returned to an appropriate behavior. A typical sequence that frequently occurs when a student is off-task is the following. They look up and see you looking at them. They return to their work for a few seconds and then look up again. If you are no longer paying attention, they will resume their conversation. However, if your eyes are still focused on them, they decide they had better remain working.

Gestures

Gestures or *kinesics* refers to body language. They are more direct nonverbal ways of communicating. Experienced teachers learn that teaching involves an element of conducting. Just as a musical conductor uses gestures to communicate with the orchestra, the experienced teacher learns to use gestures to communicate with students. Hand signals may indicate the need to quiet down, the need to stop all activity and focus attention on the teacher, or the approval of desired behavior. Head movements are used to designate approval or disapproval of student activity. Gestures are effective communication devices that can be used without interfering with the regular flow of classroom activities. Holding up your hand as a stop signal, pointing down in the direction of the work they are supposed to be doing, placing your hands on your hips while taking a stiff body posture, leaning toward the student, pointing to the clock, all send clear messages to the student. Without words they communicate your expectations to the student.

Proximity Control

Proximity control refers to controlling behavior by being in the area where the inappropriate behavior is occurring. You have probably discovered that it is hard to misbehave when the teacher is standing next to you. Suppose you are in the middle of a lesson and you notice a couple of students who are off-task in one part of the room. Move casually to this part of the room while continuing with your teaching. It may be that none of the other students are aware of the reason for your movement. However, you can be sure that the misbehaving students know why you are there. If you feel a need for added emphasis, place your hand on the desk or on the back of the chair. This leaves no doubt in the mind of the student that you mean business. Establishing eye contact and giving a disapproving look will also add emphasis. You are saying to the student, "I know what is going on and I want it stopped." Teacher movement around the classroom is an important part of management and is useful in both preventing problems and stopping minor behavior problems that may occur.

Removing Distractions in an Unobtrusive Manner

There are times when students may have objects that are drawing their attention away from the lesson or have the potential to be a distraction to others. The trick is to remove the item without engaging in a power struggle with the student. The item can then be returned at the end of the period or the end of the day. Sometimes simply just stating, "I'll keep this safe until after the lesson" can do this. A teacher who observed a student reading a comic book used a more creative approach. She slowly moved to the area while continuing her lesson. She then took the comic book out of the student's hands and used it to illustrate a point she was trying to make in the lesson. When she was done she placed the comic book on her desk and kept on with the lesson. She not only removed the object in an unobtrusive way, she captured the attention of the students with her illustration! The problem was efficiently solved without a word. The student was left with no opportunity to protest and had no option but to pay attention.

Waiting for Compliance

Another effective nonverbal approach is to simply stop what you are doing and wait until everyone is back on-task before you continue. This is often a good choice when several students are off-task. During a lesson, simply stop talking, put on a disapproving facial expression, and wait. At the beginning of a lesson you should have an appropriate signal that indicates that it is time to pay attention. Then wait until you have the attention of the class before beginning. You should not attempt to teach unless you have the attention of the students. To try and teach when several students are not attending basically communicates that what you are saying is unimportant. In addition, you will waste time because you will have to repeat everything for those who were not listening. Students in classrooms where teachers use this technique usually prompt others in the room to get on-task very quickly.

Low Profile Verbal Responses

If you have been unable to communicate your intentions effectively through nonverbal responses, you may need to try verbal responses. The important point to keep in mind is that you want to do this as unobtrusively as possible so that you direct a minimum amount of attention to the misbehavior. Unfortunately, there appear to be quite a few teachers who do not understand this principle. Their first verbal response is to state in a loud voice, "John, I want you to stop that right now!" The attention of the entire class is now directed toward John and the focus on the lesson is lost. If John had a need for attention, he just received a lot of it by misbehaving. In addition, John has been singled out and might feel that he has to save face by challenging the teacher with some back talk.

Using the Student's Name in the Lesson

Rather than focusing the attention of the whole class by stating, "John, I want your attention right now," a better response is to get the attention of the student by using his or her name in the context of the lesson. Suppose that the teacher was discussing the discovery of the New World and noted that John was engaged in some form of misbehavior. The teacher could respond by saying, "Now if John were a member of the crew, he would have noticed that . . ." John hears his name and looks up. You now have his attention and can use nonverbal messages to communicate to him that you are aware of his behavior without missing a beat in the lesson. This is often all that is required to change the behavior from unacceptable to acceptable.

Redirecting Student Activity

Teachers who work with younger students tend to become very adept at redirecting student activity away from undesirable behavior into more acceptable channels. When using this approach, you must be aware of the students in the classroom and respond quickly when it appears that one or more students is beginning to engage in an unacceptable activity. When you note this pattern, you simply go to the student and redirect the student to a substitute activity that is acceptable. In some instances this activity might be designed to give the student a quick break and then to get him or her back on the task. An example might be for the teacher to have the student run an errand or perform a housekeeping task that will take only a couple of minutes. When the student returns to the desk, you then take this opportunity to refocus student attention on the task that needs to be completed.

Another option might be for the student to engage in an alternative activity to accomplish the instructional goal. For example, a student might be having trouble completing a math assignment and is getting anxious and frustrated. You might simply move to the student and state, "John, could you help me by creating these problems on the place value chart?" having John use the concrete manipulatives will help change the activity while helping him complete the work.

One word of caution: Redirecting an activity should not be viewed by the students as a reward for inappropriate behavior or as a way to avoid assigned work. Redirecting student activity works best when you catch a potential problem in its beginning stages.

A Quiet Word to the Individual

This response is usually most appropriate when students are working independently. You simply go to the student and give a quiet, unemotional command. This might be as simple as "Back to work" or "Save the talking until later." The intent is to keep it soft enough that only a few nearby students are aware that you have said anything. In addition, you don't want to open the door for debate by posing a question such as, "What are you doing?" You are quietly reminding the student of acceptable behavior.

Rule Reminder

This response is useful if several students are engaged in misbehavior. When you use a rule reminder you can simply state, "Remember what our rule is about being out of our seat." Another variation might be asking a student to read the appropriate rule. The rule reminder communicates to the class that you will enforce the rules and they are being given a chance to correct their own behavior without any further consequences.

Reinforcing Appropriate Behavior

This response is most popular in the elementary school but can be effective in secondary classrooms if used wisely. It is most appropriate when there are a number of

ACTIVITY 8-1   DEALING WITH A TALKER

Keith is not really a problem student. He wants to please and is a likable student who does acceptable work. The problem is that he is a constant talker. Whenever students are working independently, he constantly talks to himself or to those around him. It is not loud talking, but it is noticeable. The behavior disturbs you, and you think it bothers those who are seated near him.

What would you do?

1. What might be causing Keith to talk?

2. Do you agree that this is a problem that requires teacher intervention?

3. What would you do to help Keith learn to control his talking?

---

students who are off-task. The technique is simply that of looking for someone in the room who is behaving and reinforcing them. For example, at the secondary level it might involve stating, "Bill, thanks for getting right to work." At the elementary level it might take the form of "I like the way group one is ready." The advantage of this technique is that it gives attention to appropriate behavior and lets students know that their good effort will be noticed.

These low profile responses are very effective in stopping incidents of misbehavior and providing students with the opportunity to self-correct. These opportunities communicate a sense of respect and trust to the students and are usually responded to very positively by students.

There are classroom conditions that enhance the success of these and other responses to inappropriate behavior in the classroom. One of the most important conditions is that of gaining the cooperation of the students. There are a number of variables that will influence the cooperation that the students will give to the teacher. For example, the way you establish and use your personal power in the classroom will either enhance or inhibit cooperation. One of the key variables in gaining cooperation is your communication style.

GAINING COOPERATION THROUGH COMMUNICATION

One of the major roadblocks to obtaining student cooperation is a breakdown in communication. Several researchers have emphasized the importance of communication in obtaining student cooperation (Ginott, 1972; Gordon, 1974; Harris, 1969; Rogers, 1969). They emphasize that the language teachers use when interacting with students sends messages that have profound effects on students' behavior and self-concepts.

The specific methods you choose when responding to inappropriate behavior will be influenced by your communication styles. In other words, it is not just what you say or do, but how you say or do it. Ginott (1972) summarized the importance of your communication style in his statement :

> *I've come to the frightening conclusion that I am the decisive element in the classroom. It is my personal approach that creates the climate . . . As a teacher, I possess tremendous power to make a child's life miserable or joyous. I can be a tool of torture or an instrument of inspiration. I can humiliate or humor, hurt or heal. In all situations, it is my response that decides whether a crisis will be escalated or deescalated and the child humanized or dehumanized (pp. 15–16).*

You have the power to establish one of two opposite communication styles. One style is a defensive style and the other is a supportive style. The supportive style is problem-oriented, spontaneous, descriptive, and empathic (Borisoff and Victor, 1998).

Problem-oriented means that the communication is clear and emphasizes a desire to cooperate to solve the problem rather than trying to control or manipulate another. Spontaneity refers to responsiveness and openness rather than a predetermined speech or the presence of hidden agendas. In other words, when interacting with students, you need to be willing to listen and be honest. Descriptive means that when you communicate with students you describe rather than judge. You also need to feel free to clearly state your ideas and concerns. This descriptive type of communication enhances understand and allows individuals to move toward resolving problems. Empathetic communication means that you make an effort to understand the student. If students feel that you are unwilling to recognize their feelings or perspectives, they will become defensive. This does not mean that you have to agree with their perspectives, but that you are willing to listen to them with an open mind and a concern for their welfare.

Barriers to a Supportive Communication Climate

The words you select and the messages you deliver are important if you are to develop a supportive climate in which students are willing to follow your leadership and cooperate. There are several types of communication that will create a defensive climate that will hinder your ability to solve problems and help students grow toward self-control (Borisoff and Victor, 1998).

Sarcasm
Sarcasm is something that should not be used in the classroom. It is often an insidious tactic for criticizing others that raises defensiveness (Borisoff and Victor, 1998). Some teachers think that it is just an expression of humor. However, it is humor at the expense of another. The person who is the target of sarcasm is often humiliated.

This undermines the trust of the students and leads to a lack of communication that does not build the openness needed for genuine problem solving. In addition, young children often do not understand sarcasm and easily misinterpret the message.

Reprisals and Threats

Reprisals and threats are forms of coercion that are probably the biggest barrier to a supportive communication climate. By their very nature, they are destructive to collaboration. Reprisals and threats are basically a person with power threatening to use that power to impose pain unless the other person conforms. They can pose a problem for you because once something is threatened, you may be challenged by the students to deliver. To not follow through on threats then begins to destroy your credibility. Reprisals and threats can turn into a no-win situation. If you follow through on threats, you harm relationships; if you do not, you lose credibility.

It is important to distinguish between helping students understand that there are consequences for violating rules, that they are choosing to experience those consequences, and reprisals and threats. What we are talking about here are those anger-driven statements that imply to the student that you will get even if they persist in their behavior. They include an element of revenge and getting even.

Rather than using reprisals and threats, calmly ask students to identify what happens when people continue to violate the rules. Inform them that they are choosing to experience those consequences if they continue. Keep the responsibility on the student and on the inappropriate behavior rather than making a threat that switches the attention to the threat and your behavior.

Hostile Questioning

It is typical for teachers to ask questions when someone has been misbehaving. However, some questions communicate a hostile intent. These questions are often loaded questions or carry an accusation. For example, "Don't you want to grow up?" carries the accusation that the person is immature. Your tone of voice and emphasis often communicate hostile intent as much as the words you use. It is okay to use questions to get information to help solve a problem. However, hostile questions are not intended to solve the problem, they are intended to put down or embarrass somebody.

Be aware that students may use hostile questions to try and deflect your focus on a problem. For example, a student might ask, "Don't you know anything about feelings?" The intent of the student is to hurt you and try to get you to second-guess your actions. Do not retaliate by returning the accusation. Take a couple of deep breaths. Wait for a moment and then refocus on the behavior of the student.

Personal Attacks

It is sometimes difficult to separate the behavior from the person. However, this is what you need to do. You need to communicate to the student that while you do not accept his or her behavior, you still care about him or her as a person. When confronted with a problem you need to avoid attacking the person. A personal attack such as, "You are just immature," will not open the door to further resolution. It will create a need for the person to defend his or her dignity and preserve his or her self-concept. Personal attacks are almost certain to generate a power struggle.

Word Choice
When involved in a conflict situation with a student you need to choose your words carefully. Be sensitive to the needs of the student and avoid highly charged words. Think about the way you want to phrase a statement to a student about a behavioral concern and try to choose words that are not likely to elicit an adverse reaction. As a teacher, you need to be sensitive to the background and the culture of your students in order to identify those words that might lead to emotional or hostile reactions.

Teacher Effectiveness Training

Another approach that emphasizes communication and how our methods of communication can create problems is the Teacher Effectiveness Training model outlined by Gordon (1974). He contends that breakdowns in teacher–student communication are a primary cause for most discipline problems. The development of appropriate communication skills is seen as essential in building bridges between the teacher and the student so that the needs of both are understood and met. When this is done, cooperation is the result, and discipline problems do not escalate into major confrontations that block learning and growth toward self-control. The basic communication skills emphasized by Gordon are those of collaboration, joint problem solving and decision making, mutual agreement, and nonpower methods of conflict resolution. Gordon's approach appears to be very useful when relatively minor problems occur and is focused on helping the student develop self-control.

Problem Ownership
One of the first steps in using Gordon's method is that of identifying problem ownership. Problem ownership is important because the response is different for student-owned problems than for teacher-owned problems. Problem ownership is determined by identifying who experiences the tangible, concrete effects. If the behavior is interfering with the teacher's ability to teach the class or meet his or her needs, then the teacher owns the problem. For example, loud talking or disruptive behavior interferes with the teacher's ability to conduct the class. In this instance the teacher is experiencing the concrete and tangible effects and therefore owns the problem. However, daydreaming or inattentiveness is not interfering with the conduct of the class and the student feels the tangible and concrete effects of the behavior. In this case, the student owns the problem.

One of the major breakdowns in communication occurs when teachers respond to student-owned problems. Teachers usually respond by using what Gordon calls the "language of unacceptance." He has grouped the unacceptable messages that teachers send in response to student-owned problems into 12 categories. The 12 types of messages listed below block communication and slow down or inhibit the process of problem resolution and learning.

1. Ordering, commanding, directing
2. Warning, threatening
3. Moralizing, preaching, giving "shoulds" and "oughts"
4. Advising, offering solutions or suggestions
5. Teaching, lecturing, giving logical arguments
6. Judging, criticizing, disagreeing, blaming
7. Name-calling, stereotyping, labeling
8. Interpreting, analyzing, diagnosing
9. Praising, agreeing, giving positive evaluations
10. Reassuring, sympathizing, consoling, supporting
11. Questioning, probing, interrogating, cross-examining
12. Withdrawing, distracting, being sarcastic, humoring, diverting

Gordon states that the first five categories offer solutions to the student's problem. The second three are judgments or put-downs, and the next two are attempts to make the problem go away. Number 11 (the most frequently used) produces defensiveness, and number 12 is an attempt by the teacher to avoid talking about the problem.

Remember that these messages set up roadblocks to communication when the student owns the problem. There are times when praising, reassuring, diagnosing, teaching, and advising are appropriate teacher behaviors. However, they are not appropriate when a student is experiencing a problem that is interfering with his or her attempts to meet needs. Perhaps an example will illustrate this point: Identify a time when you were having a personal problem and you shared your problem with one of your parents or a friend. How did the person respond and how did you feel? If the person started questioning, teaching, or diagnosing, didn't you become defensive and feel that he or she did not really understand?

Active Listening

Rather than using these 12 roadblocks to communication, Gordon suggests that we begin to use the language of acceptance. One of the key components of this language is "active listening." Active listening involves an interaction with the student in which you provide feedback to the student about your understanding of the message that the student is sending. (This is important because many verbal and nonverbal messages are unclear and easily misinterpreted, and misinterpretation can lead to communication barriers. Minor problems then have a way of turning into major ones.) Feedback can be given by stating your interpretation in a question form or by simply paraphrasing what the student has said. For example, you might respond to the daydreaming student by stating, "You're bored with this material." You could choose to paraphrase a student message by using a question that begins with the stem "Are you saying that . . . ?"

Active listening has the advantage of opening the door for additional communication about the problems while keeping the responsibility with the student. The goal of active listening is to communicate to the student that it is okay to have a problem and that the teacher is willing to listen and help find a solution. The approach seems so simple that many individuals are skeptical of the value of active listening. It is, however, a good beginning for responding to problems that are student-owned. Individuals are often amazed at how wrong their interpretation is and how easily a solution can be found once the problem is identified in a nonthreatening manner.

I-Messages

Teacher-owned problems require a different response. They are dealt with through the use of what Gordon calls "I-messages." I-messages communicate what the teacher is feeling and are characterized by the use of *I* rather than *you*. There are three parts to an I-message.

The first part involves identifying what is creating the problem in a nonblaming and nonthreatening manner. Examples of this component of I-messages might be, "When people talk while I'm talking . . . ," "When I get interrupted while giving instructions . . . ," or "When I can't find the material I left on the table. . . ."

The second component identifies the tangible and concrete effect. Examples might be "We have to stop . . . ," "We have to start over . . . ," or "We have to find new material. . . ."

In the third component of the I-message, you state your feelings. Examples might be ". . . and I feel very frustrated," ". . . and I get discouraged," ". . . and that makes me angry" or ". . . and that makes me afraid."

An example of a complete I-message is one that a teacher might use when responding to students not bringing material to class: "When individuals do not bring their material to class, time is wasted as we try to find material for them to use and I get frustrated." Note that the message is not demanding that the students change, it simply identifies the problem and the effect. It is delivered honestly and without anger or blame.

Students, like other individuals, are often so intent on getting their own needs met that they are unaware of the impact of their behavior on others. The I-message provides the student with the reason or the rationale for the displeasure of the teacher.

Many students will respond that they were unaware of the difficulties and offer solutions that are perfectly acceptable. Open communication and joint problem solving resolve the problem. This communicates a sense of respect and honesty.

Occasionally, students may get defensive when the teacher shares an I-message. Some may feel embarrassed, guilty, surprised, or even become argumentative. This usually signals to you that by confronting the problem, you have caused a problem for the student. When this occurs, you should switch to active listening. This combination of active listening and I-messages is then used to keep communication open until a resolution can be found.

ACTIVITY 8-2   GETTING STUDENT COOPERATION

You are teaching a very capable tenth-grade science class. The students are generally well behaved and do outstanding work. A number of the students, however, tend to get to class a couple of minutes after the bell rings. They are not disruptive when they enter; they just wait until the last minute to try to get to class. One day your principal observes you. He notes that four students enter the class after the bell and that you do not respond to their tardiness. In your evaluation conference he reminds you that it is a school rule for students to be in class by the time the bell rings and that he considers it a serious problem. He will monitor the problem, and if you are unable to correct it, he will assist you. You are embarrassed and upset about this issue and decide that you need to try Gordon's approach of using I-messages and active listening to try to obtain student cooperation and solve the problem.

What will you do?

1. What is the I-message that you will use to communicate the problem to the class?

2. What will you do if students become angry or defensive?

3. What are some possible actions that you might suggest to the class?

UNDERSTANDING GROUP DYNAMICS

An obvious fact is often overlooked when suggestions are made for dealing with inappropriate behavior in the classroom. That fact is that individuals behave differently in groups than they do individually (Redl and Wattenberg, 1959). Attempting to deal with students without understanding the context of the group dynamics can lead to frustration. Each group develops its own "culture." The group will attempt to influence the behavior of individuals through the imposition of rewards and sanctions in order to get individuals to subscribe to group norms and values. In fact, the rewards and the sanctions of the group may be more desirable and powerful than those of the teacher. Individuals also influence the group. They may facilitate group solidarity by following group norms or they may create disunity by rejecting them. Most teachers can tell stories of how their classroom changed dramatically with the addition or deletion of just one student. One of the interesting aspects of teaching is that each group is different. In order for you to deal effectively with behavior in the classroom you need to understand some of the group dynamics. For example, several of the low profile responses discussed earlier in the chapter will be counterproductive if used in a group in which the norms and expectations are different from those of the teacher. Waiting for compliance is a fruitless response if the norm of the group rejects learning as important. The group will reward individuals for disrupting the class and keeping the teacher from teaching. Similarly, reinforcing individuals may be counterproductive if group norms suggest that praise from the teacher is undesirable. Therefore, you need to understand group dynamics in order to choose appropriate responses.

There are several roles that can be found in many classroom groups. Those roles are leaders, instigators, clowns, scapegoats, and isolates.

Group Leaders

You need to realize that the members of the group, not the teacher, give individuals the status of leader. Leaders are key members because they often signal the norms and expectations of the group. If the group leaders are supportive of the teacher, then a positive, cooperative group dynamic is created. If, however, the teacher and the group leaders are in opposition, there will be constant conflict and behavior problems will seem to be immune to teacher intervention.

One of your first tasks should be to identify those students who have been given leadership status in the classroom. A classroom may have more than one person who is viewed as a leader. Different students might be viewed as leaders for different tasks. If the group leaders are accepting of one another, there will be good group unity. If however, they are jealous of the influence of others, there will be a lack of harmony and unity.

You can begin to identify the leaders by carefully observing the students and their reactions to one another. It does not take long to discover those students who are popular and the center of attention. When they speak, few students disagree with them.

Once you have identified the leaders, you need to consider how you might obtain their cooperation. Leaders like to lead and be recognized. You can begin to win them over by giving them some responsibility. This then means that the success of the class reflects their leadership. You may seek their suggestions when confronted with problems. This does not mean that you abdicate your responsibility and that you turn the direction of the class over to the leaders. What you want to do is to be accepted by the leaders as someone who is trustworthy and not always opposing him or her. You want to be careful not to engage them in a power struggle in front of the class or attempt to discredit them. Howell and Howell (1979) point out that attempts to discredit classroom leaders result in the loss of teacher power and credibility.

Instigators

Instigators are those individuals who lack the status and self-confidence of a leader so they work behind the scenes to plant ideas and influence the group. Instigators are those who usually cause trouble (Charles, 1992). They are afraid to take risks and try to prod others into taking the risks for them. Unfortunately, they are often successful.

Instigators have a negative influence on the group when they sow seeds of discontent and suspicion. They may plant the idea that the rules and the authority of the teacher need to be challenged or that the teacher really will not follow through on consequences. They get their satisfaction from seeing others act on their ideas while they escape any consequences. If you experience recurring conflicts in the classroom, you need to observe and see if there is an instigator at work continually stirring up the group.

When you become aware of the presence of an instigator, an effective approach is to discuss the role of instigator with the class. Role-playing activities that focus on how people can be manipulated by others and suffer adverse consequences can be helpful. Because instigators often lack the courage to step forward, confronting an instigator with your knowledge of his or her role can be effective in stopping them. Working to enhance the self-esteem of an instigator and pointing out their good ideas can help bring instigators out from behind the scenes and allows you to deal with them in a direct and positive manner.

Class Clowns

The class clown is the group entertainer. A class clown will often be a student with inferiority feelings and a high need for acceptance. Because they feel inadequate, they do not attempt to become a leader. Instead, they try to gain acceptance through humor and clowning around. Class clowns can have a useful function in providing for some comic relief and in building some group solidarity. However, they can also be destructive if they decide that their antics should be directed at disrupting the activities of the classroom. Class clowns often act on the unspoken feelings of the group and can provide you with some clues as to the unspoken feelings and anxieties of the group.

As with your strategy with the group leaders, you want to win over the class clown and use his or her humor in constructive ways. Because the goal of the clown is to get attention, you should ignore clowning activities that are unacceptable. Removing the clown from the classroom is often an effective approach because he or she loses his or her audience. You should look for opportunities to allow the class clown to demonstrate humor at appropriate times. Do not be so stern that you think there is no place for laughter in the classroom. Laughter can break the tension and provide relief. It can also make your class a place where students want to be.

Scapegoats

Scapegoats are the individuals who take the blame for everything. They have a high need for acceptance and a very poor self-concept. They attempt to gain acceptance by being willing to take the blame for any problems that occur. Unfortunately, many students are willing to let them. The scapegoat orientation can lead to a victim mentality with destructive potential. You need to be aware of the possible presence of scapegoats and refuse to fall into the trap of letting them take responsibility for all of the problems. Not only is this harmful to the individual, it prevents others from growing by allowing them to avoid responsibility.

Ignore efforts of individuals to gain acceptance from you or the group by becoming the victim or the scapegoat. Rather, provide the student with some opportunities to gain group membership through constructive activities. Find something they can do well and reinforce them for doing it. In severe cases, they may need some individual counseling. Once scapegoats learn that they can gain acceptance without being the victim, their willingness to accept blame will slowly disappear.

Teacher Roles

There are several roles that you can play in the classroom. You may choose to try to be a part of the group by being a facilitator who helps students learn, a leader promoting group welfare, a confidant who can be trusted, or an expert with valuable insight. These roles help create a positive group climate. However, you may choose not to be a member of the group and assume roles that are destructive to a positive group climate. For example, you may be the detective who is always looking for rule violators, the judge who is always evaluating the worth of the students, the boss who is trying to control everything, or the victim who is an easy target for hostility. These roles place students and teachers in adversarial roles in which they are always vying for power.

The roles you choose to play will have a profound impact on the group climate in the classroom. You may play all of these roles at one time or another. There are times when you must be the judge or the referee. There are other times when you

---

ACTIVITY 8-3   WHAT IS HAPPENING?

A teacher recently discussed her past year. She is experienced, with several years of successful teaching.

> *This past year was a nightmare. It seemed as if the class never came together. They were fighting with each other from the first day. They seemed to prefer arguing to having a calm classroom. I was surprised because the class was composed of a number of high achieving students and I expected to have a pleasant year. It wasn't as if they did not want to be in school. As individuals, I liked them. But, when they came together in the classroom they were always competing with each other and delighted in trying to tear each other down. By the end of the year I was totally frustrated and ready to quit.*

What is your reaction?

1. What would you identify as the problem?

2. What might be some actions that you would suggest to this teacher?

may need to be a detective or the boss. However, you need to make sure that you perform these roles in a fair and just manner, one that does not lead to an abuse of your power as teacher.

Finally, you need to remember that being a leader in the group is a role that is earned. The students will expect you to be a leader. However, your position will be lost unless you use your power wisely and earn the respect and loyalty of the students. You earn this loyalty by being a good teacher and a trustworthy individual.

SUMMARY

The majority of incidents of misbehavior that occur in the classroom are minor. The responses you choose to use will have an impact in teaching students self-control, or in turning a minor problem into a major one. When responding to problems, you need to keep the major responsibility for correcting the behavior on the student, respect their dignity, and try to handle the problem so that it does not disrupt the entire class.

There are a number of low profile and unobtrusive actions you can take that are appropriate for dealing with minor problems. Those low profile techniques do not require a great deal of teacher effort, yet are very effective. They provide an opportunity for the student to self-correct and therefore develop increased self-control.

Helping students learn self-control begins with you. You should be a model of self-control and model how to cope with problems if you are to expect students to acquire these skills. As the classroom leader, you also must take responsibility for ensuring that the classroom climate and the communication patterns are those that facilitate a supportive communication climate. Low profile methods may have the opposite of the intended effect if you have not established a cooperative atmosphere.

There are several barriers to creating a supportive communication climate. Those barriers include using sarcasm, hostile questions, poor word choice, and personal attacks. In the heat of a classroom event it is often easy to fall into one of these patterns. Understanding the destructive nature of these actions can help you avoid them.

Teacher Effective Training provides some concrete techniques keeping communication open and for communicating messages of acceptance. These include the use of active listening and I-messages. The use of these two approaches is related to problem ownership or who is feeling the concrete effects of the behavior.

An understanding of the conditions that assist you in understanding why some problems might be occurring and in deciding which approach to use requires an understanding of group dynamics. Because people behave differently in groups than they do individually, it is important for you to consider the impact of the group on the behavior of the individual. Group dynamics can also explain why some actions might work with some students and not with others. Understanding group dynamics can also help you purposefully determine the roles you want to play in the classroom.

SUGGESTED APPLICATIONS

1. Observe in a classroom. Make an observation tool with two columns. On one side keep track of the minor discipline problems that occur in the classroom. On the other side keep track of what you consider major discipline problems. What percentage of the problems were minor and what percentage was major? Did the teacher respond to the problems differently? What were the techniques most often used by the teacher?

2. Work with two peers in a small group. Each of you should identify a typical classroom problem, such as inattention or talking. One person should play the role of the students, another the teacher, and the third an observer. The teacher should use active listening and I-messages in order to clarify the nature of the problem and arrive at a possible solution. The third individual should provide feedback to the person role-playing the teacher on the effectiveness and proper use of active listening and I-messages.

3. Interview at least one or two students who are currently having difficulty in school. Ask them to identify what they believe to be the causes of their difficulties. How many of the causes are attributed to internal and how many are attributed to external factors? Do these students perceive a relationship between their behavior and the consequences of their behavior? Design a plan or a list of suggestions that you might use as a teacher to help the students solve their problems.

4. Watch a group of individuals working together. Can you identify the leaders? What behaviors characterize the leader? What happens if there is more than one person who wants to be the leader?

5. Using your own experience as a student, see if you can identify students who served as leaders, instigators, class clowns, and scapegoats. How was each of these viewed by the rest of the group? Brainstorm with peers ways that teachers might react to students playing these different roles in order to develop a more positive classroom climate.

SUGGESTED READINGS

Borisoff, D. and Victor, D. A. (1998). *Conflict management: A communication skills approach,* 2nd Ed. Boston: Allyn and Bacon.
Charles, C. M. (1992). *Building classroom discipline,* 4th Ed. White Plains, NY: Longman.
Ginott, H. G. (1972). *Teacher and child.* New York: Avon Books.
Gordon, T. (1974). *Teacher effectiveness training.* New York: David McKay.

Harris, T. (1969). *I'm OK—you're OK: A practical guide to transactional analysis*. New York: Harper & Row.

Howell, R. G. and Howell, P. L. (1979). *Discipline in the classroom: Solving the teaching puzzle*. Reston, VA: Reston.

Redl, F. and Wattenberg, W. (1959). *Mental hygiene in teaching*. New York: Harcourt, Brace and World.

Rogers, C. (1969). *Freedom to learn*. Columbus, OH: Merrill.

Weinstein, C. S. and Mignano, A. J., Jr. (1993). *Elementary classroom management: Lessons from research and practice*. New York: McGraw Hill.

9 Direct Teacher Intervention

Chapter Objectives

After reading this chapter you should be able to:

- State the role of teacher assertiveness in dealing with inappropriate behavior
- Define how to establish the link between behavior and consequences
- Explain the difference between logical and natural consequences
- Define a number of teacher responses that can be used when responding to more difficult problems
- Explain the four mistaken goals for behavior and how to identify and respond to each of them

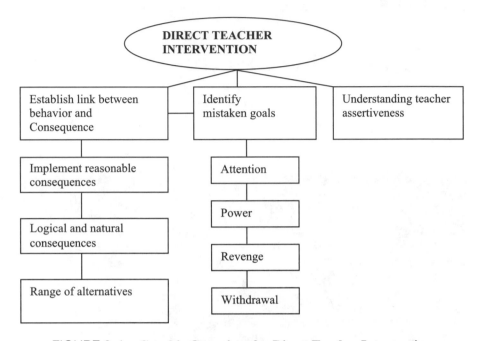

FIGURE 9-1   **Graphic Organizer for Direct Teacher Intervention**

There will always be those students who lack self-control or who meet their needs through misbehavior. These students cause you anxiety and sleepless nights. It does not do much good to wish that they would disappear. It seems that these are the students that never miss a day of school! Low profile responses to the misbehavior of these students do not seem to have much impact. What is required is more direct and forceful teacher action. When the behavior is disrupting the class, it must be stopped, and stopped quickly. More intrusive actions that require teacher assertiveness are called for. Remember that the majority of the problems you face in the classroom will be relatively minor. However, it is the relatively few serious ones that interfere with our teaching and the satisfactions we derive from it.

Several potential problems are associated with more direct and intrusive teacher intervention. First, these actions take more time and thought. Often, they cannot be implemented as easily as the low profile approaches. You may need to diagnose what is causing the problem and implement an approach that requires persistence on your part. Misbehaving students have often learned that misbehavior will result in their needs being met. When you attempt to stop this misbehavior, they will persist. Correcting this behavior and helping students grow toward self-control may require repeated interventions over a considerable period of time.

DISCIPLINE SCENARIO 9-1　**Louis's Defiance**

Pat Taylor thinks that the class would be a good class if it were not for Louis. Louis is a teacher's worst nightmare. He constantly challenges and tests the authority of Pat. When an assignment is given, he is likely to blurt out, "Who cares about this stuff?" If Pat corrects him, he usually responds with, "You can't make me." His defiant attitude and constant disruption seem to create a constant war of nerves in the class.

What do you think?

1. Would you be threatened by a student like Louis?

2. Why do you think Louis might be responding this way?

3. What consequences would you apply when Louis does challenge the teacher?

Another potential problem is that these interventions create conditions that can result in power struggles. These tests of will can easily frustrate you and interfere with the goal of helping the student acquire self-control.

We also need to be careful that these teacher interventions do not remove responsibility from the student. For these reasons, direct teacher intervention and demonstrations that include use of teacher authority and power need to be exercised carefully and with good judgment.

This chapter addresses the next category in developing a range of alternative responses. As you think about the alternative responses, there are some basic factors you must consider. You may need to help students understand the linkage between their behavior and consequences, identify their purposes for misbehaving, and consider how to use logical and natural consequences. Because the behavior you are responding to is more serious, more depth is required in understanding how to respond.

TEACHER ASSERTIVENESS

Many new teachers have difficulty with the concept of teacher assertiveness. They are uncertain as to how assertive they should be in the classroom. Some new teachers err on the side of nonassertiveness. There are several reasons for this. Some are fearful of student rejection. They are afraid that firm actions will cause the students to dislike them. Some of these teachers believe that if they are caring enough and present interesting lessons, misbehavior will disappear. Others have some deep philosophical questions regarding their role as a teacher. They are uncertain about the rights of a teacher to place demands on the students and believe that uses of teacher power are unethical or inappropriate.

Other new teachers err on the side of being too assertive. They have heard stories of uncontrolled classrooms and are insecure regarding their ability to handle the problems that might occur. They have been told not to smile until Christmas and to make sure they establish their authority in the classroom from day one. These teachers try to start out being "tough." They develop what might be termed a "hostile" response style (Canter and Canter, 1976). What is the proper level of assertiveness? How can you find that line between a firm, fair teacher who does not abuse power and a hostile one who sees a challenge to authority in every behavior?

A major issue facing contemporary teachers is a sense of powerlessness. People are not bashful about making proposals to improve education without consulting teachers. Teachers often feel as if they have little power in influencing the major decisions that affect their lives. There is a long list of reasons why these feelings of powerlessness exist. Parents are more likely to challenge teacher authority, the status of teachers has dropped, lawsuits have increased, and the role of the teacher has become less well defined. These factors cause confusion among the teaching ranks. Some fear that they will be second-guessed no matter what they do. Therefore, some are fearful of reprimanding students or demanding appropriate behavior in the classroom.

During the latter part of the 1970s, the Canters developed the Assertive Discipline model. This model was widely accepted by many teachers, in part because it did address the issue of teacher powerlessness. The Canters state that it is acceptable for you to be assertive and demand that students behave appropriately and you should not feel guilty for doing so.

Teachers do have a right, and a professional obligation, to act when students are behaving in ways that are self-destructive or interfere with the rights of others to learn. You have an obligation to maintain a learning environment in which it is possible for students to feel safe and to learn. Student behavior that threatens these conditions must be stopped, and stopped quickly. Stopping the behavior and communicating clear messages about teacher expectations are the beginning steps in creating an environment in which students achieve success and learn self-control.

The Canters call this type of teacher response to misbehavior the "assertive" response style, a style that involves clear and firm communication to the students about behavioral expectations and the resulting consequences if they are not followed. The assertive teacher is one who is willing to consistently follow words with actions.

Because the use of an assertive teaching style involves the use of teacher power, it may create power struggles between the teacher and the student and result in anger and hostility. Glasser (1965) provides some interesting advice in dealing with this anger. He states that adults must be willing to endure the anger that sometimes results when students are held responsible for their actions. He further contends that holding a student responsible will never permanently alienate the student. Parents and teachers are familiar with this behavior. Youngsters who are angry threaten to withhold their love and affection unless they are allowed to get their own way. Adults who give in to this threat are not doing their children any favors. Dealing with problems in a firm manner and holding the students accountable will teach them that they can be responsible. In the long run, relationships are improved.

Dreikurs (1968) adds another dimension. He asks the question, "Who do we discipline?" The answer he provides is that we discipline those we care about. I care about my children and want them to learn self-control as a foundation for future relationships and success. Therefore, I am willing to engage in the sometimes uncomfortable activity of trying to stop their self-destructive behavior. In the classroom, students often view your firmness as the actions of someone who cares enough to say "no."

In summary, it is okay for you to be assertive, as long as that assertiveness does not result in a hostile teaching style. You need to keep in mind your reasons for being assertive. You are trying to help the student and create a foundation for success. You are not being assertive just to fulfill your own unmet power needs or satisfy a selfish desire to get your own way. To be consistent, you should also recognize the right of the students to be assertive if they feel that you are not being responsible.

UNDERSTANDING THE LINK BETWEEN BEHAVIOR AND CONSEQUENCES

It is difficult for some adults to understand that some misbehavior exists because students have never considered the link between their actions and the consequences they experience. They attribute the difficulties they experience to things such as "bad luck" or "The teacher doesn't like me." In other words they are not responsible; someone else is responsible. Establishing this link between behavior and consequences was the focus of Glasser's book, *Reality Therapy* (1965). His later works have built on and extended this approach to the schools.

The basic principles around which Glasser has built his response to discipline problems are powerful yet simple. First of all, he believes that all behavior is a matter of choice. Individuals choose to behave the way they do. Good behavior is the result of good choices and bad behavior is the result of bad choices. Many individuals attempt to justify their choices by focusing on the past and events in their past. In essence, they are looking for excuses for their behavior. However, Glasser points out that we live in the present and must face the reality of the consequences of our behavior (Glasser, 1965). A student may have had a less than desirable home life but, although regrettable, it still does not excuse him or her from behaving responsibly. Because behavior is a matter of choice and individuals have rational minds and are able to choose, they can understand acceptable behavior and can choose to behave appropriately.

Individuals should also learn that their behavior produces consequences, and should they choose to behave inappropriately, they will face the consequences of that behavior. Glasser (1969) states that a teacher should not attempt to manipulate circumstances so that a student does not experience the reasonable consequences of behavior.

It is not enough for students to face the reality of their behavior; they must also learn how to fulfill their needs in satisfactory and productive ways. One of the reasons that individuals behave in unproductive ways is that they have not learned how to fulfill their needs in responsible ways. This failure leads to low self-esteem and self-worth. These feelings produce a failure identity, which then leads individuals to behave in irresponsible ways that do not help them fulfill their needs. Glasser believes that the school and teachers have an important role to play in helping students to learn social responsibility and to develop a success identity.

A prerequisite for success in using the Glasser approach is for the teacher to be warm, personal, and willing to be involved. Glasser notes that many students have not learned how to be responsible because they have not been involved with responsible and caring adults (Glasser, 1965). Therefore, the first step in the implementation of the Glasser approach is for the teacher to establish a warm and caring interpersonal environment. If this dimension is missing, the approach becomes a mechanical exercise with little chance of success.

Implementing the Process

The process of helping students understand the linkage between behavior and consequences begins with a teacher–student conference. If inappropriate behavior occurs at a time when you cannot have an immediate conference with a student, Glasser recommends sending them to a time-out spot in the classroom. This action is intended to stop the interruption until you can take the time to have a conference. This conference should be conducted in private, in a businesslike environment free from anger and hostility. When conducting the conference, there are several steps that you should follow.

Ask Student to Describe Behavior

This is an important first step that is missed by many teachers and should be done first before the student is sent to any time-out area. It is implemented by simply asking the question, "What are you doing?" The purpose of asking students to describe what they are doing is to get them to recognize that it is their action that is triggering the action. If students are sent to the time-out area, you then begin the conference by asking, "What were you doing?" The place where many teachers make a mistake is, rather than asking the student to describe the behavior, they ask "Why?" Their first response is "Why are you out of your seat?" "Why are you not paying attention?" The *why* question opens the door for rationalization and excuses. You then get yourself engaged in a debate about the behavior. You do not want to allow students to shift the blame to something else. You want them to recognize that they are responsible for their actions. Only when a student accepts responsibility for a behavior can the process of change begin to occur.

Some students will seek to avoid responsibility by trying to avoid the question. A common response is "Nothing." When this happens, you should simply repeat the question. Another avoidance technique is to identify another behavior. For example, a student might state, "I'm sitting in my seat." When this happens, you follow this up with, "What else are you doing?" If, after about three attempts the student refuses to identify the behavior, then you identify it for him or her. Do this very directly and without a display of emotion of emotion or anger. State, "I saw you . . ."

Another student response is to try and sidetrack you by providing an excuse. A student will often try to shift the responsibility to someone else. For example, a student might respond, "Well, Mary needed a pencil" or " Bill asked me a question." When this occurs, both ignore the answer and ask again, "What were you doing?" or accept the answer by stating, "I understand, but what were *you* doing?"

Get the Student to Identify the Consequences
Once the inappropriate behavior has been identified, ask, "What happens when people do that?" Your intent is to establish a clear link between the behavior and the consequences. They need to see that it is their behavior that is leading to the consequence and not the whims of a vindictive or angry teacher. An understanding of the link makes it possible for students to comprehend that their behavior is a matter of choice and the consequences that they experience are also a matter of choice. This step works well if you have developed a set of rules and procedures you follow in the class and have either identified or discussed the possible consequences for violations.

If a student refuses to identify consequences of responses with the typical, "I don't know," you can follow up with a suggestion of two or three suitable alternatives. This leads naturally into the next step.

Have the Student Make a Value Judgment about the Behavior
This step follows the identification of consequences by asking, "Is that what you want to happen to you?" The purpose of getting the students to make a value judgment is to attempt to get them to see that inappropriate behavior is harming, not helping, their efforts to meet their needs. Something we forget is that there is only one person who can change a behavior; that is the student. In order to do that students must recognize that their behavior is counterproductive. Glasser suggests that teachers can help students do this by asking them, "How is this behavior helping you?" or "How is the behavior helping others?" The latter question is often used to help students realize that they must demonstrate responsibility by fulfilling their needs in ways that do not interfere with the ability of others to fulfill theirs.

If a student responds to the question about consequences with the remark "Yeah, that's okay with me," don't get angry just say, "Okay," and implement the consequences. More often than not the student is simply bluffing and trying to get you angry so that they can rationalize that it is your anger and not their behavior that is causing them difficulty.

Develop a Plan with the Student for Changing the Behavior
When students respond that they do not want the consequences that follow the behavior or they recognize that the behavior is not helping them, then the door is open

ACTIVITY 9-1 DON'T BE SO SOFT!

You are a new teacher and you are having some difficulty with some of the students in your class. Every time you attempt to discipline them they get angry and claim that you are being unfair and are just picking on them. You encounter Glasser's ideas about getting the students to recognize the link between their choices and the consequences.

You go and get some advice from the school principal. The principal says, "You are just being overly sensitive. Like most new teachers you are being too soft and are worrying too much about what the students think. I think you will just be wasting your time trying to talk with them. Just get tough and lay down the law. Anytime someone misbehaves come down hard on them. Don't waste your breath or time trying to discuss things with them."

What do you think?

1. How do you react to the principal's statement?

2. Do you think there is any validity in the statement?

3. What would you say to the principal so that you could respond to problems in a way that you feel is right, yet would not result in your being considered unreceptive to suggestions?

————

to develop a plan with them. The purpose of this step is to help students establish a plan that will help them fulfill needs in a productive way. This step can be implemented simply by asking the student, "What kind of plan could we work out so that this will not happen again?" If a student is reluctant to answer, you might simply state, "You think about it and I will return in a few minutes and discuss it." You should not accept superficial answers. Pursue the development of a plan by asking students why they think this will work and what should be done if it does not. Once again the purpose is to keep responsibility with the student. Therefore, you must resist the temptation to force a plan on him or her. The student must make a commitment to the plan, and this commitment may be only a superficial one if the student believes he or she has no choice but to follow your plan. You can offer support by providing some suggestions and asking how you can help.

The plans that are made should be very simple and short-term. Initial plans for students who are chronic behavior problems might cover one period or one day. The intent is for the student to be successful in completing the plan. It is unproductive to have students spell out a complicated plan that covers an entire semester. They will not be successful and therefore will not learn responsibility. You might need to remind the student of the plan from time to time and might also need to evaluate the success of the plan with the student. If the student violates the plan, then the teacher and the student have another conference and develop a new plan. It may well be that several plans will need to be developed before the student realizes that the teacher means business and a plan is developed that is successful.

Invoke Reasonable Consequences

The development of a plan does not preclude the administration of reasonable consequences. A student who has violated a rule and misbehaved needs to realize that reasonable consequences do follow. The consequences for misbehavior should be undesirable or unpleasant to the student but should not be punishing or harmful. However, it is of equal importance that desirable and pleasant events also follow when students do behave. This helps them learn that they can experience desirable and pleasant events or undesirable and unpleasant events by their choice of behavior. This gives them a sense of power and control over what happens to them and leads to increased self-control.

IMPLEMENTING REASONABLE CONSEQUENCES

The next question that arises is, what are reasonable consequences? Some useful principles for answering this question are found in the work of Dreikurs (1968). Driekurs advocates the use of logical or natural consequences.

Logical and Natural Consequences

Implementing logical and natural consequences is another important step in helping students understand the link between behavior and consequences and to keep the responsibility for the consequences with the student rather than the teacher. Logical and natural consequences are those consequences that are directly related to the nature of the misbehavior. Natural and logical consequences are not punishments.

Driekurs (1968) points out that there is a fine line between natural and logical consequences and punishment. However, he contends that students will quickly understand the difference. Although both punishment and consequences may have results that are undesirable for the offender, the difference is that natural and logical consequences have a direct relationship to the offense, whereas punishment is arbitrary and unrelated.

Natural consequences are defined as the natural outcomes of events without the intervention of another (Driekurs, Grunwald, and Pepper, 1982). For example, a student who runs in the hall may fall and skin a knee. The injury is a natural consequence of not following a safe practice; the consequence was not planned or arranged by another. Another example of a natural consequence in school might be when a tardy student misses a positive event that occurs at the beginning of the period. You do not threaten, scold, or argue with students. You simply inform the student that you are sorry that they missed the activity by being tardy. When a student experiences a consequence, you may regret that it happened but should not attempt allow the student to avoid the loss or add additional punishments.

One of the problems with natural consequences is that many of the misbehaviors that occur in school do not have natural consequences. In addition, some consequences are too dangerous and therefore should not be allowed to occur. For example, a student running in the hall may run into an unopened door and experience severe injury. Although the student would probably learn to exercise more self-control the next time, you must do more than warn the student of the possibility of severe injury. This is where logical consequences are useful.

Logical consequences are those events that are guided and arranged by another (Dreikurs, Grunwald, and Pepper, 1982). However, they must have a logical relationship to the misbehavior and must be understood by the student. Otherwise, they may be viewed as the arbitrary imposition of punishment by a more powerful adult. For example, a student who is tardy for class may not experience a natural consequence because he or she did not miss something they desired. They could be punished by being sent to the office or kept after school. However, these punishments have little direct relationship to the nature of the offense. In the application of logical consequences, the student who is late would be required to make up the missed time on his or her own time. A secondary level student might be expected to make up the time during some of his or her free time or after school. In an elementary classroom this works well if you have some optional "fun" time during the day. Rather than engaging in this optional activity, the student must make up missed time. If the whole class does not get to work promptly they don't get dismissed promptly. If students are constantly getting in trouble on the playground, then a logical consequence would be that they can't go to the playground with the others. They may be isolated at some supervised spot. Students who run in the hall and pose a danger to others must walk with the teacher.

It is important to apply logical consequences in a consistent, matter-of-fact manner, and to make sure that the student understands the link between his or her actions and the consequence. You may need to tell them, "Because you run in the hall and I am afraid you will get hurt or hurt someone else, you must walk with me." If logical consequences are applied inconsistently, students are deprived of the opportunity to understand the link between their behavior and the consequences for those actions. As a result, their growth toward self-control is hindered.

One final comment on the use of logical consequences: They should also apply to you. For example, if you cause the class to be late for recess or dismissal, then the class should be given some additional time as compensation. If you fail to return student papers in a timely manner, you might be required to add points to those papers. The universal application of logical consequences is uncomfortable for many teachers. However, it does provide good modeling behavior for students and can go far in defusing the anger that may occur when a student has to experience an unpleasant consequence.

In summary, an important step in helping students learn self-control is helping them understand the link between behavior and consequences. This can be accomplished

ACTIVITY 9-2   HILDA'S DESTRUCTIVE BEHAVIOR

Hilda comes from a large family. There is some evidence to suggest that she has been an abused child. She rarely disrupts class but destroys the property of others when she is not watched closely. One day she got hold of a set of new pencils that one boy had brought to school and proceeded to break each of them into small pieces. On another occasion she defaced one of the bulletin boards that displayed student work. On the playground and after school she frequently hits and hurts younger students.

What would you do?

1. Why do you think Hilda behaves this way?

2. How might you use logical and natural consequences in this situation?

3. What might be some natural or logical consequences that you could use?

---

through the conference suggested by Glasser and by implementing natural and logical consequences, rather than arbitrary punishments. The application of logical consequences to everyone in the classroom, including the teacher, also has the effect of creating a more positive and democratic climate in which all individuals are free to learn from their mistakes.

IDENTIFYING ALTERNATIVE CONSEQUENCES

A major difficulty for many new or inexperienced teachers is in the identification of reasonable and logical consequences. Both Glasser and Dreikurs imply that there is no one consequence that will work in all situations. As with the development of low profile responses, you need to develop a set of alternative consequences that can assist you in making appropriate decisions. The consequences you develop need to be comfortable for you. If you do not feel comfortable with the consequences, you will be reluctant to enforce them and run the risk of being inconsistent in your actions. As you begin to develop experience you need to creatively design consequences that meet the needs of your unique situation.

The following is a list of some alternative responses from which you might choose. The responses in this category require more effort and planning than do those in the previous chapter. These responses should be used when other, low profile responses have not had the desired effect or when the problem is serious enough to warrant a more direct and intrusive response.

Beginning with these suggestions and expanding the list can provide you with a good foundation for developing a discipline plan and some security. Because the classroom is so fast-paced and spontaneous, inexperienced teachers often are at a loss as to how to respond when a more serious problem does arise. You can help prevent this problem by giving some careful consideration to some alternative choices and developing a list of your own.

Responding with Clarity and Firmness

Verbal responses are typical teacher reactions to student misbehavior. However, if you observe in classrooms for any length of time, you will discover that many of these verbal responses seem to be ineffective. A teacher will verbally reprimand a student and, while the student may stop for a short while, soon he or she is once again engaged in the inappropriate behavior and the teacher again makes a verbal response. In fact, in some classrooms the entire lesson is filled with intrusive verbal reprimands. There are several potential problems associated with these verbal responses. They tend to put the student on the spot, draw attention to the misbehavior, and set the stage for a power struggle. Therefore, verbal responses should be used with caution.

There are times when a verbal response is appropriate and necessary. However, it is important to note the characteristics of verbal responses. Ineffective verbal responses have several characteristics. Most of them are general and negative. Examples of these are: "Class, get back in your chairs right now!" or "Stop that talking!" The verbal responses of other teachers tend to be almost apologetic. "Please be quiet" or "I would appreciate your cooperation" are examples.

There are several things that you can do to increase the effectiveness of verbal responses. First, you need to deliver the message in a businesslike manner. Anger, verbal abuse, name-calling, shouting, and sarcasm should be avoided. They only cause resentment and set the stage for retaliation. Your messages should contain two important elements. They should be delivered with clarity and with firmness (Kounin, 1970).

Clarity involves identifying who is misbehaving, what that person is doing, and what he or she should be doing instead. A verbal message involving clarity would be as follows, "Betty, stop your talking and begin working on your math problems." This message indicates that Betty is the target, her talking is the inappropriate behavior, and working on the math problems is the acceptable alternative. In this message there is no question about for whom the message is intended and what she needs to do.

Firmness means using a tone of voice and body language to indicate that you mean business. As you deliver the message, you should make eye contact with the student, begin moving toward the student, maintain a rather stiff and erect posture, and make sure that your facial expressions are consistent with your intent. In other words, don't be smiling and laughing! If you are, the student will receive a mixed message and, by interpreting your nonverbal behavior, conclude that you are insincere and will continue the misbehavior and force you to take an even more intrusive approach. Then when you do, the student feels betrayed.

In summary, learn to use verbal responses sparingly. If you do, they will have more impact when you do use them. Deliver them in a businesslike manner and use clarity and firmness to maximize their effectiveness.

Verbal Limit Setting

Verbal limit setting is an effective means for responding to many of those problems that did not cease when you used low profile approaches. The intent of verbal limit setting is to convey to the students that they have reached the limit and continuance will result in consequences they do not want to experience. Jones (1987) calls limit setting the gentle use of personal power. You are exercising the personal power that you have as a teacher but you are doing so in an assertive, yet gentle manner. Jones emphasizes the importance of staying calm during the verbal limit setting. He points out that emotions are contagious. If you are upset, the student will be upset. If you remain calm, the student will remain calm. Clarity and firmness are also important conditions when using limit setting.

Jones defines limit setting as involving three components: moving in, dealing with back talk, and moving out. A prerequisite to limit setting is being aware of behavior throughout the classroom. This is the "withitness" described by Kounin (1970). Once you have identified one or more off-task students who seem to ignore your low profile attempts to get them back to work, you initiate the steps of limit setting.

Moving In

The first step in moving in is to stop what you are doing. If you are working with the total class, you can stop by just stating to the class, "Excuse me, class." If you are working with a student, tell the student you will be right back. Next, making sure your body language communicates disapproval, face the students directly so that your body language communicates a full commitment to dealing with the problem. Take a couple of deep breaths to relax yourself and call their names in an unemotional or bland manner. The reason you take a couple of deep breaths is to calm yourself. You do not want to communicate anger because this will only trigger anger in the student. Jones points out that anger will send a shot of adrenaline in the bloodstream that will not dissipate for approximately 28 minutes. This adrenaline will make it more difficult for them to concentrate and stay on-task.

Next walk calmly to the student's desk. Do not stop to answer questions or deal with other problems. You want the students to know that they have your undivided attention and you mean business. When you arrive at his or her desk, keep your body posture erect, establish eye contact, and take a couple more deep breaths. Once again, this will help calm you, will give the students time to think and make a decision, and will help them remain calm. Do not say anything. If the student makes a commitment to return to work, you can then skip to the moving out phase.

If the student does not make an obvious commitment to return to work, you will need to provide a physical and verbal prompt. The physical prompt involves bending at the waist, placing one hand on their desk and using your other hand to indicate what the student should be doing. This might involve placing a pencil in his or her hand, moving the work to a direct location in front of him or her, or removing a distracting object. The verbal prompt is a command or directive telling the student exactly what to do in one or two sentences. If the student still does not respond, place both of your hands on opposite sides of the desk and maintain eye contact. Remain leaning over until the student begins to work. Watch for several seconds after he or she begins working and then start the moving out phase.

Back Talk

There are some students who will attempt to display their own power and take control of the situation through back talk. Back talk is defined as a verbal statement intended to change the subject, divert your attention from the behavior, and to get off the hook. Therefore, back talk does not need to take the form of a hostile or confrontational statement. It can even be a compliment. For example, a student might try to divert your attention with the statement, "I really like your dress." Other examples might be displaying of helplessness, denial, blaming other students, accusing the teacher of incompetence, insulting the teacher, or profanity. All varieties have the same purpose; they are diversionary topics designed to elicit a reaction from you that will change the focus. If this does not work, some students will resort to crying.

Jones points out that back talk will starve if not fed. The student wants to elicit a response from you and a response that will take responsibility off of him or her and place it back on you. You want to keep the responsibility on the student and you can best do this by staying quiet.

Jones suggests that the first step in dealing with back talk is "camping out." In camping out you slowly place all of your weight on your elbow. This decreases the proximity between you and the student. Take a couple more deep breaths to assist you in remaining calm, look at the student with an air of indifference or boredom, and wait for the student to run out of gas. When the student stops and is looking at you, maintain eye contact, repeat your verbal prompt and be quiet. This communicates to the student that you were not listening and efforts to divert your attention have failed.

Moving Out

The intent of moving out is to communicate to the student that you intend for the student to stay on-task and you will follow through. The first step in moving out begins when the student returns to work. Thank the student for returning to work, take a couple more deep breaths, and stay in place to watch him or her work for a few seconds. If you move out too rapidly, the student will often go off-task just as rapidly. You want to convey to the student that you will invest whatever time is necessary to insure a return to work. Once he or she begins working, stand slowly but do not walk away. Monitor the behavior for a few more seconds and then either walk away or turn to another student.

If a second student was involved, you now turn to the second student and repeat any steps in the moving in, back talk, and moving out steps that are necessary to make sure that the student is on-task. The important point is for you to deal with each student independently.

After thanking the student, return to the front of the room, turn, take a couple more deep breaths and look at the student and, if possible, make eye contact. If the student is giving signs of not being fully committed to the work, wait a bit longer at this point. If everything is back in order, return to the task you were working on. However, make sure you keep the student in your field of vision.

Jones states that this whole process needs to be a deliberate one that is much more slowly paced than is normal in the classroom. He notes that the most difficult task seems to be taking two deep breaths before each move. This should take about 15 seconds. This is important because it helps keep you calm, helps you keep your composure, and sets an appropriate pace.

Loss of Privileges

The loss of privileges can be an especially effective consequence. However, it will work only if students have some privileges to lose, and if there are privileges that students desire. Unfortunately, many secondary school students are given few privileges and therefore have nothing to lose. A wise teacher will begin at the first of the year to identify some privileges that are desired by the students. For example, some secondary school teachers have discovered that students like to listen to music while they are engaged in seatwork. This is a privilege that can be withheld as a consequence of misbehavior. Others might include being allowed free time or being the first in line for lunch. Some schools consider extracurricular activities a privilege and participation depends on appropriate behavior.

One elementary teacher had a particularly difficult group of students. She identified an activity that they enjoyed and informed them that they would be able to participate in that activity for a few minutes at the end of the day. However, time wasted for misbehavior would be deducted from this time. When the group leader tested the system and realized that wasted time did mean a loss of the privilege, the class put pressure on each other to follow the rules. In a short time the problems almost totally disappeared (Jones, 1987).

There are abundant activities that elementary school teachers can use for privileges. Most elementary school students enjoy serving as teacher helpers and monitors. Loss of the classroom job for a short time is often effective. Choice of a recess activity or being made the captain of a team or custodian of the playground equipment are other highly valued privileges that can be awarded for good behavior or withheld for misbehavior.

Students enjoy having privileges. Often the threat of a loss of a privilege is enough to stop a behavior and allow the students the opportunity to consider the consequences of their actions. Some teachers do not seem to understand this and overlook this consequence.

Cost–Benefit Analysis

Many behaviors that cause teachers difficulty can be handled rather easily by letting students know that there is a cost associated with their choice. For example, teachers are often at a loss regarding what to do with constant requests to go to the restroom. You are torn between feeling that it is cruel to deny students permission if they really need to visit the bathroom. However, there is a sneaking suspicion that perhaps the request is really an attempt to avoid work. The solution to this dilemma is to place the choice on the student. You do this by associating a cost with the privilege. For example, a student requests permission to visit the restroom. You give him or her a cheerful "sure" while you reach down and click a stopwatch. "What are you doing?" asks the student. "Keeping track of the time you miss. You can make it up at the end of class" (Jones, 1987). The student is now provided with a clear choice. If he or she needs to visit the restroom, they will do so. If, however, it was only an excuse to take a break, it has not worked and they will be expected to make up the time. This clear cost–benefit choice is consistent with logical consequences and keeps responsibility with the students.

Similar costs might be associated with students who seem to need to sharpen a pencil constantly. Again, you want the student to be able to write, yet you are concerned that it is only an excuse to be up and moving around the classroom. One cost–benefit choice that frequently works is to not allow pencil sharpening during class. Instead, keep a good supply of short, grubby pencils in a container on your desk. If someone needs a sharp pencil and they do not have one, they trade the broken pencil for one of the sharp ones in the container. They have to pay a cost in trading a good-looking pencil for a grubby one, so they will only do this if necessary.

In the elementary grades cost–benefit analysis works with the all too prevalent activity of tattletales. Students need to learn that if there is a serious problem, you do need to hear about it. However, many of the stories you hear are attempts to get attention. A useful practice is to tell those who wish to tell on someone else that if they will sit down and write out the complaint along with a suggestion on how to fix it, you will then discuss it with them. They then make the choice; if it is something that is important to them, they will take the time to write the complaint.

Time-Out

Time-out is a popular response to inappropriate behavior. It involves setting aside a time-out area in the classroom. It might be a desk or a chair in an area that is not near other students. The purpose of time-out is to move the student to an area where he or she will not be able to continue to disturb others. This is not intended as a punishment but as a place where students can sit until the teacher has an opportunity to talk with them. Students stay in the time-out area until you have time to meet with them individually. When you do meet with them you ask if they are ready to return to the class.

They are allowed to return only when they give a verbal plan for how they will change their behavior. This is an effective approach if the behavior is disruptive to other students and the teacher is engaged in a lesson and cannot take the time for a response like limit setting.

Time-out is employed by telling a student to take a seat in the time-out area. The student goes to this area and remains there until you have an opportunity to meet with him or her and discuss whether or not he or she is ready to return to the group (Glasser, 1977). The student should be given time to think about the behavior and to calm down before the conference. In other words, you do not need to hurry to have the conference. Most students do enjoy being a part of the group and isolation is not a desirable state. Most students will choose to return to the group.

An alternative time-out use is for the student to take the time-out in another classroom. This can be effective in the elementary school where a student is sent to another room, generally a classroom of students a couple of years younger or older than the student. This use of time-out should be reserved for those times when the behavior is a serious disruption and nothing else seems to be working. In order to use this you do need to have an agreement with another teacher. The student goes to this room and is given a quiet place to sit and do work. Elementary students do not like being away from their friends and spending a considerable amount of time in another room generally puts them in the mood to negotiate a return.

Secondary schools sometimes have a time-out room where students from different classes can be sent if they are misbehaving. Some schools use a time-out area in the office as a consequence for more serious offenses. Once again, this action needs the cooperation of the school administration and should be done infrequently and only after other approaches have been tried.

Removing students from the classroom has a couple of purposes. First it communicates to the student that you are serious about enforcing the rules and you will not allow anyone to interfere with the learning of other students. Secondly, time away from the classroom allows for a cooling off period for both the teacher and the student when a power struggle has erupted. This decreases the probability that you will act out of anger and do something that will only make the problem worse. It also allows you the opportunity to gain control of the rest of the class and get them calmed and back on-task.

One word of caution: Never send students to the hall, the playground, or to an area where they will not be under the direct observation of another person. If students are not in a place where they can be easily observed, they may engage in dangerous activity or even the leave the school grounds. This places you under enormous legal risk.

Rearranging the Environment

If misbehavior persists, it might be necessary to consider altering the classroom environment in order to remove distractions and make it easier for the students to exercise

ACTIVITY 9-3 CLASSROOM SEATING

Maria Shelton believes in allowing students to choose where they want to sit in the classroom. She thinks that junior high students are old enough to be treated like adults and that they will respond in a positive manner if she does so. However, she does have some problems. Many of the students have trouble getting started at the beginning of a period because they are busy socializing. She finds that it takes her several minutes to get the class started. In addition, she does have considerable talking during class as students talk with their neighbors.

What do you think?

1. Do you agree with her reasoning about allowing students to select their own seats?

2. Do you think the problems are serious enough for her to take action?

3. What do you think she could do to be consistent with her beliefs and yet solve the problems?

---

self-control. For example, some students sitting near each other are just not able to refrain from talking or bothering each other. A solution might be to assign seats that are not near each other. Another solution might be to move the students closer to the teacher and into the action zone so they can be easily monitored.

You might want to look for aspects of the environment that might be the cause of the difficulty. Is the student close to the door and tempted to interact with those passing by in the hallway? Is he or she in a position so that they can distracted by what is outside the windows? Perhaps they are too near the major traffic center in the classroom and they are tempted to interact with everyone who passes by. Sitting near the teacher's desk might distract some students because they have to listen in on every conversation of the teacher.

Teacher–Student Conference

After students are sent to a time-out area, or if a problem seems to be recurring, it is time for a conference with the student. The conference is best done in a spot away from the ears of others in the classroom. It needs to be one-on-one with the student. You want to approach the conference calmly. Do not have a conference when you are angry. Make it very clear at the beginning that the purpose of the conference is to try and arrive at a solution to the problem.

During this conference you need to apply active listening and use I-messages as discussed in the previous chapter. You will also want to make sure that you focus on helping the student identify the relationship between his or her behavior and the consequence. Apply the questions suggested by Glasser earlier in this chapter. You need to get the student to do most of the talking. Ask, What is the problem? What suggestions do you have for preventing the problem? What can I do to help you? What do you think I should do the next time this happens? If the student is reluctant to talk, make some suggestions that you do not think he or she would like. When they protest, then ask him or her to supply an alternative. Be very firm and do not let the student get by with superficial responses. For example, if he or she states, "I just won't do that any more," respond with, "That is not good enough, what if you forget?"

You need to be open to suggestions by the student and not be defensive. The student might have a good point. In a conference I once had with a student he informed me that I wasn't teaching content that was of interest to him. He was right! We made a deal that I would work to find material that interested him and he would work to stay on-task. It worked and the problem was solved.

Teaching Students to Modify Their Own Behavior

Some students have difficulty with self-control. They do not engage in serious misbehavior, just numerous incidents of minor misbehavior. A useful response is to help these students monitor their own behavior and learn how to take appropriate action to prevent getting into trouble. Several studies have shown that teaching students to monitor their own behavior is effective and has several advantages (McLaughlin, 1976). One advantage is that the student becomes more aware of his or her behavior and the control of the behavior is left with the student. Another advantage is that it relieves the teacher from always playing the role of the enforcer.

There are several methods you can use to teach students to monitor their own behavior. One technique is to provide the students with a series of questions they can learn to ask themselves when they are faced with temptation or when they begin to feel anxious or angry. The questions might include:

- What is causing me to feel this way?
- What will happen if I don't control myself?
- Is this what I want to happen?
- What can I do to calm down and gain control?

In response to the last questions you might work with the student to identify acceptable responses. For example, some students might be given the freedom to choose to go to the time out area for a short time voluntarily. They might be allowed to put their head down and think of favorite activities or happy thoughts. They could learn to count to a certain number and when they begin to relax and calm down, they resume work.

Another method is to have students keep their own record of their behavior. For example, they can keep a tally of every time they get out of their seat or every time

TABLE 9-1 **A Selection of Direct Teacher Interventions**

Conditions: Use alternatives that are logical or natural and help students understand the relationship between behavior and consequence.

Responding with Clarity and Firmness
Verbal Limit Setting
   Moving In
   Responding to Back Talk
   Moving Out
Loss of Privileges
Cost–Benefit Analysis
Time-Out
Rearranging the Environment
Teacher–Student Conference
Teaching the Student to Modify Own Behavior

they talk without permission. You can help by reminding the student when to record something. Some students respond positively to this approach. At the conclusion of a given period of time, you and the student can review the records. Some students are surprised at the prevalence of the behavior. You can then allow the student to set some goals and decide how they will reward themselves when they improve.

Implementing self-monitoring requires more than just talking about it. It requires that you model and demonstrate the technique. For example, you might model the self-verbalization technique for the students and even use it by asking the questions out loud when you begin to feel anxious or angry. You can also keep tallies of things you would like to change. For example, you might have a verbal speech habit such as saying *okay* too much. You can inform the class about what you are doing and keep a tally sheet on your desk. As they see you modeling the technique, they will learn how to apply it to their lives.

MISTAKEN GOALS

Deciding on responses to more serious or persistent behavior problems is more effective if you understand why the student is acting in a particular way. If you do not understand what the student is trying to accomplish, you may respond in ways that will be counterproductive. Dreikurs states that every action of a student has a purpose (Dreikurs, Grunwald, and Pepper, 1982). The basic purpose is to attain status and feel significant. However, some students do not attain acceptance through acceptable actions and develop the belief that the only way to gain recognition is through misbehavior. Therefore, their behavior is motivated by what Dreikurs terms *mistaken goals.*

Defining Mistaken Goals

Dreikurs identified four types of mistaken goals. These goals are at the root of most misbehavior. Those four mistaken goals are attention, power, revenge, and withdrawal. Because the individual has learned through past experiences the actions that he or she can take that are most likely to achieve his or her mistaken goal, his or her behavior will elicit a reaction from you that is consistent with that goal. Therefore, you cannot count on your immediate reaction to be the correct one. More than likely your first reaction will only reinforce the student in using misbehavior as a way of achieving the mistaken goals. Understanding each of these four goals will help you avoid this trap.

Attention-Seeking

Attention-seeking is a common goal for most people. Individuals want to be noticed. They want to feel that they are significant enough to capture the attention of others. Most of us know that one of the most humiliating and infuriating events is to be ignored, and we have learned that we can capture attention by performing in ways that are socially acceptable. For example, many students learn that they will gain the attention and affection of significant others by doing well in school.

However, students who are frustrated in their attempts to do well in school or who do not receive attention regardless of their efforts soon give up and seek other methods for attracting attention. These methods include misbehaviors designed to get the attention of the teacher and other students. Unaware teachers often provide reinforcement for this behavior. A student has a need to get attention so he or she gets out of his or her seat and wanders around the classroom. You loudly reprimand the student in front of the class and tell him or her to sit down. You think that you have punished the student when, in fact, you have provided what is desired, attention. Some students will go to great lengths to get attention. Understanding this point helps explain why misbehaving students sometimes ask, " What do you get for being good? Everybody knows me." Remember that attention-seeking individuals prefer humiliation and punishment to being ignored.

Power-Seeking

We all have a need to feel that we have some personal power, that we have at least some control over our environment. People who have been frustrated in gaining power through acceptable means usually seek power and, therefore, a feeling of significance through socially unacceptable means. Through their inappropriate behavior, these individuals are seeking to prove that no one can make them act in a certain way. As they frustrate others, especially parents and teachers, they are demonstrating power and their power needs are being reinforced. They may try to accomplish this goal through defiance, deliberate disobedience, arguing, crying, acting stubborn, or throwing a temper tantrum. These reactions only cause more frustration for you and present a challenge that few teachers seem able to resist.

The goal of the student is to engage the adult in a power struggle. Regardless of the outcome of the power struggle, engaging the teacher demonstrates that he or she has power. As a teacher, you may be tempted to meet the challenge issued by these power-seeking students. However, it is a no-win situation for you. Just to engage the student in the power struggle reinforces his or her mistaken idea about how to get power. It is difficult for a teacher to really win a power struggle. The student has a lot more time to try and find ways of rendering the teacher powerless and they seldom play by the rules. If you respond by demonstrating your power and think that you have prevailed and have taught the student a lesson, the lesson he or she has learned is that power is what matters most. In addition, you have created conditions for the student to move toward a more serious goal, getting revenge.

Revenge

The anger and the frustration that usually follow power struggles leads to revenge. When students feel hurt and angry or believe that people have been unfair to them, they try to get even. Their reasoning is that they have been hurt and therefore they have the right to hurt others. They are reinforced in their efforts when they see others hurt.

These students are convinced that no one likes them or believes they are significant. Therefore, their behavior is not their fault, but it is caused by the way others treat them. Because the student bent on revenge does hurt other people and does cause hostility, the retaliation of others in response to their behavior is taken as proof that they were right in the first place. No one likes them, and they have a right to strike out.

The revenge-seeking student is one of your most difficult challenges. Students who have revenge as a goal have serious problems and it is not likely that they will change quickly. As a teacher you are a convenient target. You need to realize that you may not be the cause of the behavior but only provide an easy target. This type of goal is also difficult for many teachers to handle because students do make them feel bad and take much of the joy out of teaching. I have seen teachers driven from the classroom in tears by revenge-seeking students. Because you are hurt by revenge-seeking students you may fall into the trap of striking back and trying to get even with the student. This will be ineffective and set the stage for further confrontations because it provides justification to the student for his or her continued acts of revenge.

Withdrawal

Some students who are unable to achieve a sense of significance through acceptable means may become so discouraged that they simply give up. It is much better for them to withdraw, not to even try than to fail and again be proven insignificant. As a defense mechanism to avoid even trying a task, these students will hide behind a display of inadequacy. They will go to great lengths to discourage the teacher from attempting to help them. Like the revengeful student, this student has serious problems and causes a great deal of frustration among teachers.

Unfortunately, it is easier for you to give up on students who display inadequacy than to persist. Consequently, they do not receive the help they need, they do not make progress, and this confirms what they thought all along: They are insignificant and inadequate.

Identifying Mistaken Goals

Teachers who are unaware of the goal that a student is trying to achieve may behave in ways that reinforce the student's attempts to feel significant and powerful through inappropriate behavior. Therefore, the first step in taking corrective action is to identify the goal of the student.

Dreikurs, Grunwald, and Pepper (1982) identify two basic ways that the teacher can identify a student's goal. The most reliable indicator is your immediate reaction to the behavior. If you feel a need to yell at or nag a student, the goal is usually attention. If your first reaction is that the student is challenging or testing your authority, then the goal is usually power. A first reaction of feeling hurt or defeated often indicates that the goal of the student is to get revenge. Feeling frustrated to the point of throwing up your hands and leaving the child alone is usually an indication that the student is seeking to be left alone through a display of inadequacy. In all of these situations, the first reaction of the teacher is the wrong one.

A second indication of the student's goal is through the student's response to correction. If the student stops a behavior when reprimanded but then starts again after a short time, attention is the probable goal. If the student becomes defiant when reprimanded and continues to misbehave, the goal is probably that of power. A student who becomes abusive and angry when reprimanded and who complains that he or she is being picked on and unjustly accused is often seeking revenge. A student who is passive and does nothing when reprimanded is usually demonstrating a sense of inadequacy and simply wants to be left alone.

Responding to Mistaken Goals

Merely identifying the goal is not enough. You need to have a plan of action that will help the student move away from these mistaken notions and toward self-control. As stated above, it is usually the wrong response to act according to your first impulse because that is exactly the reaction the behavior is designed to elicit.

Dreikurs et al. (1982) recommend that a first step in dealing with a student who is misbehaving is to disclose the goal to the student and to observe the reaction. The disclosure needs to be done in a matter-of-fact, nonthreatening manner and never as an accusation. Therefore, the disclosure is best not done when you are angry. Disclosing the goal has the effect of opening up communication between you and the student. In addition, most students are unaware of the goals that they may be pursuing through their misbehavior, and disclosing their mistaken goals helps them understand their behavior and be more purposeful in becoming more productive.

The process of disclosing the goal to the student is best done by using simple questioning techniques. You begin by asking the student if he or she is interested in knowing the reason for his or her behavior. If the student replies in the affirmative, then continue with a follow-up question. If the student says no, you simply respond by saying, "I would like to tell you what I think," and then continue with the follow-up question.

The follow-up questions usually start with the stem "Could it be that . . . ?" For example, follow-up questions intended to reveal a goal of attention-getting might be phrased, "Could it be that you would like me to pay you more attention?" or "Could it be that you want me to come and help you more?" Questions intended to reveal the goal of power could be phrased, "Could it be that you want to show me that I cannot make you behave?" or "Could it be that you want to be the boss?" Revenge goals could be revealed through "Could it be that you want to hurt me or others?" or "Could it be that you want to try to get even?" Inadequacy might be addressed through the question, "Could it be that you want to be left alone because you are afraid to fail?" or "Could it be that you want to be left alone because you don't think you can win?"

Dreikurs states that you can often tell when the goal has been correctly identified by the student's reaction to the question. Although the student may answer "no," a recognition reflex such as a grin, embarrassed laughter, or body language indicating some discomfort usually confirms that you have hit the target.

There are several other responses that can be used when students are misbehaving. These vary according to the goal that the students are attempting to achieve. One basic principle that should be followed when responding to incidents of misbehavior is not to follow the first impulse. Rather, you should do something that is very different and unexpected.

Responding to Attention-Seeking

A first attempt at dealing with attention-seeking behavior is refusing to give attention to inappropriate behavior and giving attention to students when they are behaving. However, ignoring a behavior once is not likely to result in the desired change. The student has had years of gaining attention through misbehavior and one time will not be enough to result in a change. However, persistence will pay off, and the incidents of inappropriate behavior will begin to diminish.

In some situations, ignoring the behavior is not possible. Instead, other actions might be useful. One action would be to have a personal conference with the student. During this conference you should discuss the situation with the student in a calm, but firm, manner. Identify the goal for the student and suggest you work out a plan. In working out the plan you might ask the student how many times attention is desired during the period or the day. Each time that the student misbehaves in an effort to gain attention the teacher can merely state, "John, that's one," "John, that's two." This procedure shows the student the number of times he or she is actually seeking attention in unproductive ways.

The number of incidents is often surprising to the student and he or she will choose to make changes. However, if the incidents continue, the student may be seeking power and the teacher may need to use other responses. The use of logical consequences, such as having the student make up the time that is spent disrupting the class, may be productive.

Responding to Power-Seeking

Many teachers find it very difficult to avoid a power struggle with a student. The culture of education is steeped with an autocratic tradition that the teacher is to be obeyed and his or her authority may not be challenged. Students, however, do not share this tradition. Those who are power hungry take great delight in drawing teachers into power struggles.

You need to realize that drawing a line and challenging a student to defy teacher authority is asking for trouble. It is much easier simply to refuse to engage in a power struggle. Often, an unexpected sympathetic or friendly reaction to a student who is trying to gain power is enough to stop the behavior. For example, the teacher might respond with statements such as, "I'm sorry that you feel so alone and powerless" or "I know you are feeling angry but will this help you feel better?"

Another response is to simply admit that the student cannot be forced to behave. Admitting that the teacher has limited power and refusing to rise to the challenge often takes all of the fun out of attempting to engage the teacher in a power struggle. What you want to do is to place the emphasis on things over which you do have control. You may not be able to make students stay in their chairs, but you do have control over who stays in the classroom. You simply state, "You are right, I cannot make you behave. However, if you want to continue your behavior, you will do it elsewhere." Removing the student from the situation, and thus from the audience, is often enough to stop the behavior.

Responding to Revenge-Seeking

Students who are attempting to achieve revenge are students with serious problems. They are hurting inside and are looking for an excuse to explode. A major step in dealing with such a student is to change the relationship between you and the student, and, if possible, work on the relationship between the student and the rest of the class.

One of the important ingredients in changing the teacher–student relationship is to treat the student with respect. This is very difficult to do when a student is often treating you in an abusive manner that may cause emotional discomfort. However, you are the professional and have an ethical obligation to take charge of the situation. You should never pursue the same mistaken goal by trying to get revenge on a misbehaving student. This justifies the behavior of the student and communicates that revenge is acceptable.

You should try and treat revenge-seeking incidents in a matter-of-fact manner. Even though you are upset, it is important to communicate to the student that you have self-control and will not retaliate. Removing the student from the situation in a quiet and nonthreatening manner provides the student with an opportunity to cool down. You can discuss the situation with the student by identifying the goal the student was pursuing and then asking the student to apologize or make restitution. You can offer to help the student anytime he or she is feeling angry and resentful. The security a confident and assertive teacher provides to students produces a calming effect on them, removing much of the anger that is seething inside. They begin to realize that not everyone is against them and that they do have some worth.

Discussion with the entire class may be needed. The purpose of these class discussions should not be to place blame but rather to help the class understand how their treatment affects others. Role-playing situations may be especially helpful in stimulating a discussion about feelings, anger, and revenge. This understanding can then be applied to create an environment in which individuals are accepting of each other and the need for power struggles and revenge is eliminated.

Most students who are seeking revenge feel very much alone and on the outside. You may need to help them work to gain group acceptance. Talking with the student and helping the student understand the impact of his or her behavior on others might do this. The students might simply be deficient in social skills and not understand the relationship between their behavior and the reactions of others. You need to model and teach appropriate social skills for dealing with anger and hurt. Helping the student gain acceptance can also be accomplished by finding something he or she can do well and focusing on that ability or skill. Many disruptive students have been completely changed by a teacher who was interested enough in them to discover their talents and to consider them worthwhile. Once the teacher accepts the student, the class soon follows.

Responding to Withdrawal

Students who display inadequacy and try to withdraw are students who are extremely discouraged and have given up. Overcoming this discouragement is a major task for the teacher. Once again the student who is displaying inadequacy is a student with serious problems and must not be ignored.

A beginning step in overcoming displays of inadequacy is never to give up on the student. Communicating to the student a sense of optimism and celebrating every success, no matter how minor, are important ingredients. This also means that you must be careful not to place the student in high-risk situations. When activities and tasks are presented to this student, they need to be broken down into small steps so that the student does not feel overwhelmed.

Placing students in cooperative learning groups in which they are working with others and their failures are not spotlighted is also a useful approach in overcoming the discouragement that students displaying inadequacy feel. Helping such a student,

ACTIVITY 9-4   FRUSTRATING FRANK

Frank is not an especially troublesome student. In fact, he is extremely passive and apathetic. He doesn't do any work and at the end of the class period will turn in a blank piece of paper with his name on it. Getting low grades does not seem to disturb him. When you try to help him he just shrugs his shoulders and says, "I don't care."

What would you do?

1. What mistaken goals do you think account for Frank's behavior?

2. What would you do to try to get him to do some work?

---

like helping the student seeking revenge, is a time-consuming process, and immediate results should not be expected.

SUMMARY

Some students do not respond to less intrusive measures. When this occurs in the classroom, you must realize that it is permissible to be assertive and to expect that a student will obey. You should not think that you have no rights, nor should misbehaving students interfere with your right to teach and the right of others to learn.

Several steps can be taken in response to these more serious incidents. Dreikurs and associates (1982) have provided teachers with helpful ways of identifying the goals that students might be pursuing so that teachers do not inadvertently fall into the trap of continuing to reinforce students' behavior. Once these goals have been identified, teachers can then take some action. Dreikurs suggests that revealing the goal to the student, not responding to the first impulse but doing something unexpected, and implementing logical consequences are productive ways of changing the behavior and the goals that the student is pursuing.

Glasser (1965) has made a sound contribution by suggesting a specific approach to help students understand the link between their behavior and the consequences. They need to realize that when rules are violated, regardless of the reason, they should expect consequences. This process involves identifying what the student was doing, making a value judgment about the behavior, identifying reasonable consequences, making a plan, and implementing reasonable consequences. Teachers need to be warm and supportive individuals who model self-control for the student and who are persistent in their efforts.

Another step is to develop a list of possible consequences. The development of this hierarchy can provide you with a sense of security when you enter the classroom because you have already considered some potential actions that you can take.

SUGGESTED APPLICATIONS

1. Interview several teachers about assertiveness. Do they agree that teachers generally have not been assertive enough? How can teachers demonstrate assertiveness without alienating students and parents? Do principals support teacher assertiveness?

2. Observe in a classroom and see if you can identify students who might be pursuing the mistaken goals of attention, power, revenge, and withdrawal.

3. Reread Discipline Scenario 9-1. After reading the chapter, how have your responses changed from your responses when you first read it?

4. Continue to develop your list of alternative consequences. Add ones from this chapter that you feel comfortable using and add any others that interest you. How would your consequences fit the natural and logical definitions?

SUGGESTED READINGS

Canter, L. and Canter, M. (1976). *Assertive discipline: A take charge approach for today's educator.* Santa Monica, CA: Canter and Associates.

Dreikurs, R. (1968). *Psychology in the classroom,* 2nd Ed. New York: Harper & Row.

Dreikurs, R., Grunwald, B., and Pepper, F. (1982). *Maintaining sanity in the classroom: Classroom management techniques,* 3rd Ed. New York: Harper & Row.

Jones, F. (1987). *Positive classroom discipline.* New York: McGraw Hill.

Glasser, W. (1965). *Reality therapy: A new approach to psychiatry.* New York: Harper & Row.

Glasser, W. (1969). *Schools without failure.* New York: Harper & Row.

Glasser, W. (1977). 10 steps to good discipline. *Today's Education* 66, 60–63.

Kounin, J. (1970). *Discipline and group management in classrooms.* New York: Holt, Rinehart and Winston.

McLaughlin, T. (1976). Self-control in the classroom. *Review of Educational Research* 46(4), 631–663.

CHAPTER

10 Responding to Persistent Misbehavior

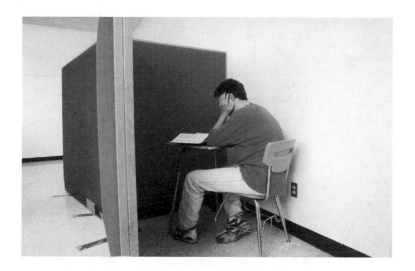

Chapter Objectives

After reading this chapter you should be able to:

- Identify how to use detention effectively
- Describe how to conduct an effective parent conference
- State how to seek outside assistance
- Apply behavior modification to change a specific behavior

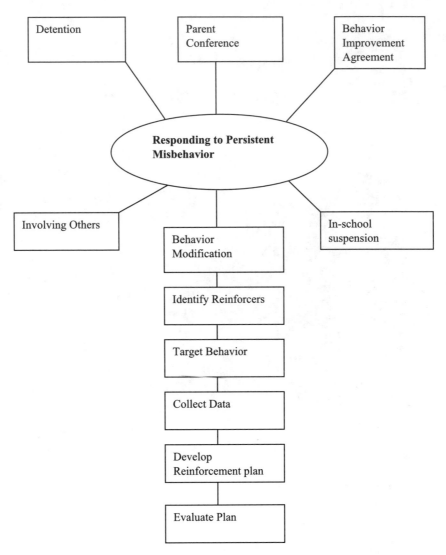

FIGURE 10-1   **Graphic Organizer for Responding to Persistent Misbehavior**

Applying the ideas covered in the earlier chapters will help prevent and eliminate most of the problems with misbehavior. However, some students demonstrate patterns of persistent misbehavior. Fortunately, the number of these students is relatively small. Most teachers and administrators claim that only about 5 percent of the students demonstrate this frustrating pattern of behavior. These students are considered serious, or chronic, discipline problems. They usually have a long history of problem behavior and the causes of the misbehavior are often very serious ones. Because they have a long history of problems, working to help them will often take a considerable amount of time and effort. A principal used to remind me when I worked with this type of student, "Remember, it took them 12 years to get this way, they won't change in a week." It is these students and these problems that cause teachers the most concern. You must have a plan of how you are going to work with these students or you run the risk of having a classroom that is constantly filled with tension and anxiety and a teaching experience you would just as soon forget. These students have the potential for destroying all of the good things that do happen in the classroom. It is probably accurate to state that these students account for a good percentage of teacher burnout and disillusionment.

Some suggestions for dealing with these students will be provided in this chapter. These approaches will require considerable time and effort on your part. No quick

---

DISCIPLINE SCENARIO 10-1 **Tardy Trouble**

You are teaching a sophomore English class. One of the students in the class, Wilma, has become an especially troublesome student. She obviously dislikes school and you suspect you are not very high on her list either. When she is in class, she is a disruptive influence. She delights in making sarcastic remarks and making a display that nothing in this class is of any value. You have tried ignoring her behavior, have tried to give her attention when she does what is expected (which is seldom), you have tried individual conferences with her, and nothing seems to get through.

Today she enters the class about five minutes late. As she enters she slams the door, and noisily makes her way to an empty seat. The whole class must stop until she takes her seat. You have lost all patience with her and her attitude. You decide to confront her.

"Wilma, why are you tardy?"

"I had to go to the bathroom. You don't want me to go in here do you?"

"Wilma, I don't appreciate your attitude!"

"Well, I don't appreciate yours either so I guess we're even."

The class is sitting breathlessly, observing this encounter. You do not want to let Wilma get away with this disrespect and you certainly cannot continue to let her disrupt the class. The class is observing to see what you are going to do.

How would you respond?

1. How far do you think a teacher should go in tolerating behavior of this sort?

2. Given your knowledge of Wilma, do you think you might have responded differently to her tardiness?

3. What will you do now?

fixes are promised. It may take a long time before you begin to see progress. The rewards, however, of seeing students of this sort change their behavior and become productive and contributing members of the class make the effort worthwhile.

TEACHER RESPONSES

There are several steps that you should implement when confronted with students who demonstrate persistent and serious misbehavior. These approaches do involve a significant amount of teacher power and should be reserved only for those times when you think you have reached the end of your rope.

TABLE 10-1   **Responses to Persistent Problems**

Detention

    When will it be?

      After School

      Before School

      Lunch

    What days will be detention days?

    How long will it last?

    Who supervises the students?

Parent Conferences

    Where are they to be held?

    What is the best time to hold them?

    Are there any special concerns regarding parent conferences in the school?

    How should they be arranged?

    How long should they last?

Behavior Improvement Agreements Involving Others

    Who should be involved?

    How are they to be involved?

In-School Suspension

    What is the procedure for using in-school suspension?

    What work do students need to have?

Detention

Detention is one of the time-honored disciplinary approaches. A universal threat is "behave or you will stay after school." However, detention is often used inappropriately and is ineffective.

For elementary teachers detention requires that you also stay after school to supervise. This might mean that you are punishing yourself because you have other things to do. However, most teachers have a number of tasks to perform that will keep them after the regular school hours so this is not a serious concern. An alternative approach might be to have detention only on certain days. This will allow you to plan ahead and will make it more pleasant for you.

Some high schools have a detention hall where all students report. This makes it easier on the teacher but can also lead to abuses. Because there is little cost to the teacher, some teachers give out a detention slip for every problem. Like all other approaches, when detention is overused, it loses its effectiveness.

There are several potential problems with detention. First there is a logistical problem; students who ride the school bus cannot be forced to miss the bus unless alternative transportation is provided. Therefore, it is generally best to notify the parents before the student serves detention. They can then arrange for alternative transportation. Another alternative is to have detention during lunch. This requires that students eat in a spot that is separated from others and miss the socialization that often occurs during lunch.

Secondly, detention may not be viewed by the students as necessarily bad. It might actually be preferable to going home to an empty house. This is especially the case if you are not careful about how you implement detention. Some teachers keep the students after school and then have them assist them around the room. For some students this added attention and an opportunity to have some time with the teacher is a reward.

Third, if detention is made too unpleasant it may cause resentment and anger. This may then produce a student who will seek ways of getting revenge. The best approach is to keep the students in the room or the detention hall and not allow them to interact with anyone. They may be required to complete work they missed because of their behavior. However, you want to make sure that it is not work that requires your help or attention.

One elementary school developed an interesting alternative to detention. They established what they called a "Kindness Club." The Kindness Club was based on the idea of traffic school. Some of the teachers thought that students might need to be taught appropriate behavior. The Kindness Club is an after-school activity that lasts for four weeks. The school district did provide a late bus as alternative transportation for these students and others who were engaged in a variety of after-school activities. Students who had a certain number of rule violations were referred to the club. Although it was originally intended to be a form of punishment, a creative teacher turned it into a positive activity. The teacher developed a specific curriculum designed to teach responsibility, anger control, and conflict resolution. Problems and alternative methods of resolution are discussed. Role-playing is used to help students test different ideas and try to understand different perspectives. At the end of the month the students develop a plan for how they will avoid trouble. The last class session includes a "graduation ceremony" in which students are recognized for their growth.

Prior to admission to the Kindness Club the teacher meets with the parents and the parents sign an agreement insuring that the student will attend. One unexcused absence and the student is dropped. Because there is a useful and relevant curriculum, the students want to attend and attendance is seldom a problem. The club has had a positive influence on the school and has been accepted by both the students and the parents.

Parent–Teacher Conference

If a student is demonstrating persistent misbehavior, it is time to have a parent conference. The overwhelming majority of parents do want their children to be successful in school. Therefore, properly conducted parent conferences can have a positive impact. Cooperative parents can help provide incentives and sanctions at home that can reinforce what you are trying to do at school.

However, you should not expect miracles. In fact, one of the main causes of persistent misbehavior is poor parenting skill. Some parents do not know how to cope with the behavior of their child and may have even given up. However, if nothing else, a parent conference does serve an important function: It notifies the parents that a problem exists so that if more serious action is implemented, they will have been informed and given an opportunity to respond.

Parent conferences are most effective if there has been a positive relationship established between the teacher and the parent. Elementary teachers, with fewer students, find it easier to do this. In addition, the parents of elementary children are a little more eager to participate in the school. Secondary teachers have more students and generally do not make as much effort to get to know the parents. However, efforts to meet parents and establish some positive contact with them will enhance the probability that a parent conference will be successful.

There are some perspectives and skills that will help you conduct successful parent conferences. It is important to step back and consider the perspective of the parent. Most parents have considerable ego invested in their child. They often take criticism of their child as implied criticism of them, and failure of their child as a personal failure as a parent. Teachers who approach the parent conference with a blaming or hostile attitude will usually find that the parents are also hostile and defensive. Parents want teachers that are concerned about their child. You need to make sure that your concern for the child permeates the conference.

You also need to remember that many times parents approach such a meeting with teachers with considerable anxiety and fear. This is often because most of the contact they have had with the school has been negative. They have only heard from the school when the news is bad. Parents of students who have a history of difficulty have probably had several parent conferences and they have probably had some negative experiences that cause them to look forward to a conference with a definite lack of enthusiasm.

What this implies for you is that you need to approach parent conferences with positive comments on students as well as comments on their behavior. Be honest, open, and demonstrate understanding and warmth. Do not be hasty in making judgments and treat parents with respect. Allow them opportunities to share their perspectives and do not be too quick to become defensive. You want to communicate to parents that you are having the conference because you are both interested in the welfare of the student. The purpose of the conference is to see how you might work together to increase the probabilities of success.

Before having a parent conference dealing with inappropriate behavior, you need to do some homework. One of the most important aspects of that homework is to keep and gather records regarding the problems that have occurred and what you have done. When you begin to encounter more serious discipline problems, you should begin keeping anecdotal records. These need not be elaborate. Keeping a blank set of cards or a notebook handy is helpful. You can make three columns that you can quickly fill in. The first column would include the date and the time, the second an exact description of the behavior (do not editorialize), and the third is your response. Do not make judgments, just record incidents.

You should also gather information about the student from permanent records. Have there been past parent conferences with other teachers? Has there been a history of academic difficulty? Have there been some traumatic events in the past that might have influenced the student and the parents' attitude? You should be as knowledgeable as possible about the student and the family before entering the conference. This will communicate to the parent that you are a professional and you have taken this conference seriously.

When conducting the conference, have it in a comfortable spot. Do not make a parent sit in a chair designed for a primary grade student. You want to develop a cordial and friendly, yet businesslike, atmosphere for the conference. You want to maintain your poise and be very professional in your demeanor. This is not the place for gossip or small talk. Start the conference on a positive note and inform the parent that you are concerned about the student and you are seeking their advice and assistance. Do not be "preachy." State very simply that you are having a problem, state the problem and ask the parent if he or she can offer any insight as to why the problem is occurring and any suggestions on how it might be approached.

Do not dominate the conference; allow ample opportunities for the parents to participate. If the parent is critical of you, clarify his or her criticism and express your interest in learning from your mistakes, but refocus the discussion on the student. A major part of your role in a parent conference is to keep it focused and not allow it to drift into criticism of you, other teachers, or the curriculum. The focus is on the student, his or her behavior, and how you can help the student. You may find it helpful to take some notes on the parents' comments. This indicates to them that you are listening and taking their comments seriously.

You should enter the conference with some clear goals of what you want to accomplish and some ideas of what you would like from the parent. After the parent has had an opportunity to share you might then suggest what you think the parent can do to help. This is especially useful when a parent expresses frustration and resignation.

TABLE 10-2 **Parent Conference Worksheet**

Student: _____ Conference Date: _____ Time: _____

Parent's Name: _____

Other important information:

Specific problem to be discussed:

Goals for the conference:

Strengths of the student to share:

Questions you want to ask:

Suggestions for the parent:

Conference summary:

Follow-up actions:

ACTIVITY 10-1   CONDUCTING A PARENT CONFERENCE

John is a sixth-grade student who is causing considerable difficulty in the classroom. He has considerable ability but does not appear interested in using it. He almost never does homework, and his work in class is poorly done and exhibits only a half-hearted attempt. He has been late to school on several occasions and has been non-committal in conferences with him. A former teacher reports that the parents are somewhat hostile toward the school. They seem to have the attitude that the teachers are incompetent to begin with and have singled out John to pick on.

Plan for a parent conference

1. What needs to be done in planning for this parent conference?

2. What would be most important for the teacher to communicate during this conference? How could that be done?

3. What should be the goals of this conference?

Remember that they have taken their time to come to the school. One of the worst things that can happen is for them to leave feeling like the conference has been a waste of time or that the only reason for the conference was so that you could express your frustration to them.

Provide plenty of time for a conference and do not rush it. You should also make sure that the parent has your undivided attention. However, do not prolong the conference beyond what is necessary. Always end the conference on a hopeful note. End by summarizing what has been said and reviewing what you have agreed to do and what the parent has agreed to do. Identify how you are going to report progress to the parent. Let the parent know how he or she can contact you should he or she have further questions.

After a conference you need to review and write down what was agreed on. You need to make sure that you follow up on the suggestions. In a few days you may want to contact the parent with a report and ask if he or she has any further questions. Conferences conducted in this manner have a good chance of developing the parent as an ally and increasing the chances of changing student behavior

Behavior Improvement Agreements

Behavior improvement agreements are written agreements between the teacher and the student. When other less formal techniques have failed, the teacher and the student together list the behaviors that need to stop (Queen, Blackwelder, and Mallen, 1997). If there are several behaviors, it is best to try and identify one or two of the key behaviors for the focus. Do not try to change everything at one time. You can then identify the consequences that will follow if the agreement is broken. You and the student both sign the agreement and each gets a copy. It might be appropriate to send a copy of the agreement to the parents and to file one with the school principal. Queen, Blackwelder and Mallen suggest that it is most effective if the student actually writes out the agreement in his or her own words.

The advantage of the behavior improvement agreement is that it makes very clear and specific what the student can expect if his or her behavior continues. The formal, written nature of the agreement also communicates the seriousness of the problem. In addition, having a written record of the agreement is very useful if the agreement is broken and further action is needed.

The behavior improvement agreement should be fair and should be something with which the student can have success. It may well be that a student who has a history of behavior problems will not take the first agreement seriously. If he or she does not, he or she should experience the consequences that were specified and then another conference should be held to work out another agreement. If, after several attempts, the student does not fulfill the agreements then additional action needs to be taken.

TABLE 10-3 **Behavior Improvement Agreement**

Student:_____

Teacher: _____

Date: _____

We have both agreed to follow this plan in order to improve the learning environment.

I _____, agree to do the following in order to improve my behavior:
　　　　　(Student)

I _____, promise to assist by doing the following:
　　　　　(Teacher)

Failure to fulfill this agreement will result in the following consequences:

Signatures:

_____   _____
　　　　　(Student)   (Teacher)

Involving Others

For those few students who continue to violate behavioral improvement agreements or when all other efforts seem to fail, it is time to involve other professionals in the school. You are not a psychologist or psychiatrist and you cannot be expected to solve all problems. You should not be reluctant to seek help. Some problems are just too serious for you and seeking outside assistance is not a sign of failure. It is the professional thing to do.

Allowing a student to continue on a path of self-destruction is not professional or compassionate. The student may need help, and need it quickly. Not seeking help under the mistaken notion that it is your personal failure can lead to tragedy. You must always consider the welfare of the student over your professional ego.

The beginning step in seeking additional assistance should be to consult with the school principal or the school counselor. At this point you should be able to document specific problems, conferences you have had with parents, behavior improvement agreements that have been broken, and any other actions you have taken. The step of involving others means that this is a serious problem. Teachers who feel that the school administrator does not back them up are often those who do not have documentation. Poor record keeping can lead to difficulties down the road if the problems become very serious and additional action is needed. Teachers and administrators can be embarrassed when challenged by parents and even attorneys if they have no records to back up their actions. When school administrators are presented with a wealth of supporting data, they usually take the issue seriously.

Present the material to the administrator and ask him or her for advice regarding the next step. The administrator might give you some specific suggestions that you can try. Take those suggestions, try them, and continue to document their success. If there is no improvement, then you need to take your documentation back to the administrator.

At this point some schools convene a committee to review the problem. This committee might consist of you, the principal, the counselor or the school psychologist, and any other relevant individuals. In order for the committee to be effective you need to have good records. You will need to present a complete overview to the committee. You need to present all of the data that you have gathered for the committee to review. They may then recommend additional steps. One such step might be for the principal or the counselor to observe the student in the classroom. This does not always work because the students are usually on their best behavior when someone else is in the classroom. Another action might be for the committee to have a conference with the parent. Additional psychological testing or even a referral to community agencies might be in order.

Involving these other professionals is an important step in finding a solution. If more serious action, such as suspension or expulsion, is needed, this committee is an absolute necessity.

In-School Suspension

In-school suspension is a schoolwide disciplinary response and students are placed in in-school suspension only after consultation with others, such as the principal, and this is identified as an appropriate next step. Because it is a severe measure, it must be reserved for only the most serious problems.

In-school suspension tends to be more common in secondary schools. These schools have a separate room set aside that is supervised by a paraprofessional or a teacher with good management skills. I know of one high school in which the supervisor is a retired Marine Drill Sergeant! Students who repeatedly interfere with the instructional program or who pose a threat to other students are placed in the in-school suspension room. Students generally start the in-school suspension only at the beginning of the school day so that there are not disruptions during the day. Students stay in the room all day until they are willing to contract with the teacher and the school principal, indicating that they are willing to cooperate and return to the classroom. If they never agree, they may stay in the room for the rest of the term. This usually does not happen because students are social and want to interact with their friends. Their stay in the room is usually no more than a day or two.

Students in the room are not allowed to socialize with each other. They are often placed at desks that are at a significant distance from others. They are often not allowed to take breaks with other students and may even be required to eat lunch apart from others with no socializing. Work for them to do is delivered to the room so that they are not allowed to wander around the school gathering assignments.

In-school suspension does require considerable commitment from the teachers and administrators to make it work. It will require effort from you to deliver material for the student to the person in charge. This means an extra effort to gather together books and materials, and requires extra planning. Therefore, it should be reserved for only those rare occasions when there appear to be no other alternatives.

BEHAVIOR MODIFICATION

Behavior modification is an approach that can be used with a variety of behaviors, from those that are minor to those that are serious. Because the use of behavior modification does involve considerable planning and effort, it is often reserved for the more serious and persistent problems. Behavior modification is commonly used in special education settings when there are more serious and persistent problems.

Behavior modification does provide you with some powerful tools in understanding and changing student behavior. However, it is an approach that is often misunderstood and misapplied. Many critics see it as mechanistic and cold, a dangerous form of manipulation that bribes individuals to change their behavior by offering them a reward for behaving.

A basic assumption of behavior modification is that all behavior, thoughts, and feelings are learned. This learning is the function of reinforcements and punishments or the associations that an individual makes with desirable or undesirable consequences (Hyman, 1997). For example, a person who receives attention when a particular behavior occurs soon links that behavior with attention. If attention is something that is perceived as desirable, the probability that the behavior will be repeated is increased. Similarly, a young child who touches a hot stove soon associates the hot stove with pain, and the probability that the child will repeat the behavior is decreased. Therefore, a person's behavior at any given time is the product of past reinforcements and the contingencies in the present environment.

Thoughts, feelings, emotions, internal motivation, and expectations for success are all considered irrelevant concerns because you can do nothing to change the internal psychological state of the learner (Stipek, 1988). In addition, behaviorists do not think that you should count on the students developing a flash of insight as to why they misbehave and deciding to change. Rather, it is your responsibility to alter the classroom environment so that those things that are reinforcing student misbehavior are removed and reinforcement is provided for appropriate behavior.

Behavior modification is based on the principle of reinforcement. This principle is a part of the operant conditioning theory of Skinner (1971). The principle of reinforcement states that behavior that achieves desirable consequences has a greater probability of being repeated. As a given behavior achieves desirable outcomes, the behavior is strengthened or reinforced. On the other hand, behavior that is not followed by desirable consequences is weakened and is less likely to be repeated. Those things in the environment that are desired by individuals are called reinforcers. It is important to note that, by definition, anything that strengthens a behavior or increases the probability of recurrence is a reinforcer.

Reinforcers

There are two basic types of reinforcers, positive and negative. Positive reinforcers are those things that an individual desires. For example, if an individual wants attention, then attention is a positive reinforcer. Negative reinforcers are frequently misunderstood in that they are confused with punishment. Remember that a reinforcer strengthens a behavior or increases the probability that it will be repeated. Punishment does not have this effect. Negative reinforcement is the avoidance of an unpleasant consequence. For example, why do individuals take out the garbage, a rather unpleasant task that has little appeal to most people? They perform this low interest task in order to avoid something even more unpleasant: The aroma that will fill the house if garbage is not removed. You might use negative reinforcement in the classroom by allowing students to avoid an activity viewed as unpleasant as a contingency for a desirable activity. For example, a student who behaves appropriately may be allowed to skip doing homework.

Unwittingly, teachers often use negative reinforcement in the classroom and end up strengthening undesirable behaviors. An example might be a teacher who sends a student to sit in the hall for misbehaving. The student may be seeking to avoid something that is perceived as even more unpleasant, working on a boring or threatening assignment. Sitting in the hall might be more interesting and less threatening to the student. Therefore, the next time he or she wishes to avoid an unpleasant or threatening assignment, misbehavior is likely to occur. Because negative reinforcement tends to reinforce escape or avoidance behavior, it should be used sparingly. For example, students who are allowed to skip homework are able to avoid an activity that will provide them with practice and the learning of study habits that might be important for future success. The major emphasis of a reinforcement program in the classroom, therefore, should be on positive reinforcers.

Positive reinforcers are those things that have sufficient value to the student that he or she is willing to put forth effort to earn them. Several categories of positive reinforcers are available for use by the teacher. These include social reinforcers, symbolic reinforcers, activity reinforcers, and token reinforcers.

Social Reinforcers

Social reinforcers are those positive events, such as praise, words of approval, smiles, laughter, or physical contact, such as a pat on the back, that occur during social interaction (Gallagher, 1980). Social reinforcement is relatively easy to use because it does not take a great deal of effort or involve any cost to the teacher. For social reinforcers to be effective, they must be given consistently and honestly. Teachers who give insincere or undeserved praise learn that its effectiveness as a reinforcer soon disappears. In addition, the teacher should make a conscious effort to apply social reinforcers consistently enough to affect behavior. Occasional praise or comment is likely to have minimal impact on behavior.

Some individuals will try very hard to obtain social reinforcers. However, students who have a long history of failure and problem behavior may not find social approval strong enough to result in a change in behavior. In addition, social reinforcers need to be administered by someone who is a significant other to the student. Individuals who like their teacher may work very hard to obtain social reinforcers from him or her. However, those who are not positive about the teacher may find that the social approval of peers for disobeying the teacher is much more desirable than social reinforcers administered by the teacher.

Symbolic Reinforcers

Symbolic reinforcers are such things as stamps, checks, happy faces, gold stars, or a grade given to the student to designate approval. Symbolic reinforcers are often quite useful with young children. A happy face or a gold star is highly prized and will have a direct effect on the behavior of the student.

The most commonly used symbolic reinforcer in the classroom is the grade. However, grades have drawbacks as effective reinforcers. Grades are often not given immediately and are not tied to a specific behavior. Therefore, their value in reinforcing a specific behavior is lost. In addition, young children may not have learned the cultural value of grades and therefore do not place high value on them.

Students who have a history of low grades do not believe that a high grade can be earned and therefore will not try. The effectiveness of grades as reinforcers declines during early adolescence and especially among those students who are alienated (Stipek, 1988).

Activity Reinforcers

Activities that individuals like to do can be used to reinforce behavior. Good examples are attempts to link participation in extracurricular activities with classroom performance. Students are allowed to participate in a high-interest activity only after they have performed well in other areas. Elementary school teachers are using this form of reinforcement when they allow students to tell a joke to the class or to choose where they would like to sit when they behave in an appropriate manner. Parents are using activity reinforcers when they make a high-interest activity, such as viewing a favorite television show, contingent on completing homework or performing required chores.

TABLE 10-4   **Sample Activity Reinforcers**

Getting to use puzzles
Earning extra free time
Going to lunch early
Assisting the teacher
Listening to music during independent work
Running errands
Supervising the lab
Taking care of materials/equipment
Using the computer
Taking care of VCR
Serving as team captain
Reading a book
Watching TV
Seeing a movie
Tutoring other students
Free time in library
Free time in commons area
Attending or skipping an assembly
Choosing elective free time activity
Going first
Work in school office
Choosing a game for recess

Token Reinforcers

Teachers faced with the impracticality of other types of reinforcers might try token reinforcers. Token reinforcers include items such as chips or stamps that can be turned in to the teacher in exchange for an activity or a reinforcer that the student desires. An application of token reinforcement commonly used is in the form of contracts or contingency management systems. In these approaches, the teacher and the student work out an agreement. Once the student has obtained a given number of tokens for good behavior, he or she may then engage in some activity or obtain some prize that is desired.

Some Qualifiers in the Use of Behavior Modification

A couple of problems must be considered when applying behavior modification in classroom settings. One relates to the identification of effective reinforcers. Keep in mind that the reinforcer must be something that the student wants. Student and teacher perceptions about what is desirable are sometimes very different. Thus, teachers may think that the environment has been arranged for desirable events to occur while students see them as undesirable events. For example, one teacher who had fond remembrances of games played during recess in elementary school attempted to use increased recess time as a reinforcer. However, several students who did not possess much athletic skill viewed the increased time as additional opportunity for humiliation and therefore punishment. Rather than improving their behavior, increased game time led to an increase in the disruptive behavior of these students.

In addition, what is reinforcing for one individual in the classroom might not be reinforcing for another. One might desire attention and enjoy being on center stage, while others might be uncomfortable with the attention and would seek to avoid it. Implementing a behavior modification program for a large number of students in a given class can then pose the significant problem of identifying reinforcers for each student in the classroom. Some reinforcers are effective for many students but it is unlikely that any one reinforcer will be appropriate for all. Therefore, behavior modification works best when you can identify specific students and provide reinforcers that would be effective for them.

A second issue relating to the use of reinforcers in the classroom is that the reinforcers generally available to the teacher may not be very powerful. Some of the more powerful ones, such as food and water, cannot be ethically applied to the classroom. For example, you cannot make lunch or a drink of water contingent on good behavior. Some teachers do use treats, such as popcorn, as reinforcers. They are not as powerful because they are generally things that an individual can do without.

Several methods are useful in identifying appropriate reinforcers for a student. One method is to ask students to identify their preferences. Many of them will be open and will share their preferences with you. Talking to students often reveals interests and hobbies that may not have surfaced in the classroom. This information can be helpful when choosing activities that might serve as reinforcers.

ACTIVITY 10-2 THE CLASSROOM LEADER

Steve is one of the most popular students in the tenth grade. He is a personable, handsome boy with good athletic skills. However, Steve is not academically oriented. He frequently jokes and makes distracting comments when the teacher is speaking. During seatwork he talks and seldom gets on-task. Because he is one of the leaders, the rest of the class follows his example. This has made teaching the class extremely difficult.

What would you do?

1. Do you think behavior modification would work with Steve?

2. What specific behaviors would you identify to increase or decrease?

3. What reinforcers might you try with Steve?

Observing students in a variety of settings is another way to identify reinforcers. The activities that individuals engage in during their free time is frequently a good indication of those activities that the individuals find reinforcing. You can take some of these activities and test them as possible reinforcers.

A key element after choosing reinforcers is to keep data on their effectiveness. The teacher needs to know how often a particular reinforcer is used and the effects of the reinforcer on the subsequent behavior of the student. The reinforcers that the teacher thought would work well may not be as powerful as first thought. Therefore, you might need to engage in additional observation and study in order to identify more powerful reinforcers. In addition, students may grow tired of the same reinforcers and stop responding to them. Therefore, you may need to change the reinforcers periodically.

Implementing Behavior Modification

Implementing behavior modification takes some planning and does follow some specific steps. There are two major steps in the process: identifying the behavior to be changed, and developing a plan (Charles, 1992).

Targeting the Specific Behavior to Be Changed

A key element in the application of behavior modification in the classroom is the identification of the specific behavior to be changed. Frequently teachers are not specific enough in pinpointing the behaviors they want to change. They tend to make statements such as, "He is hyperactive" or "She needs to learn to be respectful." What does "being respectful" involve? Does it mean they do not interrupt others? Does it mean sharing with others? These statements are too broad and do not give enough guidance.

When trying to identify target behaviors you need to identify observable, measurable behaviors in such a way that two people would agree when they occur or do not occur. For example, being respectful requires interpretation and two people might have difficulty identifying when a student is being disrespectful. They could however, agree on the times when the student interrupts another. You may also need to change your statement from a negative to a positive one that indicates what you want the student to do instead. For example, if the problem is the student being constantly out of his or her seat, then the behavior you want to increase is the amount of time spent in the seat. This is important because it helps clarify your expectations and identify behaviors you want to reinforce. Just performing this step helps teachers become more effective problem solvers. The precise definitions of acceptable behaviors and those to be reinforced are key in the success of a behavior modification plan.

Data Collection

The next step in the process is that of gathering data regarding the frequency of occurrence. This requires that you observe the student for a period of time to determine if the behavior is serious enough to warrant an intervention (Kerr and Nelson, 1998). The data gathering can present a problem for a busy teacher who is trying to attend to the needs of 30 or more students. One approach would be to use another observer, such as an instructional aide, to observe the student and record the frequency of the behavior you want to change. If you believe the student is out of his or her chair too much, have an instructional aide observe for several days and record the exact number of times the student is out of the chair.

Another approach is to observe a student only during those times when the behavior is most likely to occur. For example, you might choose to observe the student during independent work times to record the number of times the student is off-task. A third option might be to choose several random times during the day when you will observe and take data. Again, you should do this over several days so that you get a good average. It is usually helpful to develop some observation form or checklist that you can use to tally every instance of the behavior that you see.

Reinforcement Schedules

Once you have identified and gathered data on the target behaviors, you now need to decide on the reinforcers that you will use and how you will provide them. To be effective, the reinforcers need to be employed as soon as possible after the behavior. During the beginning stages of the plan, the behavior should be reinforced every time the behavior is demonstrated. Again, this poses a heavy burden for a teacher who is attempting to manage a classroom of 30 or more students at one time.

There are a couple of options that you can try. Once again you could use an instructional aide to monitor student behavior and provide reinforcers during those times when the teacher is otherwise occupied. A token system might work best, with the assistant providing a token every time the student demonstrates the behavior.

If an instructional aide is not available, you can set aside a specific time when your attention will be focused on the behavior of the student. This is especially useful if you can identify specific times during the day or class period when the student is most likely to cause difficulty. For example, if the student seems to demonstrate the inappropriate behavior more during those times when he or she is working independently, then you concentrate on observing that student and providing reinforcement for appropriate behavior.

You will need to make a decision about your reinforcement schedule. For example, if you are going to reinforce the student for staying on-task, how frequently will you provide reinforcers? You might decide that you will provide a token or other reinforcer every three minutes the student is on-task. The interval you choose will be related to the severity of the problem and the ability of the student. If the student has a great deal of difficulty with self-control, then a short interval might be necessary. Determining how frequently you will reinforce the behavior and how long you will try the plan is based on the behavior you are trying to change and the frequency of occurrence. Those behaviors that occur frequently, and therefore can be reinforced frequently, will show results much more rapidly than those that occur only a few times during an observation or reinforcement interval. For example, if you are reinforcing a behavior that occurs frequently during the course of a school day, you are likely to see more immediate improvement than if you are reinforcing one that occurs only a couple of times each day.

One question that is often asked is whether other students will react negatively if one student is receiving reinforcement and attention and the others are not. The answer is yes, they will, if good behavior is not normally rewarded and the classroom climate is one in which positive reinforcement is scarce. However, if positive reinforcement is common and students are getting their attention needs met, then there will be no problem. Students are quick to recognize when another student is having difficulty and they accept your efforts as being designed to help that student. The more intense attention paid to a specific individual for a short period of time will not be resented. They appreciate your efforts to make the classroom a better place for everyone.

After the initial program is started and the desired behavior is beginning to occur regularly, the reinforcement schedule is changed so that reinforcement is provided less frequently. The best reinforcement schedule now is an intermittent one in which the student does not know when a reinforcer might be given. Once this stage has been reached, the use of behavior modification with a given student becomes relatively simple. The main issue here is to make sure that reinforcers are given occasionally and are not totally eliminated.

Evaluating the Effectiveness of the Plan
The precision of behavior modification in identifying the behavior to be changed makes it possible to evaluate the effectiveness of the program with a given student. This is an advantage that behavior modification has over other approaches to dealing

with inappropriate behavior. You can gather data to indicate the effectiveness of the plan. If it is not working, then changes can be made.

You pinpointed the specific behavior you wanted to change and have gathered data about the frequency of the behavior during the first stage of starting the behavior modification program. This what is normally called *baseline data.*

Evaluating the effectiveness of the intervention program then takes place after the reinforcement program has been in operation for some time. You discontinue the formal reinforcement program and once again tally the occurrences of the focus behavior. This should be done in much the same manner that the baseline data were gathered. After a few observations, average occurrence of the behavior is determined and compared with the baseline data. This comparison can help you determine the effectiveness of the intervention program. If there has been little or no change in the frequency of occurrence, you may need to consider changing the reinforcers or the reinforcement schedule. If the behavior is changing at an acceptable rate, you then resume the intervention plan. Remember that if the reinforcements stop altogether, the old patterns are likely to recur.

Elimination of Inappropriate Behavior

Your goal is to eliminate the inappropriate behavior and replace it with desirable behavior. Reinforcing the desired behavior is intended to teach the desired behavior. Often, the most difficult component is eliminating the undesirable behavior. An important step in this process is the precise identification of behaviors that you wish to eliminate. Once again, vague definitions, such as "hyperactive," "aggressive," "immature," or "disrespectful," are not enough. You must precisely identify those behaviors that led to the conclusion that the student is too aggressive, immature, or hostile.

The purpose of this precise identification is to assist you in problem solving so that the frequency of undesirable behaviors can be reduced. According to the principle of reinforcement, something must be reinforcing the behavior in order for it to continue. If it were not being reinforced, it would gradually disappear. You can begin your problem solving by asking, "What could be reinforcing this behavior?" It might be your actions or those of the rest of the class that is reinforcing this behavior and keeping it going.

Withholding Reinforcement

The inappropriate behavior would not continue unless it was resulting in some payoff for the student. Therefore, the beginning step in weakening a behavior or decreasing its frequency is to try and withhold reinforcement for that behavior. For example, if you are giving attention to misbehavior, it might be your attention that is reinforcing the behavior. You may then need to try and ignore inappropriate behavior and provide attention when the behavior is appropriate. However, there might be other reinforcers in the environment, such as other students.

An example might be helpful in clarifying this point. One teacher of behaviorally disordered students had a student who frequently threw temper tantrums in the classroom. As she searched for possible explanations for the behavior, she hypothesized that the attention of the other students was reinforcing the behavior. As long as they gave the student attention for his temper tantrum, it would continue. Her problem was to try and figure out how to remove this reinforcement. She accomplished this by providing students with tokens for ignoring the boy the next time he threw a tantrum. The next time the boy threw a tantrum, she quickly went around the room and provided tokens to those students who continued working. She gave them the token and said, "Thanks for ignoring Johnny." In this way she changed the environment by removing the reinforcer for the temper tantrum: student attention. After two or three more tantrums, Johnny realized that his behavior was not gaining him anything he desired: Students were ignoring him and he was not receiving any tokens. In a short while, the temper tantrums ceased. She had learned that attention was a powerful reinforcer for this boy. Therefore, she could now provide lots of attention for appropriate behavior as a replacement for the tantrums.

This illustration brings up an important point that is often lost in classroom applications of behavior modification. You are not the only person who may be providing reinforcement in the classroom. An entire classroom of individuals, and in some cases individuals outside the classroom, might be providing reinforcers for a particular behavior. In fact, some of these individuals, powerful peers or parents, are able to provide more powerful reinforcers than you are providing. Therefore, withholding reinforcers may have little impact on behavior. For this reason, the advice of well-meaning individuals to "ignore a behavior and it will soon cease" often is ineffective. It is not the approval or reinforcement of the teacher that the student desires, but reinforcement from some other source.

Administering Punishment

A second way that behavior is weakened is through the use of punishment. Punishment is defined as something that is undesirable, painful, or discomforting that results from a misbehavior. Because it is an undesirable outcome of behavior, punishment weakens or decreases the probability that a behavior will recur. Punishment can be quite effective for stopping an unwanted behavior. However, behavior modification theorists are reluctant to advocate the use of punishment because it may have several undesirable side effects.

Punishment may actually reinforce undesirable behavior rather than decrease it. This may occur because your perceptions may be different from those of the student. You may think that sending a student out of the room is punishment while the student views escaping a boring lesson as reinforcement. A student who receives little attention at home would see any type of attention, even punishment, as preferable to being ignored.

Another potential problem is that while punishment may stop inappropriate behaviors, it does not teach appropriate ones. Unless appropriate behaviors are taught, other undesirable behaviors are likely to take the place of the behavior that

ACTIVITY 10-3   KEEPING SUSAN UNDER CONTROL

Susan seems to be in perpetual motion. She is unable to stay in her seat and do her own work and is constantly bothering others. She always has to get a book, sharpen her pencil, or get a drink. The teacher has tried taking away privileges, putting her name on the board, and keeping her after school. Nothing seems to work.

Apply behavior modification to this problem:

1. What behaviors would you identify for change?

2. What process could you use to gather data about her behavior?

3. What might be some possible reinforcers you might use?

4. What would be your reinforcement schedule?

---

was punished. Therefore, in order to be effective, punishment needs to be combined with positive reinforcement of appropriate behaviors.

A third potential drawback in the use of punishment is that it may produce long-lasting fears and anxieties that can interfere with performance. This is especially true if students believe that the punishment inflicted is unfair or malicious. They blame the teacher for the punishment and associate the punishment with the teacher rather than with the inappropriate behavior. Too much reliance on punishment in the classroom can result in a negative atmosphere that is harmful to teacher–student communication and to the teaching and learning process.

Other criticisms of the use of punishment center on the claim that the use of punishment serves as a model for aggressive behavior and that it teaches students that the infliction of pain is an acceptable means of settling interpersonal problems. Although this claim is not universally held, it is a valid concern that must be taken seriously. Teachers are significant others in the lives of many students and do serve as role models. Consequently, you must be concerned about what you are teaching through your actions.

In summary, the use of punishment is effective for stopping a behavior and is appropriately used when the behavior is dangerous or when very few appropriate behaviors seem to exist for the teacher to reinforce. It is only a beginning point to gain control until appropriate behavior can be developed and reinforced (Gallagher, 1980).

Advantages of Behavior Modification Approaches

Behavior modification approaches provide a teacher with a systematic plan for attacking a particular discipline problem. A consistent theory underlying behavior modification provides some basic principles that can be applied to solving a specific problem.

Behavior modification seems to be especially useful for working with students who persist in misbehavior so that the time needed to implement it is justified. This will also reduce your work by allowing you to focus your attention on a few students rather than trying to implement the plan with the entire class.

Behavioral approaches are popular because they place primary responsibility and authority with the teacher for dealing with discipline problems. Some teachers like the approach because it places them in control; some administrators tend to favor the approach because it makes it easier to hold the teacher accountable. The student's background, home life, emotional state, and attitudes are irrelevant. If the teacher applies the right reinforcements in the proper manner, then the behavior will change. This serves as an antidote to the professed helplessness of some teachers to control the behavior of the students in their classroom.

Disadvantages of Behavior Modification Approaches

One of the most important disadvantages of behavior modification is that the emphasis on external controls may interfere with the development of self-control. Some studies (Kohlberg, 1970; Selman, 1980) seem to indicate that a primary emphasis on external rewards inhibits individual development of higher levels of moral development. There is also some evidence that an overreliance on extrinsic rewards may interfere with the attainment of important educational objectives. Several studies indicate that rewards have a negative impact on the willingness of students to attempt difficult or challenging tasks (Stipek, 1988). Other studies indicate that the use of extrinsic rewards may also have a negative effect on student motivation (Doyle, 1986). Students who are already interested in a task become less interested when external rewards are provided to them for engaging in the task.

Another major disadvantage of behavior modification approaches is that effects may be short-term. Rewards may be effective in eliciting the desired behavior only under conditions in which the rewards are present (Stipek, 1988). The behavioral change may not transfer to situations outside the classroom or to other classrooms where the rewards are not present. Because accepting challenges and attempting difficult tasks are important educational outcomes, an overreliance on extrinsic rewards should be avoided.

Another major concern is that the emphasis on observable student behavior may keep the teacher from identifying how the problem behavior might be prevented in the first place. Many of the problems can be traced to poor teaching methods, poor interpersonal skills, or inappropriate exercise of teacher power. The inappropriate behaviors might be student attempts to cope with boredom, anxiety, or anger. Unless these conditions are addressed, there is little chance that behavior modification will have the desired effects. The attention to modification of student behavior might be misplaced. Rather than attempting to modify the behavior of the students, perhaps the behavior of the teacher needs to be modified.

SUMMARY

Responding to persistent misbehavior places more demands on planning and teacher time. Therefore, these responses need to be reserved for those few students who do not respond to less intrusive methods.

One of the most common approaches to this class of behavior problems is detention. However, detention is often used inappropriately and becomes ineffective. Detention might be reinforcing for some students who would rather spend the time at school with the teacher than to spend time at home.

Many teachers fear parent conferences. In order to increase the potential for productive parent conferences you need to spend time planning for them. You need to have data on the behavior of the student and to approach the parents in a warm, yet professional, manner. You need to recognize the perspective of the parents and make sure you do not imply criticism of them as a parent.

Persistent problems may require involving others. Some schools use disciplinary committees to review especially difficult cases. This committee may offer insights that can help you deal with the problem or may recommend alternative placements or actions that are beyond the authority of an individual teacher.

In-school suspension is an approach that is generally used in secondary schools, where they have the resources to hire someone to supervise students who are removed from the classroom for some period of time. In-school suspension must not become just a place where students are able to avoid class work and escape to visit with friends. It needs to be a place where they do work and their interaction with others is limited.

Behavior modification can be used for nearly any problem that might occur in the classroom. However, because it requires a considerable amount of teacher time and effort it is best used for more serious problems. Behavior modification is based on the principle of reinforcement. Understanding this principle can be helpful in problem solving even if you do not use the formal steps of the behavior modification process. One of the basic principles that you can use is to remember to reinforce those behaviors that you want and to withhold reinforcement for inappropriate behavior. If you can identify what is reinforcing inappropriate behavior and remove that reinforcement, there is a good probability that you will be able to eliminate that behavior.

SUGGESTED APPLICATIONS

1. Interview some teachers and get their advice on conducting parent conferences. Do they generally find parents cooperative? What are the typical problems that they encounter? What have they found most effective?

2. Discuss with a local school principal how he or she handles persistent discipline problems. Does he or she use disciplinary committees? If so, what is the purpose

of the committee? What sort of data does the committee want from a teacher? What actions do these committees usually take? Does the school have in-school suspension? How does it work?

3. Conduct an experiment with behavior modification. Identify a behavior of a friend, spouse, or child you would like to change. This might be a behavior you want to decrease or one you want to increase. Define the behavior precisely, gather some baseline data, decide on a reinforcement plan, implement your plan, and then evaluate it to find out if it was effective.

4. Check a nearby school to see if anyone is using behavior modification. You may find it in a special education classroom. Observe in the classroom and see how it is applied. Write up your observations and identify what you believe to be the strengths and weaknesses of the approach.

SUGGESTED READINGS

Charles, C. M. (1992). *Building classroom discipline,* 4th Ed. White Plains, NY: Longman.

Doyle, W. (1986). Classroom organization and management. In *Handbook of research in teaching,* 3rd Ed. Wittrock, M. (ed.). New York: Macmillan, 392–431.

Gallagher, J. (1980). *Changing behavior: How and why.* Morristown, NJ: Silver Burdett.

Hyman, I. A. (1997). *School discipline and school violence: The teacher variance approach.* Boston: Allyn and Bacon.

Kerr, M. M. and Nelson, C. M. (1998). *Strategies for managing behavior problems in the classroom,* 3rd Ed. Upper Saddle River, NJ: Merrill/Prentice-Hall.

Kohlberg, L. (1970). Stage and sequence: The cognitive-developmental approach to socialization. In *Handbook of socialization theory and research,* D. Goslind (ed.). Chicago: Rand McNally.

Queen, J. A., Blackwelder, B. B. and Mallen, L. P. (1997). *Responsible classroom management for teachers and students.* Upper Saddle River, NJ: Merrill/Prentice-Hall.

Selman, R. (1980). *The growth of interpersonal understanding: Developmental and clinical analyses.* New York: Academic Press.

Skinner, B. F. (1971). *The technology of teaching.* New York: Appleton/Century/Crofts.

Stipek, B. (1988). *Motivation to learn: From theory to practice.* Englewood Cliffs, NJ: Prentice-Hall.

11 Responding to Serious Behavior Problems

Chapter Objectives

After reading this chapter you should be able to:

- Identify causes of attendance problems
- Describe measures that can help prevent cheating
- State the seriousness of vandalism
- List steps you can take to stop aggression between students
- Define what can be done to help prevent violence against teachers
- Describe what can be done to prevent and respond to substance abuse

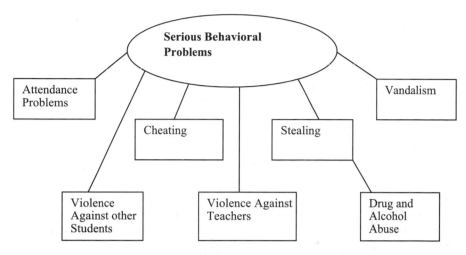

FIGURE 11-1 **Graphic Organizer for Responding to Serious Problems**

A popular misconception is that severe and serious misbehavior is commonplace in schools across the United States. One might get the impression from media coverage that schools are filled with drugs, alcohol, vandalism, and violence. Media images highlight schools with metal detectors at each door and security personnel patrolling the halls. The impression is created that this is a new phenomenon. However, disorder and violence have been characteristics of schools throughout history. Schoolchildren in seventeenth-century France carried weapons and were feared by schoolmates and ordinary citizens. Between 1775 and 1836 English students participated in mutinies, brawls, and beatings of teachers on a regular basis. U.S. schools have not been without their episodes of violence by students and parents (Hyman, 1997). Although school crime and violence is a serious problem that does require the attention of the public, the number of incidents of serious and violent behavior has remained fairly stable over the past couple of decades.

To be sure, there are schools where violence and fear do dominate. However, those are the exception rather than the rule. One study reported that seven out of ten high school teachers felt they had substantial or complete control over their students. Only one percent believed they had no control (Hyman, 1997). One recent study revealed that parents and students believe that their school provides a safe and secure environment. A majority of the students have never been victims of violent behavior or been physically hurt around school. However, a sizable number of students, 44 percent, reported that over a one-month period they had personal experiences with angry scenes or confrontations (Metropolitan Life Insurance Company, 1994).

Although these episodes are relatively rare in the majority of the classrooms across the United States, you do need to be prepared to deal with them when they occur. Any amount of violence in the school is too much. The potential for harm and the disruption of the educational environment is too great. They cannot be ignored. Because these are serious problems, responses to these problems are serious ones. They require considerable thought and must be applied carefully. There are no easy solutions. However, it has been my experience in working with special programs involving violent students that their behavior is often a desperate plea for help. They want someone to notice they are in trouble and help them. They just do not know how to ask for or receive help in socially acceptable ways.

Serious problems in the classroom may be the result of problems that exist outside the classroom. Many problems have their roots in larger societal concerns. Crime, drugs, and antisocial behavior in society will lead to the occurrence of these problems in schools. However, you must not use this as an excuse for not acting or attempting to find a solution. It only means that the problems will be more difficult to solve and that the involvement of the entire school and even the community might be required in order to make significant progress.

This chapter provides suggestions for dealing with those problems that interfere with developing and maintaining a positive classroom environment: persistent attendance problems, cheating, stealing, vandalism, violence, and substance abuse.

DISCIPLINE SCENARIO 11-1   **The Explosive Student**

Hector is a boy in your classroom. He is larger than most of the other students and has had a difficult life. Numerous moves have resulted in severe academic difficulties and left him with few friends. Most of the time he is a likable boy who tries hard. However, achieving academic success is very difficult for him. There appear to be times when his frustration becomes too great. When this happens he is likely to explode.

Today you have checked the roll and you are just getting started with the lesson. The assignment you are giving is a challenging one. Someone makes a comment to Hector and he utters several words of profanity. You quickly respond by reminding him with a firm voice that you will not tolerate that kind of language in the classroom. Hector leaps to his feet and starts swearing at you. He denounces you and the school as being worthless. He grabs a book and flings it across the classroom.

How would you respond?

1. What action would you take in response to this violent outburst?

2. What would be your major considerations?

3. What do you think could have been done to prevent this outburst?

4. What long-range plan might you put into effect to help Hector learn to control his temper and to prevent future occurrences?

ATTENDANCE PROBLEMS

Serious attendance problems that cause teachers concern are of two types: those students who are frequently tardy to class and those who are frequently absent. Frequent tardiness is often the more serious for a teacher. Just when you get the class started, the tardy student arrives to disrupt the flow of the lesson and create a disturbance. Frequent, unexcused absences are often bothersome for two reasons: First, the students are missing essential learning, and when they return, they are behind and require reteaching. Because reteaching is so time-consuming, they may not get the help they need, fail, and then become a disruptive force in the classroom. Secondly, teachers often interpret frequent absences as a statement of disinterest and low regard for the teacher and the subject. Therefore, unexcused absences are viewed as a personal affront.

Attendance problems are a major concern throughout the United States. Some inner-city schools report daily absence rates of over 50 percent, and school administrators list attendance as the most serious discipline problem (Duke and Meckel, 1984). The disruption in the learning process caused by frequent absences and tardiness is a major factor in low achievement. If serious school reform is to have an impact on student performance, the issue of school attendance must be addressed

Identifying Causes of Attendance Problems

The first step in correcting any problem is to spend time diagnosing it and identifying its causes. Time used in diagnosing these problems is time well spent because it helps school officials eliminate unproductive approaches. A variety of explanations account for persistent attendance problems. One study reported that approximately 8 percent of secondary school students stated that they stayed away from school at least one day a month because they were afraid to go to school. Lack of attendance due to fear must be dealt with very differently than lack of attendance due to apathy.

One of the major causes of attendance problems in schools is lack of student success and fear of failure. Just imagine being required to attend a job or a school where you believed you had no chance of success. After a short time, frustration and bitterness would take root. For some students, this frustration takes the form of aggression; for others, it takes the form of avoidance behaviors. Even the fear of being caught and punished for truancy is minor compared to the humiliation and fear that accompany persistent failure.

Another cause of attendance problems is apathy. Apathetic students see neither the importance nor the relevance of school. They do not enjoy school and do not believe that the school is interested in them or their success. They see the school as a cold and uncaring bureaucracy. The curriculum is not viewed as especially relevant, and teachers are individuals who are out to get students rather than help them. School rules are arbitrary and insensitive to the feelings of students. Many teachers become frustrated and unenthusiastic as they simply go about doing a job. These schools are not pleasant places. Attendance problems are a form of passive resistance to the school and school policies. Administrators and teachers need to remember that more school rules and stiffer penalties are not the answer to this problem. Rather than trying to use the stick to motivate them to attend school, a carrot is needed. The school needs to be a place where students feel that they are accepted and their needs are met. Glasser (1986) contends that most schools concentrate on teaching and directing students without taking into account whether what is done is satisfying to them. Attention needs to be directed at how we can make the school a place where students will want to come because they believe it is the best alternative for fulfilling their needs.

Teachers who experience repeated tardiness or numerous cuts need to perform some self-evaluation. Have you created a positive learning environment? Have you avoided psychological intimidation? Is your class getting started on time? Do you have interesting activities at the beginning of the lesson or are the first several minutes generally wasted with administrative chores? If students believe that they will be missing something interesting or important at the beginning of class, they will make an effort to get there on time. Do you emphasize the importance of what you are teaching and try to relate it to the previous knowledge and the interests of the students you are teaching? Are student needs being met in your room? We must not make the assumption that students accept what we are teaching as important or worthwhile. A large part of our job is to help them see the connections between their world and the world of education.

Finally, fear of violence is another major cause of attendance problems. Unfortunately, schools are places where violence does occur and they are not safe havens separate from the outside world. Changing patterns of attendance may require considerable effort to make the school a safe place. The issue of violence is dealt with later in this chapter.

Approaches to Solving Attendance Problems

The seriousness of attendance problems and the resulting loss of academic progress demand creative approaches to the issue. The search for solutions should start with the teacher and move to the school and then to the community.

The Teacher

A good beginning point for solving attendance problems is with the teacher. Your attitude and behavior might be significant contributors to the problem. This is especially true if you are experiencing burnout. Burnout leads to a lack of enthusiasm and excitement for teaching. Some teachers have lost confidence in their ability to teach a given group of students. This lack of teaching efficacy, the belief that your students cannot or will not learn, depresses your motivation. Less time is spent on planning, little attention is given to trying to plan interesting lessons, and a general feeling of hopelessness is communicated to students. Students will soon realize that a teacher has low expectations for their success and they will work to this level of expectation. The following questions might be helpful for you to consider.

1. How do you feel about teaching?
2. Do you look forward to going to school?
3. Are you interested in the subjects you are teaching?
4. Do you believe that the students in your classes are capable of learning?
5. Do you have confidence in your teaching ability?

If your answer is "no" to some of these questions, you need to consider taking action. You should seek some counseling to evaluate your career choice and decide whether or not to continue teaching. All of us will answer "no" to some of these questions at some point in our career. However, if it is a persistent problem that continues beyond a short time you need to consider your own mental health as well as the well-being of the students. Professional development activities, such as getting a mentor or buddy teacher, seeking a different grade level or assignment, or participating in worthwhile professional growth activities, might help you develop new enthusiasm and confidence. In some cases, a career change is the best resolution.

Students

Conferring with students who are chronically absent or tardy, and doing so in a way that allows them to identify the factors contributing to the problems, can be fruitful in identifying and removing causes. You may discover that the solution is a relatively easy one. For example, one high school teacher, after several confrontations with a tardy student, finally asked the student about the problem. The student had a locker in a distant corner of the school and by the time he went to his locker to get the material required for the class and returned, he was late. Circumstances prevented him from taking the material to the previous class. Allowing the student to drop off the material before going to the previous period solved the problem. The student could then come directly to class. The problem was solved and everyone was satisfied. A girl who was always late to school once bothered me. After talking with her I discovered a dysfunctional family and a courageous young girl who was trying to take care of younger siblings and get them off to school. We were able to work with social agencies to provide a home environment that solved the problem.

If the problem is related to student lack of self-control, you should not excuse persistent attendance problems. You are not doing students any favors by allowing them to develop a lack of responsibility that may hinder them for the rest of their life. Instead, be consistent in following through with consequences when students violate attendance rules. The use of logical consequences, such as making up lost time or missing out on fun or highly desired activities, is also helpful in letting students know that the you are serious about attendance and will follow through. When firm and consistent behavior is coupled with prevention, great strides can be made to diminish the occurrence of attendance problems.

CHEATING

Cheating is of universal concern. Not only is the issue an ethical one, but cheating also denigrates the importance of school tasks and interferes with valid assessments of student progress. Handling the problem of cheating can be especially difficult because it is so widespread in society. Teachers find it difficult to extol the virtues of honesty when the practices of business people and public officials regularly skirt the law.

Identifying Causes of Cheating

One of the basic causes for cheating on school tasks is fear of failure. This is especially the case with "high stakes" tests and assignments, those that carry a heavy weight in determining student success or failure. In recent years, assertions of poor education have led to the mandating of more high stakes tests. More of these tests are used to determine whether or not a student will move to the next grade or graduate. With so much riding on the outcome, it is not surprising that students find creative ways of cheating.

Another cause of cheating is that students do not perceive the relevance of school tasks. Many students see the object of education as a series of unnecessary and irrelevant hurdles to clear rather than a series of important skills that will help them throughout life. The result is that they do not understand that cheating is actually harming them. Because the tasks are perceived as being of little value, any means of passing is justified.

Cheating would drop dramatically if students really believed that an honest display of their knowledge and skill would be beneficial to them. If they felt that teachers would use the information to help them learn and achieve, then they would be less likely to provide inaccurate information to the teacher. Unfortunately, most students see school tests as the means by which the teachers label them and give grades rather than as a means of diagnosing learning difficulties in order to help them achieve success.

Approaches to Solving Cheating Problems

Unfortunately, some teachers become so obsessed with cheating that they engage in a game of "cops and robbers." The teacher is the cop who is always trying to catch the crooks. This presents a challenge for many students so they test the limits to see what they can get away with and the whole purpose of education becomes distorted. Students can be very creative in their efforts to cheat and students who want to cheat will find a way. The key to solving cheating problems is changing the attitude and the perspectives of the student and working to prevent the need for cheating.

An important aspect of prevention is to make sure that you administer fair tests and assignments. Tests that contain trick questions or that are not perceived by students to be accurate measures of important objectives communicate that you are more concerned with spreading students out on a grading curve than actually assessing their knowledge and growth. For example, I remember an undergraduate professor who took pride in testing students on trivial items with the mistaken belief that this required students to learn the material thoroughly. Students soon figured out the game and they looked for the bizarre and trivial aspects of the subject and missed the important points altogether.

Check your tests and assignments. Are they valid and worthwhile or are they exercises in busywork and trivial pursuit? Are students rewarded for effort as well as quality? Do you overemphasize competition so that students are always competing with each other? Those students who think they have little chance to win will be tempted to engage in cheating in order to get recognition.

It is also important to convince students that it is in their own best interest not to cheat. You need to clearly demonstrate to students that you use test results for their benefit. This means that tests need to be more diagnostic and the results need to be communicated clearly to students and used to increase their skill and mastery. You can demonstrate the value of accurate information by meeting with students to discuss the results of their tests and planning additional experiences that will help them master the material. When students believe that tests and assignments are useful to them, the temptation to cheat will be diminished.

The importance of any one test or assignment should be lessened. When the stakes are high and success is dependent on one or two major tasks, cheating becomes a means of self-preservation. More frequent testing and more frequent assignments help lessen the importance of the assignment or test and reduce the number of cheating incidents.

ACTIVITY 11-1 CHEATING

You are giving a test in your third period class. It is an important test that has a major influence on semester grades for the course. You have emphasized the importance of the test as a means of motivating the students. You did give them some review questions and some time to prepare for the test in class. As you are scanning the room, you notice that a couple of the girls near the back seem to be looking up frequently to check on your location. You notice a piece of paper on the desk of one of the girls. You casually walk to that area and take the paper. As you unfold it you find it contains information that might be helpful in answering some of the questions on the test.

What would you do?

1. What would be your first reaction?

2. What might be some alternatives?

3. Are there some things you could have done to lessen the probability of cheating?

When students are caught cheating on a test, a private conference is an appropriate response. Public accusations and ridicule only invite denial, defensiveness, and retaliation. In private and without anger, share the information with the student, ask for an explanation, and identify possible consequences. While consequences should be implemented, they should not overshadow the use of the conference as a way to diagnose and eliminate the causes of cheating. You may need to teach students appropriate study skills so that they come to learn that success is possible without cheating.

STEALING

Persistent loss of personal and school property leads to a serious deterioration of student and teacher morale and the creation of a climate that is not conducive to good learning or behavior. This is one of the most serious problems that teachers face. It is often difficult to handle because those who steal are often difficult to catch.

Identifying Causes of Stealing

Some students may resort to stealing because of jealousy. They believe that it is unfair that one student has objects that they covet. Other students may steal objects simply to get revenge on another student or the teacher. They feel unjustly treated by that individual, so they decide to take a prized possession in an effort to hurt him or her. Other students steal because they have low self-esteem and are trying to get attention. Students in this last category are often easy to identify because they usually make sure they get caught.

Approaches to Solving Stealing Problems

One of the first steps in solving stealing problems is to remove the temptation for stealing. When students bring prized possessions to the classroom, you can volunteer to keep them in a safe place and then return them at the end of the day or the period. Teacher belongings, such as money, should be kept in a safe place (a locked desk drawer or cabinet) to which students do not have access. When teachers leave the room, they should lock the door to prevent entry.

When there is a high incidence of stealing, class discussions dealing with value issues and respect for personal property can be helpful. Students can share their feelings and frustrations and suggest ways of solving the problem. This will be especially helpful if students believe that their best interests are threatened by stealing behavior. Use of peer influence and peer pressure to refrain from stealing is one of the most powerful approaches.

Individuals who are caught stealing need to be counseled in a private and in a nonthreatening manner. Natural consequences are appropriate measures to use with these students. They can be required to return the stolen material or to make restitution. They can then be denied access to desired objects or activities until they demonstrate responsibility. As with cheating, it is important to identify the causes for stealing and to deal with the causes rather than the symptoms.

VANDALISM

The cost of vandalism for school districts in the United States every year is enormous. In 1991, 11 percent of the elementary school principals and 14 percent of the secondary school principals reported serious or moderate levels of vandalism (Goldstein, Palumbo, Striepling, and Voutsinas, 1995). About 58 percent of the students in grades three to twelve believe that their school has, to some extent, a problem with vandalism and graffiti. There does appear to be some relationship between vandalism in the school and other serious problems in the school. In other words, vandalism might be a symptom of lack of communication and a poor educational climate (Metropolitan Life Insurance Company, 1994). Destruction of equipment and materials makes it very difficult to provide a quality education for all students.

The problem of vandalism is usually one that needs to be treated at a school or even a community level. Teachers, however, do have some responsibilities in helping prevent vandalism and in cooperating with authorities when vandalism occurs.

Identifying Causes of Vandalism

Vandalism is almost always an expression of anger and antagonism. Some of this anger and antagonism might be against society in general, and the school is an easy target. However, many acts of vandalism are expressions of anger and frustration directed at the school. This happens when the school is viewed as a threat rather than as a positive force. For example, I once participated in a community study of an inner-city school where school officials discovered that the people in the community viewed the school as a threat second only to the police department! Rather than looking at the schools as a place of help, they viewed them as places to be feared. When this climate exists, vandalism is certainly to be expected.

Approaches to Solving Vandalism Problems

The efforts of all teachers and staff are required if serious incidents of vandalism are to be prevented. An individual teacher can seldom prevent these acts. Perhaps the single most important preventive action that can be taken by a school is to build school pride. Students who are treated with respect and dignity and who feel that the school is working with them rather than against them will not vandalize.

Another effective schoolwide measure is to try to reduce "neutral turf." Neutral turf is those areas of the school, such as halls, rest rooms, and playgrounds, where there is no sense of clear ownership. These areas are not seen as the responsibility of any one person or group of individuals and are where a great deal of vandalism occurs. Assigning responsibility for these areas to specific individuals or groups can reduce neutral turf. For example, classes or teachers can be assigned the responsibility of taking care of the halls and the rest rooms close to their classroom. Students can be allowed to decorate the halls so that they have pride of ownership as well as a responsibility to keep their area clean and free of graffiti. School administrators need to be highly visible and accept responsibility for monitoring difficult neutral turf areas.

Classroom meetings to discuss incidents of vandalism and their consequences are useful in helping teachers identify the causes of vandalism and in dealing with student anger and hostility. They should be allowed to express their feelings openly without fear of retribution. Action then needs to be taken so that students believe that their feelings are respected and that they do have some outlet for their anger other than vandalism.

Students who are guilty of vandalism are best treated using natural consequences. They should be required to clean up any mess and to make restitution for any damage. Some parents try to relieve their son or daughter from responsibility by paying for damages. If possible, the students responsible should be held accountable and should make the restitution or repair the damage themselves.

Serious problems of vandalism that occur when the school is not in session might require the assistance of the local community. Community surveys to discover the attitude of the community toward the school can be helpful. Efforts can then be made to develop positive community attitudes. If the community believes that the school is their school and that it is working on their behalf, incidents of vandalism will diminish. The community needs to believe that the school is important and that everyone has a stake in maintaining it. Community meetings between school officials and community representatives in which the problem of vandalism is discussed and support from the community is solicited can be extremely helpful in solving serious vandalism problems.

VIOLENCE AGAINST OTHER STUDENTS

Violence against other students is an issue that causes considerable concern. Media attention often leaves the impression that many schools are "blackboard jungles" filled with violence. However, Hyman (1997) points out that schools are still relatively safe places when compared to the community at large. For example, the aggravated assault rate in the early 1990s per 100,000 people was 1,308 for the city of Dallas and 1,324 for the city of Los Angeles. However, the rate for the Dallas Independent School district was 16 and for the Los Angeles Unified School District was 47. Concern for violence has led to a requirement in California that all teacher preparation programs include violence prevention.

In reaction to these concerns schools have instituted a number of ways to deal with violence. These include metal detectors at doors to prevent weapons from being brought into the school, security guards in or around the school, random checks of bookbags and backpacks, dress codes that ban certain types of clothing, safety and antiviolence programs, a hotline number for students to call, strict disciplinary codes, classes on conflict resolution, and automatic suspension or expulsion for violent activities. Students state that they believe that mentoring programs, security guards, and suspension or expulsion are the most effective responses. They rate metal detectors as generally unsuccessful (Metropolitan Life Insurance Company, 1994).

Although violence does not occur at near the rate that is suggested by the media, it is a serious problem. Fear is a powerful emotion that can seriously hinder the learning process. The threat of violence is often a major concern of new and inexperienced teachers.

Identifying Causes of Violence against Students

As with any complex social issue, there are no simple answers to the causes of violence in society and schools in particular. Students are regularly exposed to violence in their community as well as on television. Fighting and aggression are frequently portrayed as an appropriate and even masculine response when an individual's self-respect is assaulted. Half of all students believe that it is impossible to walk away from an angry scene or a confrontation without fighting and many believe that an apology indicates weakness (Metropolitan Life Insurance Company, 1994). Unfortunately, the only method of conflict resolution that many students observe is fighting and aggression. This helps explain why fights between students often break out over trivial issues such as name-calling. Students see this as a direct challenge and assault to their dignity and therefore must respond with the society-sanctioned response, fighting.

One of the most common activities that promotes violence is bullying. In one study of 12th-grade students, nearly a third of the students surveyed felt so affected by bullying that they wanted to transfer to another school. Sixty-four percent of the students reported being a victim of a bully. The most common type of bullying was name-calling, followed by "cruel mind games, being pushed around, and occasional threats with a weapon" (*New York Times,* 1997).

Students identified factors that they believe contribute to violence. Most of the students believe that there would be less violence if there were more things for students to do. In addition, they believe that adults in society do not really care about what they think. As a result, almost half of the students who have been victims of violence do not talk to their parents about problems or disagreements because they do not think they care or understand. They also indicate that they do not discuss problems with teachers because they believe there is no confidentiality (26 percent), because teachers do not seem interested (24 percent), or because they do not think teachers can help them (22 percent). These same students indicate that teachers some-times treat them as numbers rather than as people (Metropolitan Life Insurance Company, 1994).

Acts of violence and bullying behavior are attempts to gain power. Power-hungry students unable to fulfill this need through constructive behavior often resort to physical aggression in an attempt to demonstrate their power. Teachers working with students who frequently engage in acts of violence against other students might note that those students involved are usually the ones who are having difficulty succeeding in other aspects of school life.

Revenge is yet another reason for acts of violence against other students. Those students who feel lonely, left out, and rejected by other students may resort to violent acts in an attempt to hurt others. They may not even strike back at those who are causing the pain, but may choose easy and convenient targets, such as weaker and more defenseless students.

Approaches to Solving Problems of Violence against Students

The data reported in the Metropolitan Life survey indicate that there are some things that can be done to prevent violence. Perhaps the most important aspect of prevention is improved communication. Teachers need to do a better of job of communicating their concern to students. They need to create opportunities for students to talk with them in confidence. Classroom and school meetings dealing with violence and alternatives to it are viewed positively by the students and could be instituted rather easily. The school needs to create an environment in which concern for students is a priority.

Students also indicate that they think swift and harsh responses, such as suspension and expulsion, are effective. Students do report that clear disciplinary codes are important. This implies that, while schools need to create a positive school atmosphere and make attempts to listen to students, they also need to respond decisively when acts of violence do occur.

There are some procedures that you can use when confronted with acts of violence, such as a fight. First of all, it is important to realize that fights often erupt when horseplay gets out of hand. This behavior often escalates into out-of-control behavior and then a fight. You need to develop an awareness of when this type of horseplay begins and step in before it gets out of hand. Intervention at this early stage can often be accomplished through humor or a response that places students in calming situations. If the situation has moved beyond the horseplay stage and individuals are having a confrontation but have not yet resorted to violence, Goldstein, Palumbo, Strieping, and Voutsinas (1995) recommend several steps.

The first step is to remove any audience that might be present. Remember that one motivation for violence is to "save face." An audience will only provide more motivation for the escalating behavior. Give the onlookers some verbal directives and get them away. The next step is to use calm talk to bring down the level of anxiety and communicate a sense of control. If you remain calm, students will have more confidence in your ability to resolve the situation. Use vocabulary and a demeanor that will defuse the situation. Talk slowly and softly and move deliberately. In other words, you do not want to begin by blaming or threatening students; this will only increase their anger and the probability of violence. You may give them some advice such as, "take 10 deep breaths" or "calm down."

If the situation remains tense, use a firm and assertive voice and deliver the "broken record" technique. The broken record technique involves repeating a student's name or a command over and over until you get his or her attention. Then give him or her a directive. This technique might go something like this, "John—, John—, John, go to the desk. John, walk to the desk." Another example might be, "Stop, stop, I said stop, both of you, stop."

Once the students have been separated, you then proceed to have a conference with each of them. Listen to what the students have to say, make them feel as if you are listening to their concerns. Use active listening to clarify what they are saying. You may indicate that you understand their frustration but do not get into a debate about who started it. Emphasize that, regardless of the causes, there are consequences. Point out the consequences for fighting, and discuss some alternatives.

If the confrontation has moved to violence and fighting, there are different steps that you need to take (Goldstein, Palumbo, Strieping, and Voutsinas, 1995). A primary consideration is that you protect yourself and others from harm. A natural tendency of teachers is to rush in and begin grabbing or separating the students. This may put you in danger.

The first step in a fight situation is to assess the situation quickly. Determine how many students are involved, the level of their anger, their size, and whether you see any weapons or objects that could be used as weapons. Is there an audience? What is the role of the audience? Is there any blood? Remember that there is always the threat of HIV. If you see blood, back off until help arrives. The next step is to call for help. Some schools have developed a planned sequence for calling for help. One suggestion might be to identify a dependable student and send the student for help. Inside the school you might be able to grab a phone and send a message to the office.

Now you may begin to move in. A first step in moving in is to try and disperse the audience. Give them some verbal commands. Be firm and give them a specific thing to do such as, "Okay, everyone, back to class." When moving in, use assertive verbal commands. This is not the time to discuss or reason, communicate with firmness and clarity that you want the fighting to stop now. Keep your voice firm but calm and do not get angry or use an angry tone. Remember that most students involved in a fight are afraid of being hurt. They may act brave but underneath they are shaking. Many of them are looking for an excuse to quit. If a teacher arrives, disperses the crowd, and takes charge, this might be all that is needed for both parties to stop without feeling as if they lost face in front of friends.

When moving in, stay alert, keep your hands up to protect yourself, and move in at about a 45-degree angle from the rear of one of the participants. This angle serves a couple of purposes. It helps you avoid getting hit if a student ducks and it makes the students aware that someone is moving in. Move in slowly, staying out of the striking range of punches until they stop. If they show no signs of letting up, you need to keep up the verbal commands, but stay out of the way until help arrives and several individuals can move in to restrain the students. If they do stop and back off a step or two, try to position yourself between the two students and give them some directives to keep them apart. Your actions will depend on your characteristics and those of the students. One teacher friend of mine with an imposing physique would step between the students and separate them with a hand on each of their chests. Students would not dare resist. However, if you are small and the combatants are large, this would not be wise.

Once the fight has been stopped, your task is not over. You need to continue to manage the situation in order to prevent a recurrence. Do not send the students to the office together or leave them so that they can start again. They need to be isolated, allowed a cooling-off period, and then be dealt with. This is where help is also useful. You may take one student and have another teacher take another student. Take them to different locations and use a calm, matter-of-fact voice to settle them down.

Because of the seriousness of violence against students, school administrators should be informed and involved in the decision about the consequences of the act. Once they arrive on the scene they can take charge of the situation and conduct conferences with the students and decide on the consequences. Fighting and aggression are serious acts and should not be tolerated in school. Therefore, the consequences

---

ACTIVITY 11-2 THE FIGHT

Tony is a rather large fifth grader. He is an older student because he has been retained once. He uses his size and age to try and intimidate the other students. He often bullies them by calling them names and threatening them. Today, in the hall outside the classroom, you hear Tony call one of the other boys a name. The other boy does not back down but returns the insult. Tony takes a swing at the boy and a fight erupts. Several punches are thrown and a desk gets knocked to the floor. The other students jump to their feet and begin yelling encouragement to the other student.

How would you respond?

1. How would you implement the steps for stopping a fight?

2. How would you react once you got the fight stopped?

3. What consequences would you implement for both of the boys?

4. Would you implement any consequences for the rest of the class?

should be serious ones. Many schools have adopted the policy of automatic suspension for any student involved in an act of violence.

Treating the causes of violence is difficult and time-consuming. There are no easy approaches that will quickly and immediately remove student anger and hostility. Those individuals who feel powerless need to be provided with some avenues for feeling important and powerful. Those who are lonely and left out need to be given some status so that the need for revenge is removed. Finally, conflict resolution and coping skills can be taught to provide students with other, more socially appropriate ways to deal with anger and fear. Indeed, for some students with a history of violence, special counseling and help from school counselors and psychologists might be required.

VIOLENCE AGAINST TEACHERS

It was a dark and cloudy evening in late November. Ms. Jones was making her way through the parking lot at the conclusion of another school day. She was thinking of all the things she had to get done that evening. She had to stop by the store, fix dinner, arrange for a neighbor to let in the washing machine repairman tomorrow, grade papers, and prepare materials for the following day. Suddenly her thoughts were disturbed by a noise behind her. As she turned, she was suddenly struck by something and knocked to the ground. Her books, papers, and purse went flying. She felt something, probably a foot, strike her in the ribs. Several other blows struck her in the back. The wind was knocked out of her, and she could feel the pain from her skinned knees and hands. There was an intense pain in her side and in her right shoulder. She heard a voice shout, "Hey, teacher, we get detention, you get lumps. You'd better back off or we'll show you who is really tough!" As she tried to raise her head, all she saw were the backs of several boys disappearing around the corner of the building.

Teachers who worry about their own safety are not in a position to deliver the best possible instruction or to interact with students in positive and constructive ways. It is important, however, for teachers to recognize that violence against them is a possibility and to learn preventive measures to protect themselves.

Identifying Causes of Violence against Teachers

One explanation of violence against teachers is that it is the final outcome of power struggles between students and teachers. Students become frustrated in their attempts to cope with teacher power, so they ultimately decide to seek revenge on the teacher. The student might feel as if he or she is backed into a corner and the only way to maintain the respect of peers is to strike out at the teacher. Another reason is that teachers, as representatives of authority, are accessible targets. Students who have hostility toward adult society in general, but find it difficult and dangerous to vent that hostility toward other symbols of authority, such as the police or their own parents, focus on the teacher. These are deeply troubled students who are bent on revenge. The teacher may not be the sole cause of the anger, but is simply a convenient target.

Approaches to Solving Problems of Violence against Teachers

Violence against teachers, like violence against students, is a serious problem that cannot be ignored. When it occurs, the consequences must be swift, and consistent with the seriousness of the offense. School authorities need to be involved immediately and, regardless of the reasons, violence cannot be excused or tolerated. Many schools have a policy that results in the automatic suspension of any student who commits an act of violence against a teacher.

Teachers can use several steps to prevent acts of violence. One of the first steps is to exercise common sense in their daily activities. For example, teachers need to make sure that they don't present themselves as easy targets for students who are seeking revenge. Precautions (such as not being alone in the classroom with doors unlocked late in the evening or not entering a volatile situation alone when students are likely to react with aggression) are necessary for personal safety.

Teachers who establish good communication with class members are often able to identify those students who have deep-seated anger and hostility. They must then communicate to these students that they care about them and are interested in helping them find ways of dealing with their feelings. Counseling and therapy or class meetings in which students are allowed to express their feelings and frustrations are possible solutions.

Perhaps the best way to prevent acts of violence against teachers is to win over the students so that students view teachers as allies rather than enemies. Students will rarely harm someone they believe is trying to help them. This means that teachers need to establish a warm, caring relationship with students. Teachers who threaten students with ultimatums implying serious consequences or who use physical force when disciplining them are inviting retaliation and violence.

Teachers who find themselves in conflict situations with students must remember that they are the trained professional in the group and that they need to take charge and find a solution that does not result in violence. Those teachers who place a priority on saving face or demonstrating their power are not creating conditions that will allow for a successful resolution. This reaction is only modeling for students that power is an appropriate method for conflict resolution. While you may have one type of power, students will retaliate with the only power they have at their disposal, physical force.

DRUG AND ALCOHOL ABUSE

Drug and alcohol abuse in the schools has received national attention as a societal problem of great proportions. According to a 1989 survey, 70 percent of the public school students and 52 percent of the private school students between the ages of 12 and 19 years reported that drugs were available at their school. In fact, many school officials report that it is one of the most serious problems they face. The negative influence of drugs on learning and on the classroom climate is well documented. Drugs in the school can be the origin of behavior problems, violence, and theft. The problem is not confined to any one type of school or to any particular grade level. Students are experimenting with drugs and alcohol at earlier ages, and suburban as well as inner-city schools are affected. Those individuals who think that they can avoid the problem by choosing to teach in only the "best" neighborhoods are being unrealistic.

Dealing with alcohol and drug abuse in the schools is further complicated by society's tendency to assign to schools the responsibility for solving complex social problems. Alcohol and drug abuse is a problem for all of society, and measures taken by schools will have limited success.

Identifying Causes of Drug and Alcohol Abuse

The causes for drug and alcohol abuse are numerous. Some individuals begin abusing drugs as a result of peer influence to be a part of the "in" group. Others take drugs as a coping mechanism for difficult life situations. Still others get involved as a symbol of rebellion. Those who tend to be more mature and who are prematurely attempting to be "adult" are also likely to engage in alcohol and drug abuse.

Many of the students who are involved in drug and alcohol abuse are those who have low self-esteem, a lack of confidence, and a perceived incompetence in dealing with reality (Hyman, 1997). School factors can contribute to drug and alcohol abuse by furthering feelings of inadequacy and insignificance. Students who do not trust school officials or who do not believe that they can trust what school officials tell them are likely to reject appeals to "just say no" and to experiment because usage is a rejection of school and school authority. Those bored with school may experiment because it involves excitement and risk-taking. Students who do not feel worthwhile or accepted by teachers may use drugs as a means of coping with rejection and a low self-concept.

Approaches to Solving Problems of Drug and Alcohol Abuse

As with most problems, the best approach to solving drug and alcohol abuse is prevention. Schools can take steps to help students feel significant, to provide them with alternative activities to help them feel competent, and to provide insight into the nature of addiction. Because of the importance of peers, group activity designed to help students deal with peer pressure is an important activity.

Drug and alcohol abuse involves both physical addiction and psychological dependency. It is important to keep these two dimensions in mind. It is difficult for schools to treat the physical addiction. School psychologists or drug counselors may be needed to help coordinate this aspect of treatment with local agencies that treat drug problems. This also requires the involvement of the family.

Dealing with such serious social problems is time-consuming and psychologically difficult. Small steps are the norm, and frequent relapses can be expected. When counseling students who may have a problem, it is important not to label the student or to fix blame. There are usually many reasons for the abuse, and fixing blame only creates defensiveness. When students learn that a teacher can be approached with a problem without fear of being put down, an important first step has been taken. School counselors and administrators may need to be brought in so that the student can be referred to individuals or agencies with the expertise to help. Because teachers are not drug counselors or trained therapists, they should not attempt to solve problems for which they are not equipped. To try to do so may only delay help that has a higher probability of success.

Many schools have instituted a "zero-tolerance" policy regarding drug and alcohol abuse. This means that the students caught with drugs or alcohol are removed and suspended from the school. If students come to school under the influence of alcohol or drugs, they need to be removed from the classroom immediately. The legal risks of

---

ACTIVITY 11-3   SUBSTANCE ABUSE

Cindy is a rather insecure ninth-grade student. You have noted that she wants very much to be a part of the in group. However, she has trouble gaining the acceptance of others. You have Cindy in your fifth period English class that meets after lunch. Today when Cindy enters the room she is acting strangely. She is talking very loudly and lacks coordination. Her conversation is incoherent and jumbled. Other students are watching her and giggling. The pupils of her eyes are dilated and you suspect she is under the influence of drugs.

What would you do?

1. What would be the first steps you would take?

2. What, if anything, would you do to try to get Cindy some help?

3. What might you do to deal with the issue of drugs with the whole class so that they would not see the problem as an amusing one?

looking the other way are too great. In addition, you are not helping the student. Many school districts have developed alternative schools as an important educational option for students who are having persistent problems with drug and alcohol addition.

In summary, drug and alcohol abuse is seldom a problem that you can solve alone. To attempt to do so may be harmful to the student. The student needs professional help and counseling as soon as possible. Your focus in the classroom needs to be on prevention. You need to be aware of the forces that might be prompting students to become involved in the drug culture and deal with those forces in an honest and open way. You need to create an environment in which students will feel significant and will feel that they can talk with you.

SUMMARY

There is a misconception that contemporary schools are filled with acts of violence and serious misbehavior. This is not the case, but every teacher needs to be prepared for those serious incidents when they do occur. Because these are serious behaviors, they often have complex causes and simple solutions are not likely. Responding to many of the serious problems requires a schoolwide or even a communitywide response.

When faced with problems of a serious nature, it is wise to try and determine the causes of the behaviors before attempting to implement a solution. Identifying the possible causes of the behavior will increase the probability of responding in ways that will have a positive impact.

SUGGESTED APPLICATIONS

1. Reflect on the various serious problems addressed in this chapter. Which are of the most concern for you? Why do they concern you? Identify a plan of action that you could take to obtain the necessary background and skill to help you become more comfortable with this type of problem.

2. Interview teachers at several different grade levels. Identify what they consider to be serious behavior problems at their grade level. How do they and how does their school respond to these serious problems?

3. Identify several articles that deal with alcohol and drug abuse in the schools. Read them, and develop a list of behavioral characteristics that can be used to identify those students who are involved in substance abuse. Identify approaches or programs that have been effective in dealing with substance abuse.

4. Research issues such as the prevalence of violence against teachers. How serious is the problem? What suggestions are given to help teachers protect themselves from violence?

SUGGESTED READINGS

Duke, D. and Meckel, A. (1984). *Teacher's guide to classroom management.* New York: Random House.

Glasser, W. (1986). *Control theory in the classroom.* New York: Harper & Row.

Goldstein, A. P., Palumbo, J., Striepling, S., and Voutsinas, A. M. (1995). *Break it up: A teacher's guide to managing student aggression.* Champaign, IL: Research Press.

Hyman, I. A. (1997). *School discipline and school violence: The teacher variance approach.* Boston: Allyn and Bacon.

Metropolitan Life Insurance Company (1994). *The American teacher, 1994.* New York: Louis Harris and Associates.

New York Times (November 26, 1997). *Bullies more of a menace than once thought.* New York: New York Times, p. B-12.

12 Teaching Conflict Resolution

Chapter Objectives

After reading this chapter you should be able to:

- State the importance of teaching conflict resolution in schools
- Explain the nature of conflict
- Define components needed in conflict resolution
- List approaches to conflict resolution
- Identify the steps of problem solving negotiations
- Explain the role of a mediator
- Define when to use arbitration
- Explain group conflict resolution

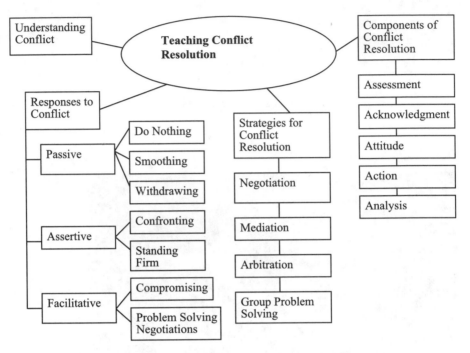

FIGURE 12-1 **Graphic Organizer for Conflict Resolution**

Conflict is a natural part of life and most of us experience some sort of conflict on a daily basis. Unfortunately, many people are terribly deficient when it comes to re-solving conflicts in a satisfactory manner. Some people will deny the existence of con-flict in the hopes that this denial will make it go away. Others will simply take flight and run away from the conflict. Still others assume the role of a victim and give in to others. Some view conflict situations as a matter of power and status and believe that they must win any conflict situation by dominating others (Lee, Pulvino, and Perrone, 1998). Inappropriate strategies for dealing with conflict usually lead to even more problems and a possible escalation to violence.

Classrooms are places where there are a variety of conflicts. One type of conflict is conflict between students as they seek to meet their own needs. When students are faced with conflicts with other students an all too common response is a fight.

Another common source of conflict is conflict between teachers and students as teachers attempt to enforce rules and promote learning. When faced with this sort of conflict, students may take flight rather than fight and find ways of avoiding the class-room or the teacher. In more serious situations they may seek retaliation or revenge and resort to verbal or physical abuse against the teacher.

These unproductive responses create an unhealthy classroom climate in which learning is difficult and the development of self-control blocked. Left unchanged, these unproductive conflict resolution approaches lead to unhealthy perspectives that can harm a person throughout life and threaten the fabric of society.

Helping students learn how to resolve conflicts constructively has been largely ignored. This is true even though teachers spend a considerable amount of time and energy dealing with destructive conflicts and in spite of research evidence that indicates that attending to constructive conflict resolution can increase classroom productivity (Johnson and Johnson, 1995). In recent years, recognition of the importance of productive conflict resolution not only to education but also to society in general has led to proposals for change. Some legislative bodies have taken actions focusing on the inclusion of conflict resolution approaches in the education of teachers. For example, the state of California recently required that all teacher preparation programs include content on dealing with violence. This follows the lead of the Texas legislature, which passed legislation mandating the teaching of conflict resolution in professional development activities (Johnson and Johnson, 1995). Conflict resolution skills are being viewed as fundamental skills needed in order to reduce violence in society.

Because classroom management and discipline is one of the key areas of conflict within a classroom, it is logical to include conflict resolution as a part of the total management and discipline plan (Johnson and Johnson, 1995). Implementing conflict resolution as a part of your total plan has several advantages. First, teaching students how to resolve conflicts can make your job easier and allow you to focus more on teaching and less on conflicts. Students will know how to resolve many problems on their own and eliminate the need for your intervention. Secondly, conflict resolution can help decrease violence, vandalism, and suspensions. Third, learning skills such as mediation and negotiation are important skills that all members of a democracy should possess in order to fulfill their citizenship responsibilities. Fourth, conflict resolution teaches listening, communication, and critical thinking skills that are basic to the goals of all of education. Fifth, learning conflict resolution provides a student with important life skills (Bodine, Crawford and Schrumpf, 1994). Finally, learning how to resolve conflicts is an important component in learning self-control.

UNDERSTANDING CONFLICT

There are several definitions of conflict. It has been described as a struggle over values, status, power, and resources or as differences between and among individuals. It may arise when one individual perceives that someone else has frustrated or is about to frustrate goal attainment. Conflict exists when incompatible activities occur. One activity interferes with or prevents another activity from occurring. These activities might originate within a person, between two or more people, or between two or more groups. Four different types of conflict that occur in the classroom are: intrapersonal, interpersonal, intragroup, and intergroup (Borisoff and Victor, 1998).

Johnson and Johnson (1995) point out that conflict is a normal and inevitable part of school life. We are often in conflict regarding our use of time, energy, or resources. We are faced with choices about how or with whom to perform tasks. Lee, Pulvino, and Perrone (1998) suggest that conflict is a part of the human condition because of many naturally occurring conditions. They note that common sources of conflict are gender, ethnicity, age, physical size, status, and socioeconomic differences. These sources of conflict often reside within individuals and their expectations of how others should believe, act, talk, and behave. This is the result of ethnocentrism, which leads us to conclude that our beliefs, thoughts, and actions are the natural and logical ones and everyone else should view things the same way.

Because conflict is a natural part of life, we should not seek to eliminate it, but expect it and learn to manage it so that individual rights and differences are acknowledged and a harmonious balance is restored (Lee, Pulvino, and Perrone, 1998). Similarly, Johnson and Johnson (1995) state that it is how conflicts are managed, and not their presence, that is important. They indicate that schools can either be "conflict negative" or "conflict positive." Conflict negative schools are schools where conflict is viewed as destructive and having no value. The goal of these schools is to eliminate, avoid, and deny the existence of conflict. Conflict positive schools are those that recognize that conflict is healthy, inevitable, and valuable. They manage conflicts so that they are used constructively to create an exciting and positive learning environment. Girard and Koch (1996) point out that most people tend to view conflict negatively. However, improving our response to conflict and learning how to resolve conflicts requires that we recognize that conflict is naturally occurring and potentially positive.

In summary, because conflict is a natural part of life, we should not seek to avoid it. We need to accept it and create "conflict positive" classrooms and schools. When we view conflict as something that is naturally occurring as a function of a number of factors, we can stop viewing it as a contest in which there must be winners and losers. If conflict is viewed as natural and potentially positive, the issue of winners and losers is not relevant because all parties in the conflict can be beneficiaries (Lee, Pulvino, and Perrone, 1998).

RESPONSES TO CONFLICT

Borisoff and Victor (1998) identify five components (or five "A's") that influence the success of conflict resolution approaches. Those five components are assessment, acknowledgment, attitude, action, and analysis. Awareness and understanding of these five components will result in increased probability that conflict resolution will be successful.

Assessment is the initial component. It involves making an assessment of the nature and the cause of the conflict and an assessment of the relationship and the traits of those involved (Borisoff and Victor, 1998). Assessment of the situation is important in order to choose an appropriate approach.

Acknowledgment requires that an individual in a conflict situation acknowledges that another person is involved. As noted earlier, because of our ethnocentrism, we often fail to recognize that another person with a different perspective and set of beliefs is involved. Until individuals are able to step back and acknowledge other perspectives, attempts at conflict resolution are not likely to be productive (Borisoff and Victor, 1998).

Attitude refers to the willingness of the participants to engage in conflict resolution. This means that those involved want to resolve the conflict, are willing to enter an encounter with an open mind, and are willing to cooperate with others. An important ingredient in helping individuals develop an attitude that will lead to the use of conflict resolution is developing a climate of trust in the classroom. Individuals in an environment that they believe to be hostile and threatening are not likely to develop an attitude that will lead to productive resolution.

Action is the integration of assessment, acknowledgment of different perspectives, and attitude. When these are considered, action can be taken. This is an especially important and difficult component because we all know that when we are confronted with a conflict situation we tend to lose self-control and act in destructive rather than productive ways. We need to attempt to take conscious control of our actions and attend to our verbal and nonverbal behaviors.

Analysis is the last component in conflict management. Analysis means considering whether or not the needs and concerns of all parties have been met, whether the proposed solutions are realistic and can be implemented effectively, and whether the relationship between those involved has been improved (Borisoff and Victor, 1998).

Keeping these five components in mind, approaches for handling conflicts can be considered. Different approaches might be chosen based on assessment, acknowledgment and attitudes. Understanding the various options and when and how to use them is important in helping individuals take actions that are likely to be productive. Specific conflict resolution approaches can be divided into three basic types: passive, assertive, and facilitative (Lee, Purvino, and Perrone, 1998).

Passive Responses

Passive approaches are neutral in nature and do not attempt to force a resolution. The main goal of a passive approach is to try and maintain the relationship between individuals and to keep the situation from escalating. Doing nothing, smoothing, and withdrawing are examples of passive approaches.

Doing Nothing

Doing nothing is really not an accurate description of this approach. It is basically a wait-and-see approach whereby overt action is delayed. To some extent this approach recognizes that not all conflicts need to be resolved. For example, it is healthy to have different political perspectives. It would be foolish to demand that all political parties resolve their conflicts.

There are times when it is best to take this neutral stance. Situations in which this approach would be appropriate are situations in which disagreements may be constructive, the individuals involved are demonstrating self-control, there is no display of excessive anger, and the situation does not appear to be escalating. This approach might be defined as "agreeing to disagree" without demanding that the other person change. We should not demand that individuals change their beliefs or values in order to remove disagreements.

If you are a third party, the wait-and-see attitude allows you time to consider options and allows individuals involved in the conflict time to reach a resolution or to reach a point where they welcome your intervention or perspectives. Many of us have observed situations in which individuals rushed in to try and help others work out a solution and ended up only making the situation worse.

If you are one of the parties involved there are several things you need to do in order to use the "doing nothing" approach. You need to observe and listen carefully and to control your emotions so your observations can be as objective as possible. This also means you need to control your verbal and nonverbal behavior. If you can maintain this low-key response, it will calm the situation and reduce tension.

Smoothing

Smoothing is another passive approach that is best used when maintaining a relationship is more important than accomplishing a goal. This is often used when you assess the situation and acknowledge that the interests of the other person might be more important than yours (Johnson and Johnson, 1995). The focus is on the other person's needs or desires.

The purpose is to avoid a confrontation by refusing to be put on the defensive or to engage in a confrontation. It takes two or more people to engage in a conflict and if one of you refuses to be drawn in, the potential for conflict is removed. It means you are willing to make your needs secondary. You may not agree with what another person is saying or doing but you are willing to suppress your feeling in order to maintain a positive relationship.

Humor is a good smoothing device. Laughter helps reduce tension and it is hard to have a confrontation when you are laughing. When using humor, however, you need to make sure you are not using sarcasm or making the other person the butt of the joke.

Another good smoothing technique is active listening. By using active listening you are allowing the person to express his or her desires without challenge. You are simply helping them clarify their feelings or beliefs. Smoothing requires that you avoid using inflammatory rhetoric or saying anything that can be interpreted as criticism.

Johnson and Johnson (1995) point out that smoothing and problem solving are the conflict management approaches most commonly used by competent managers and executives. When maintaining a relationship is important, smooth. When accomplishing a goal is important, then problem solve.

Withdrawing

All of us are familiar with conflict situations in which the anger and the emotions seem to run so high that reason and logic are lost. In this situation it might be best to withdraw. All of us can probably identify a situation in which a relationship might have been preserved or a long-term solution found if a confrontation had been terminated before it spiraled out of control and things were said or actions taken that could not be reversed. It would have been better to withdraw, let emotions cool, and reason reassert itself. It is often hard for people to do because their ego gets involved and withdrawing is viewed as a sign of weakness. Ego involvement can turn a difficult situation into an impossible one. This needs to be avoided. You need to remember that it sometimes takes more courage and wisdom to withdraw from a situation than to continue to escalate an already out-of-control one. Withdrawing is an appropriate choice if violence appears to be a possibility.

When withdrawing, individuals need to learn how to look for a quick way out and take it. It is time to stop debating and simply get away from the situation as fast as possible. Make your intentions very clear; terminate the confrontation and leave. This might be done with a simple statement such as, "We are not reaching a solution so I am leaving." Do not linger, debate, or react to insults. You may leave with the clear intention of resolving the situation at a later time.

Assertive Responses

Assertive approaches are those whereby you take action. They are useful when accomplishing a goal or an objective is more important than preserving a relationship. You need to recognize that assertive approaches do have the potential for evoking more anger and hostility. Examples of assertive techniques are confronting and standing firm.

Confronting

The confronting approach is useful when there are unresolved tensions that may be preventing goal accomplishment (Lee, Pulvino, and Perrone, 1998). This is the approach in which the focus is on getting individuals to get issues out in the open so they can be resolved. The approach requires open, honest communication and mutual respect between the participants in the conflict. Individuals involved in the confrontation also need to have enough self esteem so that they can easily accept criticism and are not threatened by confrontation (Lee, Pulvino, and Perrone, 1998).

The process of confronting requires that a level of trust be established between the disputants. If they do not trust each other, then defensiveness takes over and little can be accomplished. Care must also be taken to make sure that personal attacks and ascribing blame are avoided. The use of I-messages is a good technique for getting feelings out in the open and avoiding blaming or criticizing.

One of the first steps in the confronting process involves establishing a common goal. The individuals involved must agree on a common goal that they are working

ACTIVITY 12-1   FEUDING FRIENDS

You have two friends with whom you have a good relationship. You recently noticed that they have been cool to each other and have made excuses not to be together. One of them approached you with a concern about the situation but professed not to know the cause.

What would you do?

1. Do you think this would be a situation in which the confronting approach would be appropriate?

2. How would you implement this approach?

3. What would be the specific steps that you would follow?

———————

toward. This common goal may be the restoration of harmony or friendship. If a common goal is not accepted, the confrontation may well turn into a power struggle rather than a resolution of the differences.

Each of the participants then needs to communicate his or her concerns and problems and to attempt to view the situation from the perspective of the other. Discussion must include ample time for both sides to be stated. It is important that one side not dominate the discussion.

As individuals express their viewpoints, active listening can be used to clarify feelings. Once there is clarity of perspectives, solutions are often easily identified. These need not be win–lose solutions but ought to be ones that take into account the needs and feeling of both parties.

Standing Firm

There are times when there is no other option but to take a firm stand. This occurs when we are physically or psychologically attacked and we must stand up for our rights and needs. The goal of standing firm, however, should not be to win but to establish a balance in the situation and reduce the potential of being challenged by the person again. If you have to respond to a physical threat, it should be to use the minimal force necessary. The other party needs to be convinced that your intent is not to harm but that you will stand firm.

Lee, Pulvino, and Perrone (1998) note several components of standing firm. They suggest that it is important when standing firm to remain focused on the problem, not on your internal state or feelings. Allowing your feelings to take over may result in anger and fear, states that can escalate the situation to a major problem. You should attempt to remain as calm as possible and to acknowledge that a problem exists. Comments should be specific and focus on the present problems. Do not get sidetracked to other issues or fall into the trap of discussing past history. Physically stand your ground, make eye contact, and squarely face the other person. This helps communicate a sense of seriousness to the other person that may give him or her cause to stop for a minute and rethink his or her actions. This also puts you in a good defensive position if you face a physical confrontation.

Facilitative Responses

These are approaches that are intended to help resolve problems when the goal to be achieved and the relationship between the parties are both important (Johnson and Johnson, 1995). These approaches usually require more time and effort to implement. Examples of facilitative approaches are compromising and problem solving.

Compromising

Compromising is a time-honored approach to conflict resolution. There are times when those involved in a conflict cannot get what they want. Each person in the conflict may have to give up some part of his or her goal in order to reach an agreement. It means meeting in the middle so that both parties get something they desire. Compromises will not work if one party believes he or she has lost or that they had to do all of the compromising.

Seeking a compromise has the advantage of being a relatively quick process. It can be used when there is not enough time for problem solving approaches (Johnson and Johnson, 1995).

Problem Solving Negotiations

Problem solving is the process whereby solutions are sought that ensure that both individuals achieve their goals and have their needs met while also resolving any tension or anger. Each party maintains his or her interests and tries to reconcile them with the interests of the other.

Problem solving will only work when there is adequate time to implement the process and when there is an open and trusting environment. It will work best when participants openly share their concerns, identify their needs, wants, and possible solutions (Lee, Pulvino, and Perrone, 1998).

The process of problem solving involves the following steps:

- Defining the problem
- Brainstorming possible solutions
- Selecting a solution acceptable to both parties
- Planning what each person will do
- Implementing the plan
- Evaluating the plan

When implementing the process it is important that both individuals express what he or she needs in an open manner. Stating these needs helps each person understand what needs must be met in order to arrive at an agreeable solution. Once these needs have been stated, brainstorming can take place to identify possible solutions that might take into account the needs of both individuals. It is important not to evaluate the solutions but to try and get as many potential solutions as possible on the table. Once a number of solutions have been generated, discussion can center on the ones that both parties find acceptable that meet the needs of both. A plan then needs to be established that indicates the responsibilities of each person. It is extremely important that these responsibilities be clearly defined and understood so that there is no additional misunderstanding. The plan needs to be implemented and, at a later date, the effectiveness of the plan needs to be evaluated. If one or more of the individuals feels that the plan was not fair or that it did not resolve the situation, then other solutions need to be brainstormed and another plan selected and tried.

Each of these responses to conflicts is appropriate for a given situation. Students need to learn these different approaches and practice using them so that they will have options when confronting conflict. One especially useful strategy for teaching and practicing these approaches is role-playing. You should create a number of different conflict situations and present them to the class. Students can make choices as to the approach they think is most appropriate for that situation and then practice using it.

TABLE 12-1 **Responses to Conflict**

Type of Response	When to Use
PASSIVE RESPONSES	
Doing Nothing	Disagreement is not destructive, low anger
Smoothing	Maintaining relationship most important
Withdrawing	When the situation is threatening, out of control
ASSERTIVE RESPONSES	
Confronting	There is trust, good relationship, unspoken issues
Standing Firm	When your rights and needs are important
FACILITATIVE RESPONSES	
Compromising	When there is not much time, both willing to give
Problem Solving Negotiations	When there is adequate time and both parties are willing to participate

SOLVING CONFLICTS USING NEGOTIATION, MEDIATION, AND ARBITRATION

Negotiation, mediation, and arbitration are three fundamental processes that can be used when individuals are having conflicts with each other. Negotiation is a process in which two individuals sit down and work out a resolution together. Mediation involves a third party who assists individuals in finding a solution when they seem to be unable to do so. Arbitration also involves a third party and is usually instituted when negotiation and mediation fail (Johnson and Johnson, 1995).

Negotiation

Negotiation is an activity that we engage in throughout our lives. It is an unassisted problem solving process in which two or more people sit down voluntarily to discuss differences and to reach a joint decision. It involves a step-by-step process that uses communication and thinking skills to guide individuals toward a mutually acceptable resolution (Girard and Koch, 1996). Using negotiation skillfully is time-consuming and difficult. Students need to be taught how to negotiate.

We use negotiations constantly in a variety of situations. In fact, we are often unaware of situations in which we are engaged in negotiations. However, many people do not know how to negotiate and do it poorly (Johnson and Johnson, 1995).

Bodine, Crawford, and Schrumpf (1994) identify six steps in the negotiation process:

1. Agree to negotiate
2. Gather points of view
3. Find common interests
4. Create win–win options
5. Evaluate options
6. Develop an agreement

Agree to Negotiate

Negotiations cannot succeed unless those who are involved in the conflict are agreeable to negotiations. Negotiation works best if there is some interdependence between those involved so that they need each other in order to get their needs met. There must be some shared interest in negotiating. This shared interest might be as simple as a desire to maintain a relationship or a mutual desire to forego the consequences of continued conflict. In addition, at least some of the issues must be negotiable (Girard and Koch, 1996). If one of the parties in the dispute has such firm convictions that there is no room for movement, negotiation simply will not work. The basic ground rules for the negotiation are established during this step. Basic ground rules usually involve taking turns talking and not using name-calling or put-downs.

Gather Points of View

The next step is to gather information about the different points of view or perspectives in the dispute. To reach a satisfactory agreement each person must clearly understand the common and the opposed interests in a conflict. In order for negotiation to be successful, each person needs to be able to take the perspective of the other and understand how that conflict appears to the other. No two people will see an issue the same way and in conflict situations individuals tend to see only what they want to see (Johnson and Johnson, 1995). First, one person tells his or her point of view. The other person uses active listening to clarify points. When this person is done the second person summarizes what the first person said and then shares his or her point of view. The other person uses active listening. When the second person is finished the first person then summarizes the other's point of view. Johnson and Johnson (1995) recommend that individuals refrain from expressing approval or disapproval of the other's perspectives. They describe how he or she thinks the other person feels and ask if this is accurate. When this step is complete each person has the opportunity to share additional information or clarify what he or she said. Questions may be asked if they lead to additional clarification or understanding (Bodine, Crawford, and Schrumpf, 1994).

Finding Common Interests

This is a key step in the negotiation process. In addition to sharing their perspectives on the conflict, each person needs to be willing to state what they want or need. At this point each person should honestly describe his or her wants, needs, and feelings. They should alternate in doing this as was done in step two.

The other person has the right to refuse to meet those wants and needs if he or she believes they are destructive to his or her wants and needs. Sharing your wants does not carry with it a demand that the other needs to do exactly as you wish. Individuals at this phase should share how the other person's wants or needs are blocking what they want (Johnson and Johnson, 1995).

The focus at this stage needs to be on wants and not on positions. It is easy to get the two confused and some people become so locked into a position that they overlook options that might help them meet their needs or wants. The purpose is to try and identify some common or compatible interests. These common or compatible interests provide the basis for finding a resolution (Bodine, Crawford, and Schrumpf, 1994). At the conclusion of this step the disputants should be able to state the interests they have in common.

Creating Win–Win Options

The purpose of this step is to brainstorm options that take into account the common interests of the parties so that they both will have needs and wants met. The process involves stating any idea that comes to mind. The ideas should not be immediately evaluated or discussed. They should try to come up with as many options as possible. Bodine, Crawford, and Schrumpf (1994) suggest that together the disputants invent

ACTIVITY 12-2   THE ANGRY PARENT

A parent of one of your students has requested a conference. The parent arrives at the appointed time for the conference. You can tell by the nonverbal behavior of the parent that this is not going to be a pleasant conference. The parent starts right in questioning your teaching.

> *I am concerned about my son. I do not think you are teaching him what he needs to be successful. Rather than emphasizing the basics of math, you are engaging the class in group problem solving exercises. I agree that at some time students will need to apply what they have learned. However, they need to learn the basics and be held accountable for knowing basic mathematical processes. Working in groups allows students to avoid individual accountability and depend on someone else. I think the students need to be given hard old fashioned math problems that make them work and practice basic skills.*

How would you handle this?

1. Do you think using the negotiation process would work in this situation?

2. What would be the first thing you would do to apply the negotiation process?

3. What might be the common interests around which you could find a solution?

4. What might be some win–win solutions to this conflict?

---

at least three options. They emphasize the importance of them working together so that the more assertive person does not dominate. This must be viewed as a joint responsibility that will benefit both of them.

Evaluating Options
Once several options have been identified then the individuals work together as problem solvers to evaluate each of the options. The options should be evaluated on the basis of how they provide benefits for each party. They may elaborate on an option or combine parts of the options that were invented. Each of the options should be viewed from different perspectives and reformulated if needed. When evaluating the options they should be judged against reality. What are the strengths and weaknesses? What does each person gain and lose? How does the option maximize benefits for both parties (Johnson and Johnson, 1995)?

Creating an Agreement
At this step, individuals work together to create a mutually acceptable agreement that will help them resolve the conflict. The agreement should meet certain criteria. The

agreement should state who, what, when, where, and how for both individuals. It must meet the needs of both parties and must be viewed as fair by everyone involved. The agreement should strengthen the individuals' ability to resolve future conflicts. It is important for individuals to understand what not to do that might trigger a conflict as well as what to do to resolve those that do occur (Johnson and Johnson, 1994).

Some attempts to reach a mutual agreement will fail. When this occurs you start over with step one and once again clarify perspectives and wants. Persistence will often pay off. Johnson and Johnson (1995) suggest that students who have trouble arriving at a successful agreement might be sent to a problem solving area where they stay until they work out an agreement. They are not allowed to touch, only talk, and they are to tell you when they have reached a solution. It is important that they be praised when they are able to reach an agreement. If students cannot generate an acceptable agreement or refuse to negotiate then mediation might be implemented.

Mediation

Mediation is an extension of the negotiation process. It follows the same basic steps of the negotiation process but involves a mediator or a neutral third party who helps others resolve conflicts. Mediators do not tell others what to do or decide who is right or wrong. Mediators are facilitators who help individuals implement the process (Johnson and Johnson, 1995).

Mediation is appropriate when individuals involved in a conflict do not understand the negotiation process or when individuals are unsuccessful at it. The role of mediator is one that can be filled by you or by other adults or it can involve other students as peer mediators. Some schools have conducted workshops for students and have trained a number of students in the school to become peer mediators. These students are then available to serve as peer mediators whenever other students request them. In your classroom you might conduct peer mediation training and then each week select a couple of different students to serve as peer mediators. They get the privilege of serving as mediators for any disputes that arise. Schools using peer mediation report resolution rates of up to 95 percent (Girard and Koch, 1996).

The role of a mediator requires that he or she follow certain steps. The first step is to end any hostilities. He or she needs to remember that he or she is a mediator, not the police (Johnson and Johnson, 1995). He or she should not attempt to physically intervene if there is a fight. His or her role is to offer to help students resolve a conflict. The peer mediator might suggest to students that are having difficulties that they take a short time to cool down and then engage in mediation.

Note that the first step of mediation, like the first step of negotiation, is that the students involved must agree to mediation. The process will not work if the individuals involved do not agree to engage in mediation. Mediation should also take place in a private area away from distractions and the ears of others. The mediator should sit between the disputants. At the beginning the mediator needs to make sure that the disputants agree to the mediation process and agree to follow any ground rules that are established. The ground rules can be the same as those used in the negotiation process. Both individuals agree to take turns talking, agree to avoid name-calling and put-downs, and agree to cooperate (Bodine, Crawford, and Schrumpf, (1994). If they do not agree to these conditions, the mediation session is over. Another method of re-solving the conflict will be required.

The mediator should then review the steps of the mediation process and explain that the role of the mediator is not to take sides or to tell the disputants what to do. The individuals involved need to be asked if they have any questions and if they un-derstand the process.

One variation of the gathering of different perspectives step is to have the in-dividuals fill out a conflict form (Johnson and Johnson, 1995). On these forms the students identify who they are having a conflict with, the nature of the conflict, and what they want. Students who cannot write well can dictate their responses to the mediator. These forms can then be read or shared with the other person involved in the conflict.

The role of the mediator is to help the individuals through the process and make sure that it is fair. If students are unable to talk to each other without getting angry, the mediator may need to hold individual sessions with each person. Separate sessions may also be used if one or more of the individuals lacks trust and is unwilling to be open and honest.

During a mediation session, the mediator may need to ask clarifying and open-ended questions in order to promote communication and understanding. One tech-nique that is sometimes useful is for the mediator to have the disputants reverse perspectives. They are to take the role of the other person. This is often a useful tech-nique in solving stubborn disagreements (Johnson and Johnson, 1995). The role of the mediator is to help the participants move through the steps of sharing points of view, identifying common interests, inventing win–win solutions, evaluating solutions, and reaching an agreement.

At the end of a mediation session it is useful for both students and the mediator to all sign the agreement that they reach. The participants are told that all they should do is to inform their friends that the disagreement is ended. The mediator then keeps the agreement. If the agreement is not fulfilled, the mediator can ask the individuals to reconvene in order to reach a new agreement. If peer mediation is unsuccessful, then the problem should be referred to you. You may choose to serve as the media-tor, or to serve as an arbitrator.

Arbitration

As a teacher you have the final responsibility to resolve conflicts. If negotiation did not work, peer mediation did not work, teacher mediation did not work, then you may have to move to arbitration. If this does not work then the problem needs to be re-ferred to the school administrator.

Arbitration is a process in which a third party makes a final decision regarding the resolution of the conflict. It is not unlike what many teachers do on a daily basis. They are constantly serving as informal arbitrators for classroom conflicts. However, it will have more impact if it is formalized, used sparingly, and implemented only for the most difficult problems. Some changes can be made to alter the traditional teacher role so that the arbitration process will be more acceptable to students.

A potential shortcoming of arbitration is that responsibility to negotiate and solve the problem is shifted from those involved and the outcomes are less likely to be accepted than those that have been worked out together. In addition, the process does not help students learn conflict resolution skills (Johnson and Johnson, 1995).

Applying the arbitration process in a formal manner in the classroom will help students understand the process and increase the probability that they will accept the decisions of the arbitrator. The formal steps used in the process are the following:

1. Each individual involved in the dispute defines the problem. He or she may be asked to do this in writing if possible.
2. Each person is allowed to tell his or her side to the arbitrator without interruption from the other. If he or she has any evidence to substantiate the story, he or she is allowed to present it.
3. Each person is given the opportunity to respond to the other person's story. However, this needs to be done in an orderly fashion with each taking a turn.
4. Each person then tells the arbitrator what he or she wants and would like to see happen.
5. The arbitrator makes a decision. A wise arbitrator will try to find a win–win decision so that both individuals get some of their needs met.

In classrooms where teachers serve as mediators, they can combine mediation and arbitration. Students then know that if they do not reach a mediated decision, the teacher will impose one through arbitration. Johnson and Johnson (1995) point out that this increases the success of mediation because the students would prefer having a voice in the solution rather than allowing the teacher to impose one.

GROUP PROBLEM SOLVING

The processes of negotiation, mediation, and arbitration are best used to settle disputes between individuals. However, there are conflicts that affect the entire classroom. In these situations it is useful to use a group problem solving process (Bodine, Crawford, and Schrumpf, 1994). In a group problem solving process the teacher serves as a group facilitator to help clarify and discuss the issues involved. Bodine, Crawford, and Schrumpf (1994) suggest two basic guidelines for group problem solving:

1. The discussion should be directed toward solving the problem.
2. The solution should not include fault-finding or punishment.

If group problem solving results in punishment, then members of the group will be less open and honest in future sessions and group members will be less likely to follow through on decisions. One of the more difficult tasks for teachers in group problem solving is for them to recognize and accept their role. You should not be the one dominating the group or forcing the decision. You need to be a part of the group, a listener who is trying to get as many viewpoints as possible in front of the group for discussion.

A useful approach for group problem solving is the Classroom Meeting format outlined by Glasser (1969). Glasser defines classroom meetings as a method for getting students involved in decision making about their own education. They are intended to help students develop a sense of responsibility for what happens in the classroom or school. Glasser's basic premise is that when students are involved, believe that teachers are interested in what they have to say and are interested in them as individuals, conflicts can be resolved productively and many discipline problems will be prevented.

The format of classroom meetings involves arranging the chairs in a circle so that everyone is included. There is no front or back, and the environment is conducive to face-to-face discussion. The teacher takes one of the chairs in the circle in order to be just a part of the group. The role of the teacher is to introduce the topic and facilitate the discussion. The meeting should generally be relatively short and last from about 10 to 30 minutes. Students should be allowed to express their feelings and opinions openly and without fear of retaliation.

Glasser defines three types of classroom meetings: social problem solving, educational diagnostic, and open-ended. Social problem solving meetings focus on the problems that students are having living together in the school environment. Educational diagnostic meetings focus on the curriculum and the methods of instruction. Open-ended meetings allow students the opportunity to present topics that are of interest or concern to them.

In a social problem-solving meeting the teacher calls the students together to the discussion circle. The problem is identified and students are then prompted to discuss why they think the problem is occurring and to suggest possible solutions. It is permissible for you to introduce your point of view or to ask questions that would prompt students to consider issues they may have overlooked. However, as group facilitator, you do not want to try and lobby for your point of view. To do so will convey to the group that you are not really interested in their input and the whole process will be viewed with skepticism.

As with the mediation process, it is usually best to generate a number of possible solutions without evaluating them. After a number have been generated the students can then discuss the merits of each solution with a focus on win–win solutions. Criteria that can be used to evaluate the suggested options are:

- Is it fair to everyone?
- Can it solve the problem?
- Is it consistent with school rules and policies?

You are trying to get a group consensus about an agreement and a commitment about the solution. When you have reached a consensus, you need to restate the agreements and help clarify how the agreements will be implemented (Bodine, Crawford, and Schrumpf, 1994).

Group consensus does not mean that every single person in the group will agree or that everyone feels good about the proposed solution. Consensus means that the group has made a decision about what is best for the group rather than what is best for individuals (Bodine, Crawford, and Schrumpf, 1994). In trying to reach consensus it is unproductive if individuals within the group persist in arguing for their own point of view. It is best if they are prompted to present their position in a clear and concise manner along with the reasons why it should be supported. Others should do the same, so that when the group begins to consider options, they can carefully evaluate alternative points of view and search for a strong solution (Bodine, Crawford, and Schrumpf, 1994).

It is useful occasionally to have an open-ended classroom meeting. The meeting can be called and you can ask students to identify any problems or issues they would like to have discussed. You will frequently find concerns that you were unaware of surfacing in the meetings. It provides you with an opportunity to take some preventive actions and helps students believe that you do care about their concerns and are willing to listen.

ACTIVITY 12-3   CLASSROOM CONFLICT

You are the teacher in an upper elementary classroom. You notice that there seems to be a lot of tension between class members. You meet with a couple of students privately and ask them if there is a problem. The students tell you that they are unhappy about the way the students choose teams during recess periods. The best students are always chosen first and others feel left out and humiliated. You decide that this is a good time to have a social problem solving classroom meeting.

What would you do?

1. How would you start the meeting? How would you define the probem?

2. What steps would you follow to have a discussion of the issue?

3. What problem do you think you might have?

4. What might be some possible solutions that could be suggested?

5. What would you do if the group solutions did not agree with your ideas?

SUMMARY

Conflicts are a natural part of life. We all experience a wide variety of conflicts. What is important is not to ignore conflicts but to learn how to handle them in constructive ways. When facing a conflict situation it is useful to assess the situation, acknowledge the perspectives of the other, develop an attitude that is conducive to resolution, take action, and analyze whether or not the needs of all individuals were met and whether the actions are realistic and workable.

There are three types of responses to conflict situations: passive, assertive, and facilitative. Each type is appropriate for certain situations. They need to be taught to students and practiced so that they can learn how to apply them when needed.

Negotiation, mediation, and arbitration are formal approaches that can be taught to students to help them resolve conflicts. Schools have had considerable success in using peer mediation approaches.

When there are conflicts that affect the whole group, group problem solving is in order. The classroom meeting format of Glasser (1969) is useful for this approach.

SUGGESTED APPLICATIONS

1. Reflect on conflicts you have had in the recent past. Identify one situation in which the outcomes were positive and one situation in which the outcomes were negative. What do you think accounted for the differences in outcomes? What could you have done that might have changed the outcomes of the negative one?

2. Practice using the steps of negotiation with a friend. Pretend you have a conflict and follow the steps to try and seek resolution. After you have completed the exercise, discuss your experiences. What was uncomfortable? What steps did you think were most difficult? When do you think this process would be effective and when might it not be appropriate?

3. Create a plan for teaching members of your class to be peer mediators. What would you include in your plan? How would you implement it in the classroom?

4. Develop a discipline plan that you can use in your classroom. Be as specific as possible in outlining a plan that you will feel comfortable implementing and that is consistent with your philosophy and your personality. Consider the management dimensions covered in the first part of the text, the discipline dimensions in the second part, and the conflict resolution components of this chapter.

SUGGESTED READINGS

Bodine, R. J., Crawford, D. K., and Schrumpf, F. (1994). Creating the peaceable school: A comprehensive plan for conflict resolution. Champaign, IL: Research Press.

Borisoff, D. and Victor, D. A. (1998). *Conflict management: A communication skills approach,* 2nd Ed. Boston: Allyn and Bacon.

Girard, K. and Koch, S. J. (1996). *Conflict resolution in the schools: A manual for educators.* San Francisco: Jossey-Bass.

Glasser, W. (1969). *Schools without failure.* New York: Harper & Row.

Johnson, D. W. and Johnson, R. T. (1995). *Reducing school violence through conflict resolution.* Alexandria, VA: Association for Supervision and Curriculum Development.

Lee, J. L., Pulvino, C. J., and Perrone, P. A. (1998). *Restoring Harmony: A guide for managing conflicts in schools.* Upper Saddle River, NJ: Merrill.

Index

DATE DUE
